Montserrat
History of a Caribbean Colony

Montserrat

History of a Caribbean Colony

Second Edition

Howard A. Fergus KBE PhD

Professor of Eastern Caribbean Studies,
University of the West Indies

MACMILLAN
CARIBBEAN

Macmillan Education
Between Towns Road, Oxford OX4 3PP
A division of Macmillan Publishers Limited
Companies and representatives throughout the world

www.macmillan-caribbean.com

ISBN 0 333 99624 0

First published 2004

Designed by Susan Clarke
Typeset by EXPO Holdings, Malaysia
Illustrated by Tek Art
Cover design by Gary Fielder, AC Design
Cover photo: The Montserrat National Trust

Printed and bound in Malaysia

2007 2006 2005 2004
10 9 8 7 6 5 4 3 2 1

Contents

Acknowledgements

The author and publishers wish to thank Delena Lynch and Olga Allen for typing the manuscript and Barbara O'Leary for reading it and offering editorial suggestions. We wish also to thank Grace Cassell and V. Jane Grell and other Montserrat Public Library personnel for making useful resources available and in the case of Jane Grell for advice. Dr Riva Berleant-Schiller of the University of Connecticut supplied me with valuable material for which I am thankful.

Thanks are due to the University of the West Indies for the study/travel grant which enabled me to undertake research in London. Finally, the support and understanding of my wife Eudora during the period of research and writing are gratefully acknowledged.

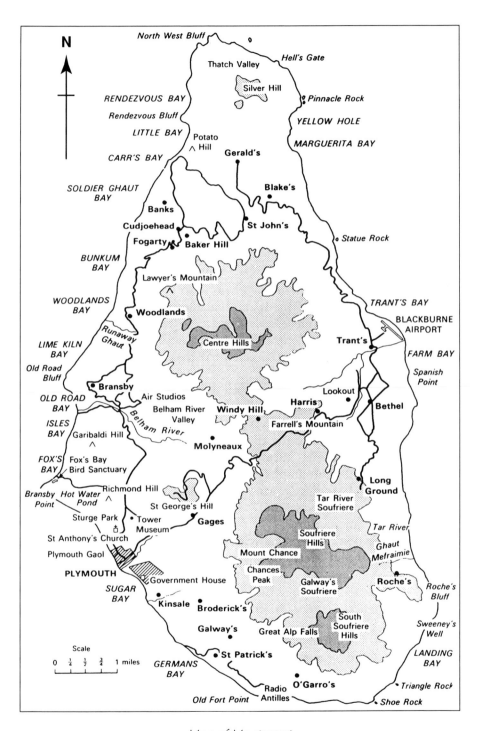

Map of Montserrat

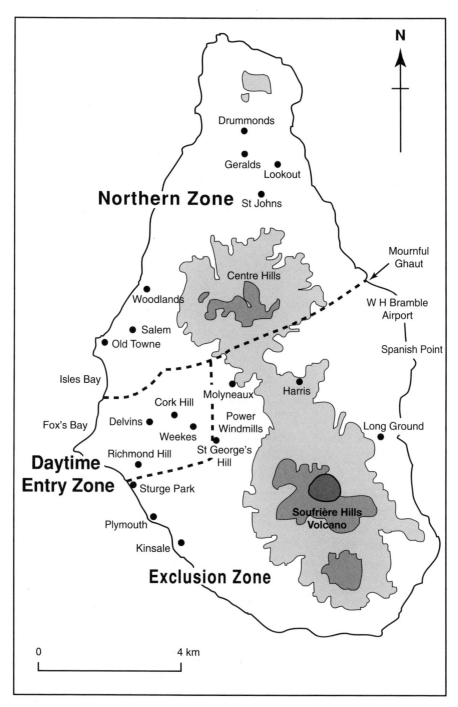

Volcano risk map showing the southern exclusion zone and the northern safe zone

List of Illustrations

List of Tables

Introduction

Purpose of the book

Advocates of unity among the former British colonies in the Caribbean usually emphasize their common history and cultural traditions. And indeed as countries of sugar, slavery and British colonialism, washed by the same Caribbean sea, the commonalities are undeniable. But equally evident is the uniqueness of each individual territory; each has its peculiar social and physical features. The Leeward Islands do not share the ethnic cleavage of Trinidad and Guyana with their large East Indian populations; Montserrat is hilly and volcanic, while Antigua, 12 air-minutes away, is mostly flat and coral; and the Caribs of St Lucia did not survive the European onslaught as they did in Dominica where some of their descendants exist at the present time.

There are common patterns, but each island has its peculiar story. This book is an attempt to study Montserrat's particular piece in the British Caribbean mosaic. Individual island studies are important because they can confirm or provide new insight on trends and identify variations on common themes. The strong Irish element in Montserrat, for instance, introduced a new facet in the social structure of a colonial society and in the discrimination and oppression endemic in that society.

With the continuing eruption of the Soufrière Hills volcano since 1995, Montserrat has added another chapter to its peculiar story. This episode not only reduced its habitable and cultivable space by almost two-thirds, but has given a new twist to its social and political history. The crisis has had a revolutionary impact on every facet of life including education, migration, social welfare, economy and politics and has provided both positive and negative lessons in disaster management and mitigation. An archipelago riddled with volcanoes is bound to have more than academic interest in this chapter of the island's story.

Even if Montserrat were to become an integral part of a mini Eastern Caribbean state or of a larger Caribbean union, Montserratians will remain in some ways a unique people. They and their forebears have occupied this giant rock as a geopolitical entity for nearly 350 years. A people's study of their written history is part of the process of discovering their identity and fostering national cohesion. A colony for over 350 years, Montserrat sorely needs that sense of identity and cohesion. Its people should be able to trace the road which they as a society have traversed unto the present and understand something of the forces that have shaped their journey and the present *locus*.

The history of the Caribbean is sometimes described as the history of sugar; by implication it is also the history of metropolitan exploitation and control. These twin factors, and more, have helped to shape Caribbean societies in their totality. For this reason, topics such as religion, education, arts and culture receive explicit attention. They are both producers and products of history; they mould and are moulded by our people.

Although over the last 25 years, the island has proved to be useful virgin territory for foreign scholars producing PhDs and other studies on various aspects of the society, no one has written a general history. Scholarly studies on the Leeward Islands such as those by Goveia[1] and Hall[2] make a very valuable contribution, but these are limited to particular periods. The present work aims to fill this obvious gap and provide, as far as possible, an analytical account of the evolution of Montserratian society from the time of European contact to the present. Information on some periods is scant and this is reflected in the work.

The only previous semblance of a general history of the island is the author's *History of Alliouagana: A Short History of Montserrat*, published in 1975. This was a very slim, rough-hewn volume based mainly on a limited number of secondary sources. The present work purports to be more authentic and comprehensive.

This book is directed to the general reader who is interested in the history of the island. But until there is a purpose-written text for schools, students of Form 3 and above should find it useful and it should prove a valuable reference text for teachers.

A note on sources

References in the book are not as numerous as they might have been if I were writing for a scholarly journal. I did not wish to blunt the appeal to the general reader by strewing the text too copiously with notes. But enough primary and secondary references are given to establish the scholarly integrity of the work and to support important conclusions and analytic statements.

The primary sources used are based mainly on documents housed at the Public Record Office at Kew Gardens, Richmond in England. These are chiefly the Colonial Office (CO) group, which deals with Montserrat, the Leeward Islands, Antigua and Montserrat, and the West Indies. Some records of the Treasury (T.71) dealing with slave registration and compensation, as well as the relevant Calendar of State Papers (CSP) were also consulted. Primary sources housed at Government House in Montserrat but managed by the Public Library were also very useful.

Some chapters benefited from valuable isolated documents. *The Sturge Family Papers*, for instance, yielded vital information on the cotton and lime industries and on the Montserrat Company which the Sturges founded. The papers were once available in Montserrat in the private possession of a grand-nephew of the famous Joseph Sturge. A *Board of Education Minutes Book (1925–1936)*, belonging to the Government House archives, provided information and insights on education at an interesting period.

The secondary sources are detailed in the Select bibliography, and only those of singular value are mentioned here. They include T. S. English's unpublished *Records of Montserrat* (1930) which is some 250 pages of typescript. It is a valuable source of information. English examined local records (including a collection of the laws of Montserrat) which have since been too badly damaged to be of much use. F. E. Peters, a pioneer Montserratian historian, wrote *A Brief History of Montserrat and her Recent Hurricanes* (1929) from his own experience and from interviews with persons who had been through the hurricanes. His work gives angles and anecdotes which escape the official reports. Two related works by Rev. A. Gwynn of Dublin, Ireland were of inestimable value in our study of the Irish in Montserrat. These are *Documents relating to the Irish in the West Indies* (1932) and 'Early Irish Emigration to the West Indies' (1929).

The Early Years of Montserrat: A Chronicle of the People Who Settled this Island, a typescript by Delores Somerville, is a mine of information on the first two centuries of the island's history, but with the emphasis on Europeans. It is written in a gossipy and familiar style, but it is based on authentic primary documents. Its usefulness, however, for scholarly purposes is limited, since she does not cite her sources. A copy is available in the Montserrat Public Library.

Two recent works merit mention because of the nature and quality of the research which produced them. One is the personally-published *Galways Plantation, Montserrat West Indies* by L. M. Pulsipher and C. M. Goodwin (1982). This is a valuable first-hand study of the economy, social structure and lifeways on a West Indian plantation. It has obvious implications for the study of history and society in the wider region. The other is a journal article, 'Free Labour and Economy in Seventeenth-Century Montserrat' (1989) by Dr Riva Berleant-Schiller. Central to this study are the *Papers* of William Stapleton, a famous seventeenth-century Governor of the Leeward Islands and a one-time Lieutenant-Governor of Montserrat. These papers are available at the Rylands Manuscript Library in Manchester.

We hope we have laid a solid foundation for later studies and the versions of emerging historians.

The physical setting

Mountainous and volcanic – these are the two words that best characterize the physical design of this $39\frac{1}{2}$ square-mile island which is variously described as 'ham-shaped', 'pear-shaped', a 'tear drop' or even as resembling 'a leg of mutton'. Situated in the inner arc of The Leeward Islands group in The Lesser Antilles, the island lies between 16° 40′ and 16° 49′ north latitude and between 60° 09′ and 62° 15′ west longitude. It is 25 miles south-west of Antigua, which is its main international transit point, and roughly the same distance north-west of French Guadeloupe, another international gateway.

Three lofty mountain ranges dominate the landscape, but the island is in fact made up of some seven masses, each representing an erupted volcano. From north to south these are: Silver Hill (1200 feet), Centre Hills (2400 feet), Garibaldi Hill (838 feet), St. George's Hill (1185 feet), Soufrière Hills (with an elevation of 3002 feet peaking at Mount Chance), South Soufrière Hills (2479 feet) and Roche's Bluff. Silver Hill was probably the first to erupt while the Soufrière Hills are the youngest.[3]

There is continual volcanic activity from many existing fumaroles. They give rise to chemical deposits, hot springs and sulphur fumes which tarnish silverware and discolour metals over a mile away. Volcanic minerals such as gypsum, alum, sulphur and iron oxides occur, but not in commercial quantities (some sulphur was collected and shipped to the United States of America in 1852). Geysers from the *soufrières* find their way to the valleys to form small boiling and bubbling lakes. Hot River on Tar River estate is an example, but the best-known is Hot Water Pond on the western coast in Plymouth. The water provides a bathing balm for rheumatism and other ailments, but only after a coin is tossed in as an oblation to the guardian spirit, according to legend.

Between 1897 and 1902 when Pelé in Martinique erupted, the island experienced frequent and unusual volcanic activity (as many as 100 tremors in a day).[4] These sparked the interest of volcanologists and geologists. Botanists were also interested in the effects of the exhalation on the vegetation. In fact, interest in and studies on the island's *soufrières* began with the visit to Soufrière and Galways of Dr N. Nugent in 1810.[5] F. A. Perret, an American volcanologist, visited in 1934 following the resumption of significant earthquake and volcanic activity. He tested water flowing from Upper Gages Soufrière and recorded temperatures of 34° to 90°. Perret was overcome by hydrogen sulphide fumes at his experimental station in Gages and had to be taken to the hospital for treatment. He noted that the gases were 'exceedingly irritating to the eyes and respiratory passages' but carried 'an odor not wholly unpleasant, of camphor-like quality'.[6]

Table 0.1 Probable eruptive sequence of Montserrat's volcanoes

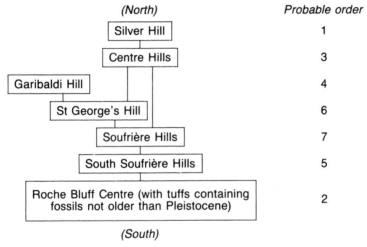

(North)	Probable order
Silver Hill	1
Centre Hills	3
Garibaldi Hill	4
St George's Hill	6
Soufrière Hills	7
South Soufrière Hills	5
Roche Bluff Centre (with tuffs containing fossils not older than Pleistocene)	2
(South)	

Source: A. G. Macgregor (1993), p. 13.

Some *soufrières* are of comparatively recent birth. The Gages *soufrière* originated in 1897 shortly after the floods of 1896, and was mildly active during the earthquake of 1898.[7] The connection between these three natural phenomena is instructive. New Cow Hill Soufrière, near Paradise ridge, was discovered as late as 1959.

The 1995–2001 volcanic eruptions not only transformed the green landscape for many a square mile around the soufrière hills, but have increased the size of the island through the deltas created by pyroclastic flows on the east and south of the island. New measurements could well reveal that the island is more than 40 square miles (103 km²). In addition some verdant valleys and ravines have become rock-strewn deserts. There is an austere beauty in the denuded landscape and the occasional glow-and-rumble from soufrière adds to this. It provides the island with a kind of natural *son et lumiére* which spectators enjoy from vantage hills like Garibaldi and Jack Boyd.

The island has 'no spacious harbours', though there are one or two small inlets on the north-western coast. This is because the hills rise sheer from the sea, producing a precipitous coastline. In the event of a violent storm, some craft still find it necessary to seek safe berth at Antigua or St. Kitts.

Another feature of the landscape is the many dry ghauts or gorges which dissect the hills. Many once carried streams, as a 1673 map reveals, and some still do so seasonally. Before the eruption Farms and Belham were more or less permanent streams but are more likely now to be periodic beds of mudflow. Tar (Hot) River in the east, always a conduit of soufrière heat and chemicals, is now smothered by its debris. Fortunately the fabled Runaway Ghaut, a draught from whose waters compels visitors to return to the island is still intact in the unmolested north of the island.

Montserrat's soils are volcanic and rocky. They are generally light and sandy on the low levels and clayey on the slopes. D. M. Lang gives us a detailed scientific study of the soils.[8] Only about 6000 acres of this hilly island are regarded as arable land. Fertility varies from area to area and erosion is a constant problem due to the steep slopes and careless agricultural practices.

The climate is tropical, with temperatures ranging from a high of 87°F in August to a low of 74°F in January and a relative humidity of between 70 and 80 per cent. The rainfall averages about 56 inches annually, but distribution is uneven throughout the island and throughout the year. The wettest months are September to December while the driest period stretches from January to July.

Natural vegetation was confined mostly to the summits of the Soufrière and Centre Hills where rain forest and elfin woodlands of mosses and lichens exist; but the Soufrière Hills are now bald. Wild palms dubbed 'mountain cabbage' abound near mountaintops, and fern groves decorate hillsides. 'Acacia savannahs' occur on lower areas, while sage bush and cacti are common around Silver Hill and South Soufrière.[9] A couple of mangrove swamps are still found along the western or leeward coast. Although the greenery has returned after the scorching winds of hurricane Hugo in 1989, the loss of large trees will be felt for several decades. The volcano too has taken its toll on the landscape on the flanks of the Soufrière Hills.

Montserrat's volcanic and mountanous landscape is sometimes referred to in a negative light. The beaches have black sand, volcanic fires smoulder and the terrain is rocky and hilly. But there is a positive side. Many enjoy bathing on black sand beneath clear water. In any case, with the current emphasis on eco-tourism, the potential for hot baths, hiking, mountain-climbing, scientific investigation, educational tours, and exploration of eco-systems is manifold. The current eruption adds an element of awe and even fear for some but it has also certainly enriched the environmental package.

J. Davy, a nineteenth-century visitor, found the Galways craters and their environs awesome and arresting:

> No island in these seas is bolder in its general aspect, more picturesque and I think I may add without exaggeration, more beautiful in the details of its scenery – indeed I might be tempted to say considering its fortunes, that it has the fatal gifts of beauty.[10]

The language is suspiciously extravagant, but Dr N. Nugent before him had described the same area as 'the most beautiful and romantic scenery'.[11] H. Coleridge also clothed the Chance's Soufrière area in poetic exuberance in 1825:

> This is a very wild and romantic scene. The whole of the bottom of the valley is broken into vast and irregular masses of clay and limestone which are scattered about in the utmost confusion, and render it a laborious task to scramble and leap from one to another. The surface of the ground is hot everywhere, and so much so near the streams of water which ran between the fragments that I could not keep my foot half a minute upon it. The water at its source boils up violently, and very gradually cools as it finds its way in a thousand meanders to the sea. A thick vapour slowly rises upwards till it meets the wind which cuts it off at a straight line and drives it down to the coast. The sides of the mounds of clay are entirely crusted with pure alum, formed by the constant action of the sulphuric acid of the water and the exhalations. In the midst of all this there is a green luxuriant vegetation of bushes and creepers; some of the flowers were marvellously beautiful, and seemed to me to be peculiar to the spot. The mountains, which rampart round this solitary glen, are of a skiey height; they appear indeed higher than they really are, for their lancet peaks are never seen except dimly and at intervals through the vast and moving masses of clouds, which are first driven from the east against the other side of the sierra, then are pressed upwards, and at last come rolling and tumbling over the summits into the vale below. The wood which clothes every inch of Chance's Mountain is soft, level and uniform, feathering him with a grasslike plumage as an Indian warrior, whilst every branch and every leaf bend devotedly forwards to the setting sun under the unceasing breath of the Trade Wind.[12]

One has to be grateful for Coleridge's elaborate description of the Chance's Soufrière for it may be decades before any recovery of the reality.

Wildlife

Montserrat's wildlife population is modest in variety. Agoutis, bats, birds, frogs and reptiles and a few species of fresh fish complete the roll. The size of the island and its distance from continents account for the paucity of animal life.

Archaeologists discovered fossils of the agouti and dog, but noted that they were not indigenous to the island.[13] The former, a game prize for dogs specially trained to sniff it out, was once important protein in the diet of some rural folks. Those that survived the chase are rarely seen, as they prefer the mountains. The fruit bat, another mammal, is reportedly also very rare.

The island's amphibians are confined to three species of frogs – the marine toad or crapaud, the tree frog and the mountain chicken. The mountain chicken (*leptodactylus fallax*) found only in Montserrat and Dominica among the Caribbean islands, is regarded in both islands as a dining delicacy. This terrestrial frog is hunted at night on mountain slopes, its natural habitat. Like the agouti and fruit bat, it is a threatened species and could disappear unless conservation measures are taken.

Jay Blankenship identified 30 land-species of birds which breed on the island.[14] The most interesting is the black and yellow oriole or tannia bird (*Icterus obert*) found only in Montserrat and now officially named as the national bird. It is mostly found at the head of the valley between Chance's and Farrell's mountains. Most islanders have never seen the national bird. Like its history, Montserrat's flora and fauna are still relatively unexplored.

1

Settlement

The slow years passed, and Cromwell's Irish came,
And found another Erin in your soil ...
Green isle of Montserrat, to-day your fame
Still rests upon the labour and the toil
With which your present settlers win their spoil
And from the earth the silky whiteness wrest
Of cotton, and the lime-trees' golden wealth
Yams and pawpaws, fruits of the far-famed West.

Spain visits

In the 1992 Columbus season, Montserrat was not without cause for celebration, but more in spite of Columbus than because of him. There are two senses in which he did not discover the island. In the first place, the concept of discovery meaning 'first-comer' is now generally discarded when applied to Columbus and the Americas. The 'new' world was not new when he came. The Amerindians had preceded him by over 1000 years, and the work of Ivan Van Sertima[1] and other scholars appears to show that Africans were in the Caribbean and Ancient America even before the Arawaks and Caribs. The list of first-comer claimants is rather long.

Columbus did not actually set foot on this 'emerald isle'. He called first at Dominica on Sunday 3 November on his second odyssey in 1493, his real destination being Hispaniola. After stopping at Marie Galante, Les Saintes and Guadeloupe, he came to Montserrat on 11 November. It was described as 'another island not very big which was twelve leagues distant'. He named it Santa Maria de Monserrate, in honour of the mountain abbey of that name outside Barcelona in Spain. (It was at this monastery that Ignatius Loyola, who founded the Jesuit order, devoted his life to the Virgin 30 years later.) The serrated outline of the island's mountains made the name suitable.

But Columbus was more interested in his fort at La Navidad, and the elusive jackpot of Cipangu, than in the emerald mountains of

Montserrat. Having performed the duty of naming it after a holy place, he moved on; gain, more than godliness, was the objective of his odyssey. He was also told by an Indian whom he had brought aboard from Guadeloupe that the Caribs had depopulated the island, so he wasted no time at Montserrat.[2] Spanish follow-up on Columbus's short sojourn in Montserrat's waters was confined to the appointment in 1520 of the island's first Governor, Antonio Serrano, whose commission included Antigua, Barbuda, Desirade, Dominica and Martinique. Like Columbus, he never set foot on Montserrat. The Arawaks and Caribs, therefore, were the only settlers who preceded the English, as far as we know. The Spanish left the name Montserrat, and in addition many of the animals and plants which they introduced to the region eventually found themselves here. Horses, donkeys, cattle, pigs, sheep, goat, dogs, cats, fowls, plantains and sugar-cane shoots are among the list. Spain also came indirectly in the form of certain diseases.

The Amerindians

Taino Indians settled on Montserrat as they did on other islands in the Lesser Antillean chain, and there is increasing material evidence of their presence.

The Amerindians of the Leeward Islands came from Venezuela, a major settlement in their trek from Asia, their original home. Archaeological research reveals that some settled at Trants on the windward coast of Montserrat around 500 BC and others on the leeward coast some time later. It is very likely that that group was preceded by the Ciboneys, a less-skilled and less culturally advanced Amerindian people.

Evidence in the form of artifacts and other recent archaeological finds throws some light on pre-Columbian life on the island. Among the relics is a clay object resembling partly a human face and partly an animal face. It was found in topsoil at Dagenham, an established prehistoric home-site. Dr Ripley Bullen of the Smithsonian Institute identified it as a modelled adorno typical of the Saladoid-Barrancoid Horizon. He suggests that the artifact is connected with the earlier movement of Indians off the mainland of South America, and closely resembles the Venezuelan pattern.[3] This therefore dates the artifact between 500 BC and AD 500 and thus points to the possibility of pre-Arawak life in Montserrat. The findings of Irving Rouse substantiate the idea of a pre-Arawak lesser Antillean people. His description of Saladoid pottery found in Guadeloupe, Montserrat's nearest neighbour to the south-east, closely resembles the Dagenham adorno. Rouse argues that Saladoid pottery is distinguishable by its bowls, which are shaped gracefully in the form of inverted bells, white-on-red painted designs and cross-hatchings in red paint.[4] The Dagenham adorno with its white-on-red design could well be the artistic effort of the Ciboneys, a Saladoid type from Venezuela.

David R. Watters identified five Amerindian habitation sites on the island, at Trants, Little Bay, Windward Bluff, Old Fort Point (in the south west corner of the island) and Dagenham Beach in Plymouth. A collection of shards, chipped stone flakes, shell tools and grindstones were discovered in varying excavations. He agrees that the ceramics at Trants support the view of Saladoid occupation around AD 200.[5] Their similarity to those found at Indian Creek in Antigua is corroborative evidence.

It is difficult to determine which of these five sites are Arawak and which are Carib. Watters himself made no effort to distinguish between Arawak and Carib sites, merely pointing out that these terms refer to language groups that are common in South America.[6] What is evident is that Amerindians inhabited the island at several points. They practised arts and crafts, raised crops, venerated their gods – a mixture of nature and ancestor worship – and buried their dead. Both the sites and the shards testify to these activities. Trants was a stable Amerindian community where up to 300 persons lived at one time according to Petersen even if the settlement was not continuous over some 2000 years of their occupation of the island. The evidence is rich in their pottery and stone tools and the remnants of their food sources – fish, shell fish, agouti, the 'rice rat', iguana and manioc or cassava. Their 'permanent' intensive settlement is also evidenced by their manufacture of stone beads in which they traded.[7] Watters' five locations are near the coast on good arable land near water-courses and are all at low elevations within easy access to the sea.

Excavations at Trants in 1995 unearthed further dramatic evidence of Amerindian occupation in the form of Amerindian skeletons. In fact the superstitious hold that the eruption of the volcano in that year was divine retribution for thus desecrating the graves of these forbears.

Earlier in this century, plantation-owner Seymour Wylde Howes collected surface artifacts and secured others from burial mounds at Trants. He unfortunately sold them to the Museum of American Indians in New York. Savage English, who saw the collection, provides us with a description which is worth quoting at some length.

Most of the Trants' finds are images of no great size, some of the best of them being quite small which very possibly may once have been *lares et penates* – household gods – mascots to use the present-day word for such things. Most of them represent human faces, and these have a decided resemblance to similar works of art from Mexico and Central America. Others are somewhat generalised four-footed creatures though among them frogs are unmistakable. And a few of them are carved from stone which certainly did not come from Montserrat or from any of the volcanic islands near it.[8]

English regards these relics 'found invariably near the sea' as Cariban. The relics and their location point to a settled farming culture characterized by a readiness for departure either in flight from enemies or in pursuit of new pastures. The Montserrat artifacts may well be a mixture of Arawak and Carib, whose cultures had some common features if only because Carib men married Arawak women. When the combative Caribs drove the Arawaks from the island they may have succeeded them not just in time but in place.

At the time of European contact, Montserrat was Carib country. It was they who gave it its first name 'Alliouagana' according to Dominican friar Father Breton. This supposedly means 'land of the prickly bush', a possible reference to a species of the aloe plant. English suggests that the Caribs preferred Guadeloupe and Dominica as permanent homes, due to the scarcity of native animals and even fish in Montserrat. This may be so, but they at least raided it periodically and sojourned there. Irish missionary Father John Stritch has left an account of a 1650 Carib raid which occurred while he was administering sacrament to Catholics in the woods. He reported that 2000 (very likely an exaggeration) 'savage Caribs', who had been waging guerilla war against the English, attacked, burning houses, killing persons and plundering shops.[9] His sympathy for the Irish, whose dispossession by the English he lamented, did not extend to the Caribs whom he bigotedly dubbed as 'savage'. The Caribs rightly regarded themselves as the dispossessed.

Carib raids on the British Leeward Islands, as well as on the neighbouring French colonies at St Christopher and Guadeloupe, forced both nations to cooperate for their mutual defence, although they were sometimes political adversaries and economic competitors. By a 1659 treaty, an alliance for offensive and defensive action against the Caribs was formed by the English and French Governors. M. Houel of Guadeloupe and Roger Osborne of Montserrat were responsible for joint action drawing on central funding at Basseterre in St Kitts.[10] This was a significant and fortunate occurrence for the colonizers, for the Caribs were not only effective warriors, but shrewd negotiators and strategists. They often played one nation off against the other, attacking one only after making peace with the other. By this means 'they politicly did maintain friendship with one of the said two nations'.[11] In addition, they enlisted the assistance of runaway slaves who had no reason to be loyal to their masters and, to the disappointment of the British, they refused to be lured by the pacifist bait of Christianity. It was a small step from Stritch's prejudiced account to castigating the Caribs as cannibals, a ploy which Akenson correctly observes was a common way of degrading one's enemies.[12]

The 1659 treaty gave Montserrat some protection, but only for a season. In 1666, the Caribs were again on the war-trail, burning and pillaging plantations, thereby setting back the young sugar industry in an island which they doubtlessly regarded as their own. Reporting on yet another raid in 1676, Governor Stapleton concluded that Indian raids were the greatest problem of the colony. Many persons were killed in this attack. After a respite of six years, the Caribs struck once more. Stapleton had anticipated the assault and had made detailed preparations to counter it. Indeed, the General Assembly was deliberating at Nevis on war strategies and on the mode of financing them, when the Indians made a surprise attack on Montserrat on 13 November 1682.

This was a devastating blow. Utilizing their well-tested guerilla tactics and their navigational skills with small boats, the Indians landed through an inlet that was inaccessible to British ships. They burned a sugar factory, killed two boys and carried off a number of slaves. In short, they deliberately struck at the source of the island's wealth. It was months (April 1683) before Stapleton could make a retaliatory pursuit, landing on Dominica, the Indian war-base. Neither the terrain nor the weather was friendly to the English. Very few Indians were killed and the 11 reported by Stapleton may have been an exaggeration, as conflicting French reports appeared to show.[13] He did, however, paralyze the Indians somewhat for the time being by destroying many of their canoes. After 1682, the Caribs abandoned the island to the Europeans. The *Stapleton Papers* on the island's public expenses for 1670–80 contain an item 'provision for soldiers and Indians'. So a few Indians were obviously in government employment, most likely as soldiers or intelligence agents.

Abiding Amerindian cultural legacy is thin. If they affected the vegetation, this was marginal; and there is no evidence as in Dominica of miscegenation, either with the Europeans or with the Africans. Apart from the name Alliouagana, used mostly by a few scholars and cultural workers, and remnants of art and pottery, all that is noticeable is a number of words that have passed into general Caribbean usage. These include cassava, guava, barbecue, hurricane, maize, potato, hammock and tobacco. These are not just words, however, but are the index of a culture. Central to that culture is the sense of struggle in defence of communal territory and personal liberty.

The Anglo-Irish settlement

In an interesting chronicle written in 1936, George I. Mendes claims that the French were the first Europeans to settle in Montserrat, though only temporarily. Escaping from St Kitts after the Spanish invasion in 1629, D'Esnambuc stopped first at Antigua, but decided, after a hurried exploration, to make for Montserrat 'whose mountainous aspect gave them some hope that they would there find some shelter in a more healthy locality'. Failing to find an inlet on the rocky eastern coast, they came to the western side and landed at Old Road Bay.[14] Mendes cites no source for this claim, but it seems plausible although in his pamphlet generally, he is wrong on some details and right on others. The French stayed long enough, it seems, to bestow on Montserrat the soubriquet 'Montpellier of the West' but apparently returned to the mother colony of St Kitts once the Spanish threat disappeared. Montserrat perhaps narrowly missed being a Gallic country.

Several groups settled in the island between 1629 and 1624 and there is no reliable evidence that 1632 was the colonizing date although this was generally accepted for centuries. There is some evidence of a possible 1629 settlement by a group of Irish who may have reached Montserrat by a somewhat circuitous route which included the Amazon, Trinidad and Surinam.[15] The 'second' group was Sir Henry Colt and his voyaging companions who left us this valuable description of his visit in 1631.

> Weddensday, 20 July. We arrived att Montserrat ye land rownd montaynous & full of woods, with noe inhabitants; yett weer ye footstepps seen of some naked men … We approchinge this ye harbar land & sea befoor we would lett fall our Anchors. All day we keep watch uppon ye mayne mast; but being cleer we come to our Anchor on ye weast side of Montserrat, in sight of Redunda our next Iland, beinge noe other then a single rock.[16]

It is not clear how Sir Henry Colt knew that the men were naked from their footsteps. We can, however, conclude that the island was without habitants in 1631, even though there was a recent Amerindian visit. Then Father Andrew White, a Jesuit priest travelling from the American colonies to England via the West Indies, made this entry in his diary for 26 January 1634: 'By noone we came before Montserrat, where is a noble plantation of Irish Catholique, whom the Virginians would not suffer to live with them because of their religion'.[17] These two accounts help us to date the English settlement of the island between late 1631 and late 1633.

It is very possible though that this wave of Virginian Catholics was preceded by settlers from neighbouring St Kitts who for the most part were similarly driven out by Protestant intolerance. They apparently had the blessings of Thomas the founder of St Kitts in 1624 who always had provisional plans for the settlement of Montserrat; when he returned home in 1625 he obtained a charter for its 'custody' along with St Christopher and Barbados.[18] It is likely that the Father White contingent was attracted to Montserrat by news of a Roman Catholic asylum in the little Antilles. Economic pull factors accounted for the presence of many Irish people in Montserrat by 1650 but it was unique among the Caribbean English colonies in having freedom of religion as a dominant motive for its establishment. St Kitts may well have arrived in 1632 but we have no documentary evidence for this.

The person responsible though for the backbone of the colony and for the 'noble plantation' which White described, was Anthony Brisket, the first Governor; and it was he who received the necessary legal authority to plant and administer this composite colony. Montserrat became a mixed colony in another sense. Later in the century a number of Roman Catholics were dispatched hither by Cromwell, the anti-papal English ruler, following his victory at Drogheda in Ireland. Many of these were forced into exile without any proper indenture. What this suggests though is that most of the settlers who came to the island did so on the basis of negotiated contracts. There were significant numbers though, whom Cromwell transported either because they were political prisoners or a financial burden on the state. The latter included orphans, widows, beggars, vagrants, social misfits and the unemployed.[19]

The exact location of the first settlement is still a matter of debate and speculation. It could have been near Carr's Bay, a good harbour far north along the leeward coast, a short distance from St Kitts, where there is also a Carr's Bay. Some regard Sugar Bay at Kinsale as the first site, since a town of that name had been prominent in the area of Irish concentration which spread from Plymouth southward to St Patrick's and the fact that the town of 'Kingsale' in Ireland was a main exit port to the new world in the 1630s gives it a good claim. There is, however, no hard evidence to support this. It is also very likely that Anthony Brisket, the first Governor, gave his name to both the first settlement and the first town. This is at Brisket Bay, which is identical to Old Road Bay, the name of another St Kitts bay. Brisket town was later renamed Stapletown, another Governor giving it his name. What seems certain is that the earlier permanent settlements were on the leeward coast stretching from Old Road River (Belham) to Kinsale.

Plymouth became the capital town early in the second half of the seventeenth century. A wall at the gaol in Plymouth still bears the inscription 'erected in 1664'. A 'Plymouth Town' is shown on a coastal map (Fig. 4) commissioned by William Stapleton in 1673, although it was situated on Dagenham beach somewhat north of the heart of the established capital. Giving the name of an English town to the capital was consistent with the policy of the time. In 1696 there were small townships at Bransby, Old Road and Carr's Bay, but these were still considered 'more remote and not so well inhabited as other parts'. They were, however, considered important enough to have a guard consisting of at least four men. At that point Kinsale, just south of Plymouth, was still a bustling town where many servants and slaves came to trade and tipple.

Irish dissidents were glad to have established Montserrat as a haven from Protestant persecution but, as we shall see later, official persecution followed them. Asylum apart, Montserrat was just another colony for metropolitan exploitation. Letters patent dated 2 July 1627[20] gave James Hay, the spendthrift Earl of Carlisle, proprietary rights over Montserrat, together with other Caribbean islands. In return, the king exacted £300 annually. The proprietors farmed out their rights to governors who themselves had to extract wealth from the inhabitants. This situation was the ideal recipe for exploitation. The burden of this pyramid of exploitation rested squarely on the indentured servants and then the slaves, literally grinding many of the latter to death.

Montserrat's first Governor, Anthony Brisket (variously spelled Bryskett, Briskett) a native of Wessex, England was of Italian ancestry, but his family had acquired property in Ireland after James I had dispossessed that country.[21] Possibly through his connection with John White of Ballyhea, County Cork, who was a surveyor in Virginia, Brisket owned property there before 1632.[22] It is not surprising therefore that his Irish colony was partly peopled with settlers from Virginia. In 1636 Brisket was in England petitioning planters and supplies to Montserrat. Charles must have been pleased to learn that he was building a church of stone and brick 'for the glory of God and your Majesty's honour'. This was the first St Anthony's Anglican church, to which Brisket probably gave his name out of vanity. He had cause to be proud of this church if its outstanding masonry and fine woodwork evident in its pews, pulpit and ceiling belonged to the first St Anthony's church. The church established the fact that Montserrat was an Irish island with an English government. Add some Scottish settlers and the scene was set for religious bigotry and ethnic strife.

Catholic or Protestant, whether they came directly from Ireland or by way of other Caribbean colonies, the vast majority of Montserratian colonists in the seventeenth century and beyond were Irish. Among these were several from the 'Galway tribes' with names like Blake, Lynch, Kirwan, Hussey, Burke, Tuite, French, Skerrett, Browne and Meade.

Graveyards in Montserrat still bear undying evidence of their adventurous and in many cases prosperous sojourn.[23] Judging from contemporary arrangements, the majority of the settlers contracted or 'indented' themselves to serve for a term of five to seven years in return for £10 to £12 in cash or in kind. This service was not comparable to black servitude and both were not part of the same continuum. Indentures were largely freely negotiated contracts between compatriots and were in fact investments. Unlike slaves who served for life and were brutally and forceably subjected to another race, they were free to go or stay at the end of their bond and their children did not inherit their status.[24]

By 1654 the characteristic colonial social structure had emerged – an Anglo-Irish planter class, a number of 'Christian' servants and a sizeable population of black slaves. In Montserrat, unlike in the other British islands, the middle group was almost all Irish. In 1649, there were over 1000 white families, most of whom were Irish, according to J. Oldmixon.[25] In that same year, the Irish element was further increased by political prisoners who were deported by Cromwell after the battle of Drogheda. In 1671, just about five years after the wasting invasion by the French and the Caribs, the number of men 'able to bear arms' was put at 1175 and there were 523 slaves.[26] In time the blacks would outnumber the whites, but not before sugar had totally transformed the economy around the end of seventeenth century.

By 1650, England had taken firm control over Montserrat and, in the view of Roman Catholic priest Father John Stritch (who would have been understandably biased), had dispossessed the Irish. It is not surprising therefore, that in 1655 Cromwell, the *enfant terrible* of the Irish, was entertained at Montserrat with marked civility by Governor Roger Osborne, on his expedition to capture Hispaniola.[27] Selection of governors was important in this Roman Catholic colony. Anthony Brisket was succeeded by his father-in-law Roger Osborne in 1649, and Brisket's son Anthony 'the second', also became Governor between 1662 and 1667. He was succeeded by William Stapleton, a former soldier 'of known valour, good conduct and great integrity, was born in Ireland and therefore understands the better to govern his country men'. Stapleton put an end to the dynastic rule of the Brisket clan and kinsfolk. But he merely replaced one dynasty with another. When he was elevated to be Governor-General of the Leeward Islands, he was succeeded by his brother Edmund, by James Cottar, a soldier colleague, and then by another brother, Redmond. In the Stapletons, the Crown made good use of a tried and trusted Irish family. The early governors were usually English or Anglo-Irish Protestants who shared English assumptions on the nature of colonial administration. The list of governors makes it clear that Montserrat was ruled for England and not as a Caribbean Irish outpost. Charles Wheler, the first Governor of the Leeward Islands, wanted all the governors of Montserrat to be English, although it was a colony of mostly Irish people.

The church was often used in the Caribbean as an instrument of colonization and even oppression. By its very existence, an established Anglican church in Montserrat was an affront to the majority of the inhabitants, who were Roman Catholics. When Father John Stritch took up office in 1651, he concluded that the Irish Roman Catholics were a persecuted sect, without any religious freedom. In fact, the island was without a Catholic priest for five years prior to his arrival. It was not until 1668 that Roman Catholic priests were permitted to minister to their community openly. Before this time, priests had to be smuggled in disguised as fishermen or, as in the case of Father Stritch, as a merchant or a wood-buyer.[28] The Irish saw English control as a dispossession and they long remembered it and the related ethnic discrimination. The petition by Nicholas Lynch and other Roman Catholics for a relief from the burden of supporting Protestant ministers drew a positive response. In 1687 the Governor of the Leeward Islands, Sir Nathaniel Johnson, *ordered* that both Catholic and Protestant clergy be paid by their vestries instead of from the national Treasury. The treatment of Roman Catholics was not consistently harsh. Governor Johnson, in particular, was noted for his impartiality in dealing with Roman Catholics.

Roger Osborne, who was somewhat Machiavellan in his approach to governance, was prepared to tolerate the Roman Catholics provided that they did not make any trouble. And he was not unaware of the secretive visits and ministrations of their priests. For their part the Catholics found it convenient to occasionally conform to Anglicanism in order to access pastoral services as well as in the interest of their own economic survival. In all likelihood there were also convenient conversions to Anglicanism for the same practical reasons including the fact that Roman Catholic priests were not available on any consistent and reliable basis. Akenson has shown that this compromise, which was consciously worked out by Governor Roger Osborne, served the island and the colonists well. Officially, Catholicism was illegal but unofficially, mass and sacraments were allowed in the shadows. In fact seventeenth century Montserrat was not a hotbed of religious fervour or object of missionary zeal. It had no resident priest until 1756 in Dominic Lynch and there was allegedly no Catholic church building until 1852 although staunch and wealthy Catholic families like the Hamiltons allowed their homes to be used as churches.[29]

In 1676, Leeward Island Governor William Stapleton reported to the Lords of Trade that the Protestant church was the 'prevalent persuasion'.

By 'prevalent' he obviously meant dominant, since at that time Catholics outnumbered Protestants six to one. And yet in 1688 efforts were being made to obtain an 'able orthodox minister according to the canons of the church of England'.[30] Both the church and the minister were still maintained at public expense. The Irish were certainly not amused that they were required to support an institution which was the cause of alienation from their original settlements in St Kitts and Virginia. Furthermore, Anglo-Irish conflicts in Britain were reflected in Anglo-Irish relationships in Montserrat. Dunn sums it up pithily when he observes that 'the Irish triton looks glum at discovering that even in the remotest corner of the Caribbees, he cannot escape English mastery'.[31]

When William Stapleton commissioned the first official census in 1678, there were 1869 Irish and 992 black slaves in a population of 3674, as Table 1.1 indicates.

Table 1.1 Census of 1678–9[32]

	Men	*Women*	*Children*	*Total*
English	346	175	240	761
Irish	769	410	690	1869
Scottish	33	6	13	52
Whites	1148	591	943	2682
Blacks	400	300	292	992

Although they were in the majority, the Irish were treated as a minority group. The English and Scots transported their differing religious beliefs and prejudices to the island, thereby adding to the climate of unease. Stapleton therefore found it necessary to pass a law to curb the tension and the threat of ethnic eruption. Thus is his oft-quoted Act to restrain

> several odious distinctions used by the English, Scotch and Irish reflecting on each other (English Dog, Scots Dog, Tory, Irish Dog, Cavalier, Roundhead, and many other opprobrious, scandalous and disgraceful terms), and therefore ordains that if any such or the like reflections are used in the island by any person, stranger or foreigner, the offenders shall be prosecuted as breakers of the public peace, and shall abide such fines or punishments as shall be imposed on them by the Governor and Council.

This law did not really address the Irish problem in any profound way and other measures had to be taken to blunt the edge of the Irish threat to the public peace. They were, it seems, generally relegated to the southern and south-eastern districts of the island where the climate was drier and the soil more arid. St Patrick's, with its large concentration of Irish, was a colony within a colony. While they may have been shoved there as part of the campaign of discrimination and marginalization, the demands of ethnic solidarity may also have led to the southern build-up.

The plight of the Irish drew sympathy and concern from other Catholic colonies in the region. The Governor of the Dominican Republic, for instance, was accused of exacerbating anti-English feelings by inciting the Irish to desert the island and escape the tyranny of the English 'heretic dogs'. The Irish, however, chose to deal differently with the problem. They preferred, if they could, to replace the Anglo-Protestant administration by one that identified closely with their religious persuasion. The many hegemonic wars fought between the French and English in and for the island gave them ample opportunity to attempt this. We turn to this matter in the next section.

Ethnic conflicts

As was observed above, the Caribs did not take kindly to their displacement by the English and they raided the colony more than once. In 1666 they added to the havoc and confusion caused by a French invasion by attacking the island 'in their pirogues' and again in 1676 when it was reported by the Irish (who were not always scrupulously objective) that they committed murders in Montserrat. The Irish, on the other hand, responded to their religious humiliation and harsh economic fortunes by rebelling and colluding with the French invaders. They rebelled in 1666, but this became swallowed up in the onset of a major French assault in which they played a vital role. This was an important episode in the history of Anglo-Irish relations in that it demonstrated the nature of the Irish threat and forced the English to devise a policy and strategies to deal with it.

The Irish provided the French with intelligence information in the war of 1665–67. With Irish guidance, the French landed at Kinsale, an Irish haunt, and thence proceeded to the English fortifications. The French General de Barre burnt and pillaged much of the island, but left the property of the Irish intact.[33] With the help of the Irish, the French captured and controlled the colony until the Treaty of Breda, which formally ended the war in 1667.

After this event the English administration could not trust the 'wicked and rebellious Irish', and Welsh and Scots were requested to make up the population shortfall and give greater ethnic balance. Stapleton's 1678 census shows no Welsh and only 52 Scots, so this particular strategy could not have been very successful. It seems as though the aim of the French was to establish a Franco-Irish colony with those Irish with whose alliance they had captured the island. Montserrat came very close to being carved into a bi-national territory as St Kitts and St Martin were.

Embittered Anglo-Irish relations in Britain, and the Irish conduct in 1666–67 caused the relationship between the English and the Irish to worsen in Montserrat. Between 1689 and 1712 the French made several sorties on the island with varying success and the Irish were instrumental in many of them. During this period the English decided to adopt the strategy of winning over the Irish by persuading them that their own security and economic interests depended on their loyalty to the British Crown. Where this failed, the administration ensured that the Irish did not 'command flags of truce' unless they were men of proven integrity, with important stakes in the colony. Lieutenant-Governor Hamilton employed similar tactics in Nevis as did his Montserratian counterpart, Hodges.[34]

Tact and diplomacy were even more necessary in dealing with the Irish as the English numbers fell. By 1689, when they outnumbered the English by three to one, they openly threatened to renounce their British allegiance and give up the island to the French. Writing from Nevis, the government seat of the Leeward Islands, John Netheway made this claim in his appeal to the King and Queen for men, arms and ammunition.[35] He may have exaggerated somewhat, but the threat was very real in this frontier society. Their treatment had made the Irish 'very turbulent and rebellious' in the words of the Governor of the Leeward Islands in 1690.

As the Lieutenant-General in 1689, Codrington appealed to Irish vested interest in the colony, which he argued would outweigh all other considerations, but he also kept the threat of military force hanging over their heads. In his view, since they were allowed to indulge in their religion and to enjoy their estates, they ought therefore to understand that they needed the protection of the English; this they could hope for only if they were loyal. They were not immune to French depredation and pillage. They could even be transported to another island, he contended. In his words, 'The French fleet cannot wait until every Dermot and Bryan has regularly packed up'.[36] This all seems logical although he may have underestimated the depth of animosity generated by the socio-religious issue.

It was expedient for Codrington to use diplomacy given the inefficient arrangement for the island's defences. But in the same breath he vowed that the Irish could expect no mercy if the British fleet came. Force was not far from his mind. Casting a double racial slur, he cynically opined than 'an assinegoe may as soon be taught logic as they (the Irish) to understand it'. He could not gamble on the cooperation of the Irish, so he made certain contingency plans. All slaves and valuable goods belonging to both English and Irish were to be taken to Nevis and Antigua and their return would be conditional on the loyalty of the owners; the English and certain Irish would be taken away, leaving an Irishman in charge of the island. The notorious British expedient of divide-and-rule was discernible in these plans, which were designed to cow the Irish into compliance as much as anything else. The strategy was successful to some extent. The captain of a vessel arrived from Cork with beef in 1689 and expressed regret that the island was ruled over by King William. Codrington promptly ordered the Governor to arrest him and there was no hostile reaction from the Irish population.[37]

This does not mean that all was well. Events such as an alleged Popish plot in England in 1687 and a series of Irish rebellions in the Leeward Islands in 1689–1712, kept Irish distrust and persecution alive in Montserrat for a long time. Punishment meted out for Irish misdemeanours was sometimes quite harsh. In 1689, a number of women were caught running away with a canoe. The Council ordered that they be given up to 39 lashes on their bare backs, complete their indenture, and then be sold for another four years as compensation to their masters.[38] Yet the mixed policy of stick and diplomacy attained some eventual success. The French invasion of 1712 was launched at Carr's Bay and Plymouth rather than Kinsale, the Irish capital further south on the leeward coast. The French army of over 3000 nevertheless carried off 1200 slaves as booty, after overpowering the English and burning the town. St Anthony's church, that first great symbol of intolerance and anti-Catholic chauvinism, was totally destroyed, as it had been in the 1667 raid. The Irish were not, however, blamed on this occasion. Indeed, in 1723, the Assembly of Montserrat, and its Romish inhabitants, were commended for loyalty to the Crown.

The Irish were still never fully trusted and continued to be denied basic civic liberties right down to the last quarter of the eighteenth century. In 1749 the Assembly passed a law which made it mandatory for all voters to take oaths of allegiance to the King and the Anglican Church. This had the effect of denying Roman Catholics an active role in the government unless they rejected the Catholic Pretender to the English throne and certain tenets of their faith.

The Catholics found this law repugnant given their large property interests, and they formally protested. Their lawyer, Martin, submitted that they had zealously defended the island, if only because they owned property and that their religion and their sympathies with the Pretender were not incompatible with loyalty to the island and its government. And, indeed, the Catholics were willing at this point to take the oath of supremacy. Pratt, the opposing counsel, argued, on the other hand, that the law was passed to protect Protestant interests lest the Roman Catholics, who compromised 80 per cent of the population and who were their avowed enemies, should dominate the colony. This was as open an admission as any of institutionalized discrimination based on the felt need for a minority to hog political power. The law was obviously a move by an Anglo-Protestant Assembly to block the road of the Irish Catholics to political power. The notion of an Anglo-Irish colony as a civil and political entity was never accepted before the first quarter of the nineteenth century.

It would be wrong, however, to convey the impression that all Irish Catholics were in conflict with the island's administration. Lawyer Martin was correct in contending that Catholics of substance were willing to compromise on religious purity in the interest of material and political advancement. The Ryan family of Cove and Palmetto Point in St Patrick's, into which the eighteenth-century diarist John Baker married, is an example. His father-in-law, Thomas Ryan, had a household of two white women, one white child and one black man, according to the 1677–78 census. In 1729 either he or his son owned a house, cattle, a mill, 18 slaves, including four children, at White River and a white household of eight, consisting of two men, one woman, two boys and three girls. He owned an estate of some 82 acres – 18 under sugar, 24 under other crops and 40 uncultivated. On it were 17 cattle, five horses, five goats and one hog, and he kept three firearms. A brother, John Ryan, was a member of the Assembly in 1678. Although he was understandably not one of the six members of the Assembly who congratulated Charles II for his escape from the Popish Plot,[39] he and his extended family were law-abiding Roman Catholics for strategic reasons. Their ample possessions gave them a stake in the island.

So far we have concentrated on the European settlers and omitted the Africans who came as slaves. While the in-fighting went on, they were producing wealth for the privileged classes. The oppression of Irish Catholics was a holiday compared to the racial misery which the slaves endured. Like the Irish, they retaliated when they could, but they were less well-equipped and they had no real allies. In Chapter 3, we shall deal with the slaves of Montserrat, to whom Montserratian playwright Edgar White once referred, in a meaningful exaggeration, as the slaves of slaves. In a later chapter also, we shall examine the Irish legacy to Montserrat.

Administration in the seventeenth century

In accordance with the letters of authority granted to the Earl of Carlisle in 1627, Montserrat's first form of government was proprietary government. In effect, King Charles I leased the administration of the colony along with

Barbados, the Windward Islands and the rest of the Leeward Islands, to the Proprietor, in return for an annual levy of £300 and one-fifth of any gold and silver discovered. As Proprietor, which literally means 'owner', he had authority to impose laws and tax the colonists for his benefit. This sounds like naked autocracy, but in theory the Proprietor was to make laws with the consent of the free inhabitants of the island. For several years this meant a small number, which excluded the Irish indentured servants.

The islands were loosely supervised from Barbados, headquarters of Carlisle's province. He sublet his authority to Governors who ruled, made laws and collected the taxes. One of the taxes due to the Proprietor was 20 pounds of tobacco per head. The overheads were heavy in these plantation colonies and in Montserrat the blacks and Irish indentured servants felt the full weight of the fleecing overclass. Using what was probably a nominated Council of an advisory nature (before 1664), the Governor administered the colony by issuing official *Orders*, as Anthony Brisket did, when in 1638 he promulgated what may have been Montserrat's first law – to ensure proper observance of Sunday.

Montserrat's first Governors were themselves estate-owners, first among equals, as it were. This presented problems when some landlords surpassed the Governor in wealth and grand living. As another planter, he became embroiled in disputes with his constituents over mundane private affairs. He sometimes did this in the guise of meting out justice. In 1654, for instance, the island's second Governor, Roger Osborne, was furious when the Anglo-Dutchman Samuel Waad inherited Anthony Brisket's estate by marrying his widow, who happened to be Osborne's sister. Osborne brought a spurious charge of mutiny against him, condemned him, ordered him to be shot, and seized his estate. Part of Waad's crime in his father's view, was that his son 'lived in better estate'[40] than the Governor. This is plausible because Waad had a very prosperous estate valued at £12 000. In addition, Osborne wanted guardianship of his sister (Elizabeth), her young son Anthony Brisket and, of course, with them the Brisket fortunes. Osborne's action was resented by many, some of whom accused him of being partial to his 'barbarous Irish' compatriots. A petition to the Lord Proprietor requested that the judicial murder be inquired into, but that the young Brisket be awarded his father's estate. The case was referred to Daniel Searle, the Governor of Barbados, for a decision, but no punishment was meted out to Osborne, who continued in his governorship. This episode gives an insight into the corrupt, callous and personal nature of gubernatorial administration in early Montserrat.

Anthony Brisket II seemed to have benefited from the Proprietor's decision. In 1666 he owned three estates – Fort House plantation of 525 acres, Waterworks of 573 acres and the third described as the South side of the River plantation (Weekes presumably) of 300 acres. He too ran into trouble, but of a different nature. When the French invaded in 1666, he accepted a commission from the French king and General De Barre to govern the island under French auspices. For this, he lost his office, and his estates were confiscated by the Crown. His plea that he reluctantly responded to the entreaty of the colonists who wanted protection from the 'fury of barbarous bloody Indians and others'[41] did not avail. Nor did his claim to special consideration based on his father's pioneering efforts in the colony, although he seemed to have given some protection to the English inhabitants from Irish attack. His sin in virtually surrendering the colony to the French was regarded as unpardonable, and he was fortunate not to have been charged with treason.

Given the economic and other woes of the governors, their conflicting interests and their lack of administrative experience, it is not surprising that the colonists were not happy with proprietary government. Besides, proprietary rights affected land tenureship, since planters could not obtain proper legal titles to their lands. In effect, the entire island had been leased to the Earl of Carlisle. The population was pleased when proprietary government was abolished and Crown Colony government was established in 1664. Although there have been occasional changes in the island's constitution, Montserrat has remained a Crown Colony ever since, sharing the dubious distinction with the British Virgin Islands, Turks and Caicos Islands, Cayman Islands and Anguilla.

Proprietary government gave way to a limited form of representative government through a Governor/Lieutenant-Governor Council and Assembly. The Governor was appointed by the King whom he represented, while the Council consisted of 12 local landowners appointed by the King on the Governor's recommendation. They were a check on his powers as well as his advisers and they also formed a kind of court of appeal.

The Assembly, the stronghold of the plantocrats, was a very important branch of the government. It was comprised of two freeholders from each parish. Members had to be Anglicans, possessing property yielding an annual income of £100, or earning a yearly income of £150, or with an annual income of £450 derived from a trade or profession practised in the island. The franchise was confined to free, white property-owners. The Assembly made laws and raised revenue to administer the territory and to pay royal levies. The limited franchise and the legislator qualifications caused representative government to resemble an oligarchy more than a democracy.

The most important source of royal revenue from the colonies was a $4\frac{1}{2}$ per cent duty on all exports. This was institutionalized in 1664, when William Willoughby persuaded each of the Leeward Islands to enact the duty. The resulting Leeward Islands Acts abolished all proprietary dues and bestowed legal titles on landowners. The duty was re-enacted in 1668 following the restoration of the island by the French, who had captured it in 1667. This revenue was too important to be left to chance or legal vagaries. Equally, private landowners wanted to be certain about the continuing legality of their freeholds.

With the institution of an Assembly, the colony was divided into four parishes or administrative districts – St Peter's, St Anthony's, St Patrick's and St George's. On the basis of these units, laws were enforced, the militia organized, public works executed and members (usually two for each district) were elected to the Assembly. St Anthony's and St Patrick's were amalgamated later to form a single parish.

This form of representative government consisting of Governor, Council and Assembly was roughly analogous to the Westminster system of King, Lords and Commons. Tensions developed between the Governor, who mainly represented metropolitan interests, and the Assembly, who championed self- and collegial interest. The slaves were without voice or advocates and sometimes some classes of Irish were just a little better off. Today, tensions continue to arise occasionally between the local government and the Westminster government, but these are never nearly as serious nor as frequent.

The administration of the island was somewhat modified in 1671 when a Leeward Act established a Leeward Island Federation, with its headquarters first in Nevis and later (1698) in Antigua. It sprang from a mutual desire on the part of the islands, on the one hand, and Barbados on the other, to be independent of each other. The Leeward Islands felt that their defence was neglected during the Dutch War (1665–67), and the Barbadians regarded the Leeward Islands as unwelcome competitors in the sugar industry. They even wished that the islands were sunk and that no more be settled.[42] This is the prelude to the long, unending and tortuous saga of British West Indian disintegration. As would obtain always, economic considerations and insular particularities loomed large.

Montserrat's behaviour gave another twist to the disintegration story. Montserratians saw Willoughby as a genuine protector, and recalled receiving aid from Barbados when the French menace confronted them. To make matters worse, the island was excluded from the de-federation and re-federation conferences establishing the new composite colony. Feelings ran so high on the matter, that 27 of the leading colonists signed a petition to formally protest the proposal. Some held the view that the 'remonstrance', as it was called, was urged by Willoughby himself, who opposed the measure. The federation, however, came into being inspite of Montserrat's stated desire for the *status quo*. It had, however, raised the important principle of the right to consultation.

In addition to the Federal Assembly, the islands shared a Governor-in-Chief, who was also Commander-in-Chief, and a judicial Court and a Court of Admiralty. The federal government reflected the oligarchic and the plantocratic nature of island governments. As Berleant-Schiller observes, Sir Charles Wheler, the first Governor-in-Chief, came with a set of objectives which matched those of the planters: 'the development of a sugar economy, a plantocracy and a slave labour force'.[43] His Council was to consist of able men of property, and the Assembly, of estate-owners and freeholders elected by freeholders in the individual islands. Council members were also required to uphold the Anglican Church. Although the term governor was sometimes loosely used in the islands, the chief executive was styled Lieutenant-Governor. William Stapleton, regarded as one of the most outstanding of Leeward Island Governors, was promoted to that position in 1672 from the Lieutenant-Governorship of Montserrat.

In the absence of the Lieutenant-Governor, the President of the Council often assumed the office of chief executive of the island. Laws made in the Assembly were reported to the Council through the Speaker for amendment or rejection. When ratified, the bills were published by a provost marshal prior to their enforcement. A copy of each law was dispatched to the Governor of the Leeward Islands who gave or secured the royal assent.

A diversionary comment on William Stapleton, the first Governor of the Leeward Islands (1672–6), seems useful here. As governors go, he was generally very able. Specifically, because of his enlightened and progressive outlook and his penchant for valuable record-keeping, we have useful knowledge of the Leeward Islands in the last quarter of the seventeenth century. Mention has already been made of the census which he undertook in 1678. Equally important, especially for the purpose of this book, is a perimeter map of Montserrat by an anonymous cartographer, which he commissioned in 1673.

Daunted by the irregular coastline and mountai͏ous interior of the island, the mapmaker had to find an unusual way ͏ capture something of the physical architecture of the island. He or ͏e linked together seven coastal perspectives as seen from a little distance off-shore. And yet, the seven profiles together suggest the outline of Montserrat. Available in the Blathwayt Atlas in the John Carter Brown Library in Providence, Rhode Island, the map has numerous details on the physical features as well as the early settlement of the island. Three towns – Plymouth, Kinsale and Stapletown – are depicted on the leeward coast, and in addition to Stapleton's *latifundia* there are 18 sugar estates and several small farms on the steep slopes of Soufrière Hills. Among the Government structures are two forts, a custom house, a church, a court house and a prison, all along the leeward coast.[44] This map is Stapleton's greatest legacy to Montserrat. In addition, his personal and semi-official papers, which are available at the Rylands Manuscript Library at the University of Manchester, contain valuable details on the public accounts of Montserrat between 1672 and 1680 and concomitantly invaluable insights into social and economic life. The papers are worth far more than their weight in gold or in sugar as the currency was in those days.

The British monarch exercised sovereign control over the island through a special committee of his Council designated mostly as the Council of Trade and Plantations. This prototype of the present Colonial office, whose name and composition varied from time to time, administered colonial affairs. One of its functions was to consider appeals from colonial courts – a development which seemed natural for a body which was at one time a committee of the Privy Council. (Appeals from Montserrat and most of ex-colonial Caribbean countries are still heard by the Privy Council, although some consideration is being given to the establishment of a Caribbean Court of Appeal.)

By 1701, Montserratian planters were hankering after the earlier days of planter-governors. They requested that the Lieutenant-Governorship be assigned to a local proprietor with vested interest in the country. Their reasoning was not based on any lofty principle of indigenization, but on the desire for cheap administration. To get an educated gentleman from England, as Governor Christopher Codrington counselled in 1691, would be a charge on the public purse, which meant the planters.[45] A planter-governor, on the other hand, would for the most part, pay his own way. Besides, the leading planters wanted to be kingmakers and brokers putting forward their own nominee as Lieutenant-Governor, expecting of course to receive patronage for their pains. Everything turned on money and profit in this materialistic and exploitative society.

By the end of the seventeenth century, Montserrat was an organized and prosperous farming colony, managed and peopled by profit-seekers, from the King to the poor white. But it had more than its share of tension caused by the fear of French invasion, and fear of Irish-Catholic rebellion, tax problems and problems of governance. Meanwhile the slaves, the most exploited sector, sought opportunities to fight back.

2

Sugar

Before sugar

As with Barbados, their surrogate 'mother' country, the Leeward Islands first turned to tobacco and other cash crops, such as indigo and cotton, for their economic fortunes. By 1650, the process by which sugar was to dominate the social and political economy of Montserrat for about 200 years had seriously started. However, tobacco and other minor crops continued to feature prominently in the island's economy until the end of the seventeenth century.

The transition from tobacco to sugar was comparatively long in Montserrat. Legal fines continued to be quoted in tobacco after 1660 and it was not until 1668 that a law first quoted the penalty in sugar. And although in that same year, a parson's payment was fixed as 1400 pounds of sugar, it was possible to give him the equivalent value in tobacco, cotton-wool or indigo. In fact, in 1684 the colony was still shipping 48 000 pounds of tobacco to England while the figure for sugar was only 200 000.[1] This means that tobacco was still the main revenue-earner in England during 1683–84.

Another source which lists the 'enumerated' commodities shipped to the United Kingdom in 1683–84 puts the figures for sugar, tobacco, cotton and indigo as 161, 327, 415 and 418 hundredweights respectively.[2] This was in addition to what was shipped to North America. So, late into the last quarter of the seventeenth century, Montserrat's 'pre-sugar' economy was still alive and well. Indeed as late as 1787, cotton fetching 2s 6d per pound still featured in the national accounts.

Table 2.1 Exports from Montserrat to England, 1683–4

No. of ships	23
Sugar (pounds)	200 170
Cotton	1 800
Indigo	41 875
Tobacco	47 500

Source: C. S. Higman (1921), p.207.

When Anthony Brisket obtained his commission from the Earl of Carlisle to settle Montserrat, his twin motives were to give his Roman Catholic compatriots freedom of worship and to traffic in tobacco. He was perhaps more successful in the latter than in the former. One can readily understand why tobacco lingered long in the Montserratian economy, for it had something to do with the particular social structure of the island and its Irishness. Most of the first landowners were English, and used Irish indentured labour on the tobacco farms, although by the middle of the century a few Irish people of means from Ireland and other Caribbean territories immigrated. In time, ex-indentured Irish joined the farming community.

Tobacco production required some skill and careful garden culture but, unlike sugar, it needed little capital outlay, a smaller labour force, and could be profitably grown by a farmer and his family on small plots. Politico-religious prejudice operated against Irish Montserratians, making it difficult for them to attract the capital necessary for sugar production, so they stuck to tobacco, cotton and indigo, the crops of poorer men. In 1680, the Montserrat Council stated that tobacco was unsuited to the island's soil. But this was merely a dishonest argument made to persuade the Lords of Trade and Plantations to liberalize the slave trade or compel the Royal African Company to supply the island with more slaves to bolster a struggling sugar industry. This was the same soil (apart from the effects of unscientific farming) which produced bumper crops of tobacco in the 1640s. In 1654 over 4500 pounds of tobacco were traded to two Dutch merchants. As Pulsipher observes, from her study of the names of the farmers provided by Gwynn,[3] the big producers, who were in the minority, bore English names, while the bulk of small producers seemed to be Anglo-Irish judging from their names.[4] Again this hints at some correlation between ethnicity, on the one hand and economic status and farming of white Montserrat, on the other.

Tobacco continued to be so important to the island's economy that in 1667 steps were taken to preserve its niche in the competitive and shrinking market. This took the form of emphasis on quality for which it had developed a good reputation. A law provided that all tobacco paid to merchants had to be in leaf-form rather than in rolls or balls. The aim was to forestall the practice of disguising inferior leaves. To reinforce the policy, supervisors were appointed and empowered to destroy all inferior tobacco found on the island. Tobacco was under attack not just on economic grounds, but on moral grounds as well, from Puritan England, and every effort was being made to protect it as an alternative cash crop for the poor Irish whites and for the general economic well-being.

From the figures presented here, indigo was evidently a very important cash crop also, for it was third in value after tobacco and sugar. And John Oldmixon informs us that Montserrat shipped very large quantities to England. Indigo was a valuable alternative for those without the means or the civic qualifications to acquire and develop the large acreage which sugar demanded. Even so, the manufacture of indigo dye, which involved soaking the wood in vats, fermentation and the application of an extracting agent, required an element of capital.

The production of ground provisions also contributed to the livelihood of poorer colonists. It did not feature in metropolitan trade figures since it was not shipped to England but there was a lively trade with Antigua and St Kitts. Subsistence ground provision farmers also enjoyed some sales on the local market.[5]

Sugar plantations

As early as 1639, tobacco prices started to fall in Warner's Leeward Islands, due partly to over-production, and measures to limit production were considered.[6] Introduced from Barbados, sugar started to take root in Montserrat in the 1640s. (As part of the solution to the dependency on tobacco, ginger seems to have been introduced around this time also.) While we have no precise date on the genesis of cane-farming in Montserrat, contemporary trading accounts help us with approximate dates.

Bridenbaugh and Bridenbaugh correctly conclude that Montserrat started to grow sugar before 1649.[7] In that year the London merchant Samuel Atkins had established a sugar venture on the island for which he required 20 horses,[8] and a court case of 1654 provides corroborative evidence. Matthew Qwynn and John Madden, who were traders to Montserrat, charged that in 1649 the Captain of a French ship, *Pelican of St Mallo*, transported to and sold in France, Montserratian merchandise of tobacco, indigo and sugar which had been destined for Galway.[9] Bills owed by Montserratians to Jacob Claus and two other merchants, Hubert Van-gagel-donve and Hance Van-dekenderth in 1654 were quoted in both tobacco and sugar. At least 14 producers were in the sugar business at that time, trading together $1741\frac{1}{2}$ pounds.[10] Sugar was still subordinate to tobacco, but the industry was now established.

These 14 producers did not include Samuel Waad, who was apparently the most prosperous planter at this time. Living in a richly-furnished stone mansion, he possessed what was described as one of the most impressive sugar works of the Caribbean. In addition to 20 000 pounds of sugar and tobacco owed to him by Roger Osborne, he had in store another 20 000 pounds.[11] He was obviously both a sugar-grower and a trader. His property, which included 70 head of cattle, 500 sheep, two horses, two colts, many pigs, 30 Christian servants and 50 slaves,[12] already had the configuration of a typical sugar plantation, with blacks outnumbering whites. Small wonder that planter-Governor Osborne envied Waad, the planter who more than anyone else symbolized Montserrat's entry into the age of sugar.

The story of sugar in the seventeenth century is not one of unbroken success. Under-capitalization, inadequate labour supply and the Irish bogey all conspired to retard the nascent industry. Irish Catholics found it difficult to acquire large land-grants because, as potential plantocrats, they were required to swear allegiance to the Anglican Church. Many who came under various forced migration schemes were not persons of means and their Irishness did not attract credit.

The link between sugar and slaves has been well established by historians. It is, however, worth emphasizing that the decision to use African slave labour was a deliberate one based on economic considerations. Simply put, it seemed more profitable to employ slave labour than free labour, because potential for exploitation was greater. This dependency on slave labour set back the Montserrat sugar industry somewhat, especially because of the monopoly of the trade by the Royal African Company with Nevis as the distributing depot. This was a bitter source of complaint by Antigua, St Kitts and Montserrat. The Montserratians complained that between 1667 and 1670 only two small slavers visited the island, bringing between them 300 slaves, half of whom were already dead. They echoed the conventional view that the slaves were essential to the development of the island.[13] It is evident that sugar was regarded as being synonymous with development.

One reason for the paucity of slaves lay in the reluctance of the Royal African Company to sell slaves in Antigua, Nevis and Montserrat. This was because of the lack of coins in these islands, which caused accounts to be kept in kind rather than coins. Not only was this cumbersome, but the Company suffered losses due to delayed payments and fluctuating prices. As Deputy-Governor, William Stapleton made a serious effort to address the currency problem in 1670 by passing a law which fixed sugar at 15 shillings per 100 pounds and determined exchange rates for the sprinkling of foreign coins which entered the island.

Emigration and war also exacerbated the human resource problem in the crucial early decades of the industry. The French raid during the Second Dutch War (1665–7) was particularly damaging. Some 600 inhabitants were taken, in addition to escaped Irish smallholders who had assisted the enemy and feared the consequences if they returned. In 1665, Cromwell's expedition to capture Hispaniola recruited 80 persons at Montserrat, thanks to the unscrupulous Governor Osborne. Montserrat could ill afford this loss. In 1678, to the disappointment of Montserrat and indeed the Jamaican administration, 25 members of the household of Captain Carroll, a planter of considerable substance, left Montserrat for England.[14] Jamaica was trying to attract such families to help in its development, and Montserrat itself felt the loss keenly. If there was no actual law here to arrest outward migration, one was at least contemplated.

In spite of all of its problems, the island became a prosperous colony by the start of the eighteenth century, based on sugar as the dominant industry. Between 1700 and 1704 it produced 1021 tons of sugar. With 2847 and 2858 tons respectively, Antigua and Nevis fared better, but Montserrat's progress was substantial considering its vicissitudes. Besides, Nevis, being the distributing slave mart for the Royal African Company in the Leeward Islands, was better supplied with slaves. By 1729, the transition from multiple small farms of the 10-acre type to *latifundia*, which were a hallmark of the plantation economy, was very much in evidence. Sugar estates of varying sizes commanded among them some 94 per cent of all lands and, even more impressively, 98.5 per cent of all the cultivated lands. On these plantations, 71.5 per cent of all the slaves were to be found.[15]

With the accumulation of wealth, plantation owners started to return home, thereby creating a typical absentee class. As Watts claims, no big planter-elite group existed in the island after the late 1730s. Even before this time, Nathaniel Webb of Somerset, who resided here between 1720 and 1736, is cited as the notable exception.[16] This explains to a large extent why sugar production started to decline after its peak-year, 1735, when 3150 tons were produced. With the departure of landowners, nearly all plantations started to operate at a loss, and consequently there was a number of estate sales.

Ironically, it was perhaps fortunate for Montserrat that the establishment of the sugar industry coincided with the administration of Governor Osborne. He earned himself an unsavoury reputation as being grasping, vicious and even dissolute, and he was a great drinker. He did not scruple to be all things to all men, provided his private interests were served. It happened that his interests in the sugar business coincided with the general interest. He could be partial to his Irish compatriots, but also lavishly entertained the agents of the anti-papist Cromwell. He ignored the embargo placed on trade with the Dutch through the Navigation Act of 1651, conducting extensive business with them himself. His colonists were free to do the same and Dutch credit and shipping were pivotal to the establishment of the Montserrat sugar industry. Osborne himself set the stage for a strong competitive ethos which may have had a positive impact on sugar. The only problem was that, with him, competition developed into corruption.

Montserrat's estates were on average smaller than those on the other Leeward Islands (some, however, spreading well over 300 acres), but in their layout and in the allotment of caneland they were generally typical. Broderick's plantation, sold by Michael White in 1766, devoted what seemed an unusually high acreage (100) to pasture and provision. The amount for cane was 200 acres. But this reduction in sugar production coincided with a period of decline in sugar fortunes on the island and the high incidence of absenteeism. About the same time, an estate formerly owned by William Irish, and named Irish Estate, had only 70 acres under cane in contrast to 180 acres given to pasture and ground provision. The details of Broderick's plantation as recorded by English are instructive.[17]

200 acres of cane-land at £60	£12 000
100 acres of pasture and provision land at £10	1000
A stone windmill	700
Boiling house and curing house	300
Refining house, stone, cockle etc.	350
Horse and mule house	250
Overseer house and kitchen	250
Still house	100
Stock house	60
Dwelling house	350
Kitchen and stewards room	150
Dining hall	150
Sick house	150
Smith house	65
Horse mill	150
7 coppers in the wall rimmed and leaded	280
A 300-gallon still cap, worm and worm tub	644
23 mules at £28	644
14 horses	450
11 heads of draught cattle	240
4 cows	40
224 negroes at £45 sterling	10 080

It is an interesting detail that in a plantation costing about £28 000 its 224 slaves, together valued at £10 080, were the item of the second highest value and were second only to 200 acres of cane-land with a value of £12 000.

Much of what is valued as pasture-land for sale purposes might well have been forest, but one can discern a trend here which indicated that the Montserrat sugar industry reached the zenith earlier than in other territories and was in decline earlier. This is the same island in which laws had to be passed in 1669 and 1693 to compel farmers to devote adequate acreage to food crops, instead of putting so much land under sugar. Greed for sugar income had caused them to grow less food and to rely instead on food imports from the North American colonies. The 1669[18] law required farmers to plant one acre of provisions for every two workers, one acre of yams for every six working slaves and one acre of corn for every four slaves. When the law was updated in 1693 it was one acre of provisions for eight slaves. Yams and corn were obviously part of the staple diet, but cassava, potatoes and plantains were essential foods. It should be recognized that these laws were not passed out of humane consideration for workers' welfare, but were dictated by economic prudence. The issue of over-reliance on imports and the need for greater self-sufficiency has a contemporary resonance. In fact, as Goveia observes, the 1693 regulation was but one clause in an Act which dealt with slave-punishment. It is her view that the measure was driven by the demands of public order rather than notions of the slave's right to sufficient food. What is certain is that by the middle of the eighteenth century the circumstances which gave rise to those provisions had changed. Sugar was in decline.

From an all-time high of 3150 tons in 1735, sugar production fell fairly steadily to only 775 tons in 1834, although there were exceptional years between, as Table 2.2 indicates.

By the end of the eighteenth century, the island was no longer ruled by the sugar monoculture, for cotton had become a substantial staple. In 1789, 2000 acres were under cotton, equal to a third of the area under sugar.[19] Bryan Edwards is not always accurate, but Goveia's figures corroborate with his on the relative acreage under cotton and sugar. According to him, between 1784 and 1788 the island's average annual produce was 2737 hogsheads of sugar, 1107 puncheons of rum and 275 bales of cotton.[20] And about the same time slave ships had actually stopped calling at Montserrat, for between 1783 and 1788, the island had a net import of fewer than 100 slaves. This symbolized the end of the dominance of sugar, although production staggered on until the early years of the twentieth century. This contrasts pointedly with most of the other British territories and certainly with the other British Leeward Islands, except the Virgin Islands, whose production was never very high, although it sometimes showed a high shipment because of smuggled sugar.

Absenteeism and war apart, a combination of factors explains the lost glory of Montserrat's sugar. One had to do with the apathy and lack of imagination of planters in the face of rising production costs and soil exhaustion; very little attention was paid to manuring. Moreover the hilly terrain made transportation between field and factory difficult and unusually dependent on human power. This meant heavy reliance on slave labour, which accounted for the high density of slaves on the island. The average number of slaves per square mile was 250[21] which meant a high production cost. (One reason why Montserratians turned to cotton was because it required fewer slaves than sugar.) An early-nineteenth-century visitor remarked on the hilly topography, and the steep and difficult roads. Canes had to be carried in large baskets on human heads and on the backs of mules, asses and horses; and sugar was sometimes similarly transported in bags to the seashore where it was put in casks.[22] The configuration of the land discouraged the use of ploughs and, in any case, Montserratian planters were never enthusiastic about ploughs even where they were usable, or in modernizing sugar production technology generally. Of the 78 sugar-mills in Montserrat in 1730, only 23 were wind-powered and three were powered by water. The other 52 were the less economical and less efficient cattle-mills. Some eighteenth-century natural disasters – a flood in 1767 and a hurricane in 1773 – also gave disastrous body blows to the ailing industry.

Table 2.2   Sugar production in Montserrat, 1697–1834

Year	Tons	Year	Tons	Year	Tons	Year	Tons
1697–98	1159	1726	1302	1754	1761	1792	1217
1699	891	1728	2537	1755	2550	1800	1875
1700	1486	1729	1816	1756	2295	1807	1507
1701	1074	1730	2338	1757	2311	1809	1096
1702	1031	1731	1662	1758	2422	1810	1928
1703	707	1732	2357	1759	1627	1814	1657
1704	809	1733	2359	1760	2569	1815	1226
1706	440	1734	1761	1761	2708	1816	1449
1707	636	1735	3150	1762	1951	1817	1560
1708	334	1736	2409	1763	2035	1818	1846
1709	471	1737	1488	1764	2773	1819	1859
1710	853	1738	2649	1765	2004	1820	1640
1711	605	1739	1805	1766	2301	1821	1664
1712	885	1740	1860	1767	1840	1822	1353
1713	1059	1741	1871	1768	2127	1823	1223
1714	468	1742	1442	1769	2556	1824	1582
1715	969	1743	2078	1770	2768	1825	982
1716	1338	1744	1936	1771	2094	1826	1524
1717	1045	1745	1643	1772	2900	1827	985
1718	1078	1746	1678	1773	1689	1828	1254
1719	1351	1747	1027	1774	2379	1829	1361
1720	1351	1748	2473	1775	1963	1830	520
1721	1106	1749	2562	1776	2168	1831	1032
1722	1444	1750	1689	1777	905	1832	1036
1723	1545	1751	1833	1778	1380	1833	1042
1724	922	1752	1160	1779	1876	1834	775
1725	1494	1753	2655	1780	1518		

Source: N. Deerr, *The History of Sugar* (1949), p.196.

War over Montserrat

Montserrat was scarcely ever regarded as a prized sugar island, but this had nothing to do with fortunes made by individual planters or with the revenues it yielded for the Crown. The chemistry of the Irish within and the French round about created a potentially troublesome situation administratively, and earned the island more ill-repute than it deserved. When Dunn refers to it as being always a backward settlement,[23] he may have accepted contemporary reports somewhat uncritically. In a dispatch to the Lords of Trade, Leeward Islands Governor William Stapleton pointed out that he and his friends had plantations and sugar works in Montserrat 'so well provided with conveniences such as waterworks that we could not find the like in any French ground'.[24] Moreover, according to Oldmixon, while the quality of Montserrat's sugar was not as good as it was in Barbados and Jamaica, it was not as 'coarse and black' as Antigua's sugar.

Stapleton may have exaggerated the island's prosperity in a bid to impress the French, for this report formed part of a proposal to cede Montserrat to them in exchange for French St Kitts. But the prospects in Montserrat were generally good in the last two decades of the seventeenth century, and Stapleton did possess thriving estates there. The proposed exchange, which did not materialize, would have solved two vexing administrative and defence problems in the sub-region – the unpredictability of the Irish in Montserrat, who were likely to collude with the French in the event of war, and the unease of dual settlements in St Kitts without secure borders. Besides, a totally English St Kitts would have been simpler to administer and defend than a truncated colony not far from a potentially rebellious Romish faction in Montserrat.

But this notion of exchange explains one reason why the capture of Montserrat was important, apart from any consideration of its size and wealth. It could be used at the post-war bargaining table, when the French and English, who were the main contenders for hegemony in the region, sat down to redistribute territories, whether in the Caribbean or elsewhere. In addition, Montserrat became part of an integrated Leeward Islands colony (1671) and an attack on the island was an attack on the colony and indeed an attack on the English. Moreover, any sugar island was a worthy object of attack; there was a competitive industry to destroy, wealth to plunder and vital human capital to pillage. Montserrat had its fair or unfair share of raids in the seventeenth and eighteenth centuries and sugar, its central concern, suffered accordingly. More leeward than Antigua, and closer to the French colonies, it was, together with Nevis and St Kitts, geographically and tactically more vulnerable to attacks than was Antigua.

The island felt the first effects of war during the Second Dutch War (1665–7) which merged into an Anglo-French duel. Fighting to gain commercial advantages rather than for territorial aggrandizement, the Dutch under De Ruyter captured 16 ships in the harbour in 1665. But this was just a prelude to the mighty martial drama of 1667 which we referred to in Chapter 1. (Some date it 1666, owing, it is thought, to a calendar confusion.) It was a carefully co-ordinated two-pronged attack, with the French landing at Sugar Bay with Irish guidance, and the Caribs from Dominica beaching at Landing Bay in the Roaches area.

Where Antigua had a fortified refuge at Monk's Hill and St Kitts had one at Brimstone Hill, Montserrat had its 'deodands'[25] at the Gardens redoubt between Galways *soufrière* and the South Hill. Led by d'Orvillier, the Caribs, whose navigational skills in rough Caribbean seas served them well in the Atlantic-driven waves at Roaches, made an effective surprise attack on the Montserrat hill of refuge. De Barre and his French contingent then converged on the English. He captured the island which he overran, sacked and burnt, destroying some 40 sugar-mills, sparing only the lives of those Irishmen who were French allies. Some of course willingly 'surrendered' to him. Over 300 English prisoners, a large number of slaves and farm animals together with the Deputy Governor himself, the second Anthony Brisket, were captured.[26]

The battle was a major setback to the island, which became totally dislocated. Indeed, for some months, it was really a French colony with Anthony Brisket administering it on behalf of the French, allegedly under duress. Some 80 Frenchmen were left by De Barre with about 500 Irish families who were obliged to swear allegiance to the French monarch. Hundreds of inhabitants fled, some in destitution, to other territories reaching even as far as Jamaica, 'with little more than their shirts'.[27] When the English recaptured the island, they deported the French and Franco-Irish as a first step in the process of recovery. The Treaty of Breda ended the war in 1667, but not the distress. It was like starting afresh and it took the island a decade before it began to thrive again, boasting a posse of 1200 fighting men in 1678.

The next major battle came in 1712 during the War of the Spanish Succession but, beginning in 1693, the island was continually harassed by the French, sometimes in the form of raids from prowling privateers. The presence of the French in any part of the Leewards was cause for alarm, given the Irish presence. A number of the Irish deserted to the French in 1689 and several were arrested and shipped off to Jamaica for trial.[28] In 1693, a French privateer succeeded in obtaining one white and 40 slaves, and four years later another made off with 10 slaves and other booty.[29] Richard Pares refers to a French attack in 1706, mainly for the purpose of capturing slaves.[30] French privateers again attacked Montserrat with six vessels in 1710, but were successfully repulsed on landing.

The defence of the island proved costly and sometimes impacted heavily on the balance sheet of property owners, especially after the economic ruin wreaked on the island in 1667. The many laws passed to deal with some aspect of defence betrayed a society under siege. In 1668 beacons or look-outs, eight-to-ten-feet high, were built and from these, cannons were fired off to signal the inhabitants to adopt a war-like posture. Mustered men had to respond readily and remain in their posted divisions. A 1672 law ordered the 'speedy' fixing of firearms. It is not clear where this new fort was built, but in 1693 the Council agreed for yet another fort to be built at Palmetto Point in the south of the island. Each family was required to send 20 slaves, providing them with the necessary tools such as shovels, bills and pick-axes on pain of penalty of an unspecified quantity of sugar for every day a slave was absent.[31] While a detachment was engaged off-island against the French in 1692, the Council was instructed to post 16 militia members on continuing guard within each of four military divisions northward with headquarters at Carr's Bay, windward with headquarters at White River, middle, and northwest. After seven days and nights they were to be relieved by another 16.

All of this activity meant interruption of economic activity and an unprofitable use of manpower. An Act of 1696 decreed that all persons between the ages of 15 and 60 had to enlist for military duty. English soldiers also brought with them a cost. Not only were they billeted in private houses, but Orders were passed for them to be paid gratuity for outstanding services to the island. The internal threat both from the Irish and the brutalized slaves, provided another reason for strong insular defence.

But this military posture and feverish defence activity did not prevent the July 1712 invasion, which was partly motivated by a desire to snatch slaves. A fleet of five ships, a Dutch 'prize', 13 sloops and small vessels commanded by Monsieur Cassart, inflicted damages estimated at £180 000 at a time when the island was experiencing some prosperity. They struck when several merchant-ships were in harbour, but there were no men-o'-war, four of which could have driven the enemy's ships 'out of the West Indies'.[32] This invasion coincided with a period of conflict and confusion within the administration and an absentee Lieutenant-Governor, John Pearne, to boot. Delayed by stormy weather, naval assistance from Barbados arrived too late to arrest the burning and plunder.

With their fortunes at stake, a number of leading citizens accepted the challenge of withstanding the French, and the devastation would have been greater without their positive intervention. Indeed George Wyke and Edward Parson, both men of substance in the colony, emerged as heroes from the fray. In the 1729 census, Wyke is listed as the planter with easily the largest property (700 acres in St Anthony's) and Edward Parson's widow owned 420 acres in the same parish, situated doubtlessly at the present Parsons. With only 60 men, Captain Wyke engaged the French at Runaway Ghaut long enough to enable the inhabitants to flee to the mountains for refuge. The ravine named Frenchman's Creek, which funnels Runaway Ghaut's waters to the sea and the remnant of a cemetery at Carr's Bay, are abiding memorials of the battle of Runaway Ghaut. With a total of about 400 men, Wyke and Parson prevented the capitulation of the island, holding out against 3500 Frenchmen until the Governor (and Captain-General) Walter Douglas arrived. They had achieved this in spite of deserters, who provided the enemy with vital intelligence.

Impressed by Parson's courageous leadership in the island's defence, the Governor elevated him to the position of Commander-in-Chief. Parson was grateful, but his response revealed that while he may have been patriotic, he was no altruist. In thanking the Governor for the new honour, he requested to be made Lieutenant-Governor of the island, so that he could command a salary. He felt that this was justly deserved since he had used his own means to equip the militia.[33] As it turned out, it was Thomas Talmack and not Parson who succeeded Pearne as Lieutenant-Governor.

A major attack on Montserrat occurred in 1782 when De Grasse compelled the island to surrender. It was to avert such a danger that a crude fort, complete with powder magazine, was hastily built at St. George's Hill, but it did not prevent the capture. The island remained in French hands, under French administration, until September 1783 when by the Treaty of Versailles it was returned to England. For some nineteen months, Montserratians were subjects of the Catholic King Louis XIV, to the delight of the Irish inhabitants, one can assume. It was the French who built two well-engineered fortifications on St George's Hill in 1782-3 – the northern or d'Abaud redoubt and the larger southern or de Bouille redoubt – named after the Governors of Guadeloupe and Martinique, respectively.[34] As it turned out, the fortified hill was used more for civil than for military purposes. After a French attack during the Napoleonic Wars in 1805, when Montserrat was bought off with a ransom, the island was unmolested. (It was from the vantage-point of St George's Hill that the cannons were sounded in the nineteenth and early twentieth centuries to announce the imminent invasion of hurricanes.)

It was not the Irish alone, however, who welcomed the French presence, which brought a respite from the trade restrictions of the Navigation Laws. All planters and merchants enjoyed a period of free trade, and plantation provisions were imported from the North American colonies. Besides, the French Governor, Joseph de Goullon, ruled benevolently and continued to use the existing Council and Assembly to pass laws in much the same way as they did under the British. The established courts also functioned as the legitimate media of justice. The island had to pay a ransom of £7500,[35] according to Alan Burns (English makes it £3000), but the benefits derived from French rule seemed to have compensated. For one thing, the French paved the main streets in Plymouth and improved the quality of public buildings. The Montserrat plantocrats anticipated the eventual termination of the French regime, so they used the opportunity to pass a number of laws to their own advantage before the appointment of the new Deputy-Governor.

Ironically, therefore, this last attack on Montserrat harboured the springs of recovery. Not so the others. They precipitated the decline of sugar and with it the value of the island, and encouraged absenteeism and sales of estates. The regime of de Goullon was too brief and detached to affect the island's culture. Very little remains as a permanent reminder of the French adventures in Montserrat, apart from a couple of grave lots (one bordering George Street, not far from the Roman Catholic Church, allegedly) and another at Carr's Bay. According to popular tradition, a stone building in Trials which once housed the indigent poor of the island was erected by the French. This has credence as the building has always been known as the 'Château'.

Sugar society

By the end of the seventeenth century when the transformation to a sugar economy was more or less complete, the island exhibited the common demographic pattern of a rich, white, powerful minority with a large slave populace at the bottom of the pile. Table 2.3 illustrates the increasing imbalance in the population.

Table 2.3   Population in Montserrat

Year	Total	Blacks	Whites	Ratio
1672		523	1175[a]	–
1678	3674	992	2682[b]	1:2.7
1689	–	–	1100	–
1707	5115	3580	1535	2:3.1
1720	5460	3772	1688	2:1
1724	5400	4400	1000	4:1
1729	6908	5858	1050	5:1

a Adult men only; b 1038 free
Source: Adapted from Berleant-Schiller (1989) p. 541, elaborated from other sources including English (1930).

Small it was, but Montserrat had its white-planter elite beginning with Samuel Waad. The persons who signed the 1668 'remonstrance' protested separation from Barbados and included names like Anthony Brisket, Thomas Roach, John Deveraux, George Wyke, Roger Bentley, David Galloway and Garret Misset, members of the white elite. Leadership in the militia further embellished the status of personalities like Captain George Wyke and Colonel Edward Parson, the former or his son advancing to the Presidency of the Council in the middle of the 1760s. There was a sharp distinction between this elite and lesser whites, although a few of the latter owned one or two slaves.

Predominantly Irish Catholics, they were either landless or cultivated small plots in steep and arid terrain, and were regarded as congenitally perfidious. Religion, politics and lack of creditworthiness combined to disqualify them for land grants. In 1678 only 26 per cent of Montserratian householders were slave-owners, in contrast to 82 per cent in Barbados in 1680.[36] These second-class whites mastered the subsistence economy, growing cash crops such as indigo, ginger, cotton, cocoa, coffee and cassava which was staple eating. They constituted a free labour force working as masons and carpenters and at a variety of other trades associated with the sugar industry, the maintenance of forts and the catering and service sector. Judging from Stapleton's documents, wages were quite low compared to the cost of living. A carpenter or a mason earned roughly 20 pounds of sugar per day. The white under-class did not have a lot to be grateful for in Montserrat in the seventeenth century, and white solidarity was not a hallmark of the society. It is not surprising that the rate of emigration of white freedmen was very high.

Social and economic rejection by the English and Anglo-Irish elite led the white servant wage-earners to liaise closely with the slaves for mutual succour. One in wretchedness, it was natural that both ethnic groups would wish to formulate common strategies for survival. This kind of solidarity was naturally a threat to the white uppercrust who moved to dismantle it, instituting a kind of apartheid by law. An Act was passed in 1682 'restraining Christians from federating with the negroes: and banning convivial association' (shades of divide and rule);[37] and a 1670 Act forbade bond and free whites to conspire with the slaves to run away. An incentive reinforced divisiveness by the offer of rewards as high as 300 pounds of sugar on the head of a runaway slave.

In an effort to arrest the decline of the white population, a law had to be passed in 1683 calculated to augment the number. For every 10 working negroes on a farm there had to be one white and, failing this, the planter had to pay a fine of 1000 pounds of muscovado sugar. It is evident that this concern over the white population was related to the defence of the island, for the sugar levy was to be invested in forts. This measure could not have been very productive, for in 1720, there were only 95 white servants on the island – 64 men, 10 women, 9 boys and 12 girls. This was a re-enactment of a previous law, but this time it had teeth. This utilitarian interest in whites led to further discrimination against slaves and underlines the racist nature of sugar society and the abiding sense of white supremacy.

Economic competition of slaves with whites came to be forbidden by law. Slaves could not ply the trades of coopers, smiths, tailors, sawyers, masons or shinglers. This economic protection for whites was veiled under a law, which ostensibly dealt with pilfering and disorderly conduct on Sundays. A 1736 law barred slaves from planting indigo, ginger, coffee, cotton and cocoa – precisely those cash crops which the 'poorer sort of people of this island'cultivated. Not only were they to lose the traditional market day, but they were banned from the lively and profitable markets of Plymouth and Kinsale.[38] Buying liquor from slaves was also forbidden. This double-barrelled attack aimed at reducing the earning of slaves, thereby reducing opportunities for manumission and consequently the chances of competing with the whites. The slaves were at the bottom of the socio-economic ladder and the system was designed to keep them there. The manumitted slave was of course free to sell his labour like the free white.

We have already established the view that plantation society was riddled with fear. As Table 2.4 shows, defence was a major item in the public expenditure in the years 1670–80. This was nearly 40 per cent of the total public liability.

Tension and fear were also evidenced in the enormous controlling and coercing power that the planters assumed over their human property – a power legitimized by the English through the absence of any central code on slave rights. It was a crude society. Making a similar point, Dunn cites

Table 2.4   Summary of public expenses, 1670–80

Military and Defence	£	*s.*	*d.*
Paid to standing guards	147	0	9
Paid to gunners	102	9	3
Ammunition	459	10	0
Repair to forts	497	10	0
Repair to prison	64	2	4
Repair of powder-house	3	9	3
Provision for soldiers and Indians	24	8	8
Total	1298	10	3

Source: Stapleton Papers, Abstract of Public Accounts, 1667–80.

the fact that cursing a Council member drew a fine of 100 pounds of sugar; in the case of a member of the Assembly it was 500 pounds.[39] In addition to the threat of raids, absenteeism and the tendency to see England or Ireland as the real home, ensured the persisting frontier nature of the society. An aim was to create wealth to fund stylish living at home.

Feasting could be lavish; the handsome sum of £18.6s.2d was spent for 'entertaining the Governor and Assembly at public meetings' in the period 1670–80. H. Coleridge wrote with relish in 1825 of the exquisite soup, the turtle entrée and the 'pure and milky' Madeira wine, which he enjoyed in Montserrat. Dressing was fine, even if climatically inappropriate. Wardrobes included black silk waistcoats, black kerseymere (woollen) waistcoats and breeches, cravats, velvet jackets, and morning sword. It is not clear how much reading was done, but a number of classical volumes formed part of the furnishings of a few homes. *Parliamentary History of England 1066–1660, Debates of the Commons 1660 to 1672* and works by Swift, Pope, Shakespeare, Congreve, Dryden and classical authors like Homer, Ovid, Cicero, Juvenal and Sallust formed part of the lists. Games like backgammon and billiards provided some recreation.

But it is apparent that under the veneer of genteel deportment and culture there was an unpolished society, characterized by excessive drinking, moral laxity and gossip. The taverns and gaming houses of Plymouth and Kinsale did not lack for clients and even the men of the cloth over-indulged to the point where Governor Stapleton described them as drunken. Significantly, though, the laws regarding drunkenness referred only to the voiceless and lowliest in the society.

The scarcity of women in Montserrat did nothing good for the tone of the society. Hilary Beckles suggests that the high percentage of women in Barbados society had a positive effect on the social culture and the development of family structures.[40] Montserrat lacked this redeeming feature. The 1677–8 census figures show only 591 white women, 300 black women, 1175 white men and 500 black men. Some households had no women at all, and yet others had one woman and two adult males. In addition to their low numbers, the uneven disposition of women in districts and households leads to unsavoury speculation about social and sexual relationships.[41] The sex imbalance led to the practice of enticing women servants away from their masters or mistresses. A law was consequently passed 'against inveigling women servants' in 1683, although it was rather vague on the penalty; it merely stated that 'any person inveigling such servants under pretence of marriage or freedom' shall be required to 'make good the service or services of such women to the speedy satisfaction of the aggrieved person'.

Sugar society in Montserrat was not without some humanitarian glimmer even though poor whites were the biggest beneficiaries. Justices of the Peace were commissioned to act as industrial relations agents. A 1673 law empowered them to regulate the wages of labourers; and in 1675 an effort was made to control the fees of doctors who were charging prohibitive fees for treating yaws, a killer among the poor whites. What may have been Montserrat's first law on poor relief demonstrated some creative foresight, but again it did not, it seems, apply to blacks. The 1683 Act was designed to take care of orphans, the old and indigent through community funds, to be administered in each parish, which would appoint an overseer for the purpose. Orphans were to be apprenticed to trades at the appropriate time; and contingency relief plans were made for destitute persons arriving on the island. Slaves were hardly 'persons' legally and were certainly not so in relation to social and humanitarian concerns. Ironically, they were the economic bedrock of sugar society.

Sugar fortunes

Many of the place names in the island derived from the names of estates which in turn took their names from prominent planters of the seventeenth and early centuries. This is one legacy of sugar. Examples include Bransby point, which was part of the estate of Ensign Bransby; Hodges Hill, linked with Anthony Hodges; Farells (Farrells), belonging to John Farrell; Parsons of Edward Parson; Frye's, from an estate belonging to William Frye; John Galloway's Galways Estate; Blakes belonging to John and other Blakes; Dominick Trant, who gave his name to Trant's Bay; Gage's Estate, associated with John Gage; and the Andrew Power cemetery in St Patrick's, a seventeenth-century gift which still carries the name of the benefactor. While not all of these made great fortunes, there are others who did, but their names were not enshrined on the already well-established estates which they bought. Some examples are Captain George Wyke, who owned 700 acres in 1729, John Bramble and Garret Misset, although Wyke and Bramble still exist as surnames.

Nicholas Tuite, John Blake and David Galway are among the seventeenth- and eighteenth-century planters who made something of a fortune here and whose names survive to the present. There are, of course, others. The tenure of Nicholas Tuite, an Irishman, was short. Born in Montserrat in 1705, in 1729 he owned 100 acres in St Patrick's and 41 slaves. (Not many farms exceeded 100 acres in St Patrick's at that time.) In addition he managed a company which traded slaves and provisions from Ireland. After a hurricane devastated his plantation, he migrated to St Croix where he amassed a large fortune, which was eventually inherited by his son who became a London banker.[42] Tuite had his beginnings in Montserrat sugar.

He was referred to as a judge in a Montserrat court in 1736, so it is most likely that it was the 1737 hurricane which brought his ruin.

Blake's Estate has a long history. The chief actor was John Blake, whose father of the same name was Mayor of Galway in 1646. He and his brother Henry emigrated to the West Indies around 1668, lived in Barbados and purchased an estate in Montserrat in 1675. Henry sold his share of the estate to John and returned to Ireland, while the latter resolved to move to Montserrat, 'and there to settle myself for some years, to the end I may in time gain something to bring me at last home'. This clear statement of intent indicates that John Blake did not come to Montserrat to find free altars. He came to seek a fortune in canes and to return home to enjoy it. Meanwhile Henry had made a fortune in Montserrat trading with Ireland in tobacco and indigo. He liquidated his debts and invested in properties at home.

As it turned out, he died in Montserrat in 1692, but not before he had played a prominent position in the island and permanently wrote his name here in place and blood as Blake's village and the yellow-brown Blakes in the northern area of Montserrat's attest.

After the French invasion of 1712, Thomas, another John and Patrick Blake are listed among the island's men of substance who affirmed their confidence in the administration of Governor Douglas. The 1729 census reveals four families of Blakes belonging to St Anthony's parish and a labourer Henry, in St Peter's, owning only 12 acres of land. He may have been the one who started the black intermarrying. (In 1815, Margaret Blake married John Griffin.) The original estate must have been outside the family, but the name was retained.

A 1924 listing of the main estates in the island included Blakes and Lookout (1000 acres) belonging to James Townsend Allen,[43] whose descendants have played a prominent role in the development of the island. Allen allegedly lost Blakes after litigation.

Galways estate has been the subject of numerous studies,[44] so a brief account will suffice here. David Galway who, like John Blake, hailed from Galway in Ireland, acquired plantation lands around 1660, and by 1668 he was recognized as being among the influential sugar-planters of the island. He was probably Protestant, since he became an officer in the militia and a member of Council, the second of which required an oath of allegiance to the Anglican church. (Some few Roman Catholics did become members of the Assembly. Indeed apart from the Governor, the members of the Leeward Islands Federal Assembly were not obliged to be Protestants.) By 1729, his son David, who inherited his property, had a plantation of 320 acres with 100 acres under cane and an animal-mill for crushing. Typically, productivity fell off under David Galway, who had not bothered to introduce windmills. His estate was nevertheless a passport to political power, for he was given authority to enforce the laws designed to control his Irish compatriots in the St Patrick's area.[45]

After the death of David Galway, the estate languished further under his grandson David and another relative, Tobias Wall Galway, between 1740 and 1760. Five years later it passed from the management of the Galways by way of lease and from their ownership by sale towards the end of the eighteenth century. It was the new owner who apparently relocated the estate, improved the technology, built its attractive Georgian great house and gave it a new era of prosperity.[46] In 1841, it was 'finely situated' in the opinion of John Davy, and was valued at £7000. The reorganized Lower Galway's estate continued to produce sugar down to the turn of the century before cotton took over in the 1920s.

Galways was a typical plantation; its fortunes amply illustrate the relationship of landed property to political power and the colonial administration's strategy of using suitably disposed Irish magnates to control their own countrymen.

Galways has gained its current prominence because the sugar-plantation ruins, which include a boiling and curing house, a warehouse, a cattle-mill, a windmill, cisterns, a manor house, a slave village and plantation artifacts, have been the subject of archaeological study for nearly 15 years.[47] The investigations have provided insights into plantation economy, lifeways and material culture and the relationships of Europeans and Africans to each other and to the environment.

The name Stapleton is no longer current, but we know that Old Town once bore the name of this seventeenth century Deputy-Governor. However, his major estate, Waterworks, still carries that name. After Samuel Waad, he was the next major Montserratian landed baron that we know of. In 1668 he acquired the 573-acre Waterworks plantation forfeited to the Crown by Anthony Brisket II, who was deemed a traitor for his behaviour during the French attack on Montserrat in 1667. This was a royal handshake to a trusted administrator who would otherwise be poorly remunerated. He added to this handsome holding with various land purchases. Altogether, he possessed:

> A certain Plantation or Parcel of land situate ... in the island of Mountserrat (viz). The Plantation Commonly called the Waterworke Plantation Containeing a Mile Square from North to a south square line, or upon ye same cross point as ye plantacons beyond Corke hill doth Run, from ye Gutt called gut hart or spring gutt. Bounded at the foot with both Rivere and Corkehill Plantacons running to the full Extent of the Mountains, Together

with all the lands above the Mill until meetes with the Windward Plantations granted formerly under Patent by my Lord WM. Willoughby to me. & also ... the woodlands on the other side of spring Gutt bounded upon the lands formerly ... granted to one Botkin and Nicholson, and alsoe all the land in the old Roade begining at the Sea side bounded with the severall windings and turneings of the River to the East and South, bounded on the North side with the Plantation of Capt. Wm. ffreeman and Capt. Jno Brambley, Containeing more or lesse [?] acres of land above Brisketts house until it meetes with the River againe, Excepting onely the lande on which the said Capt. ffreeman and Capt. Bramly have a store house built .... All that Plantation alsoe let to Mr. Tho Lee and now in his tenure and occupacon in the Parish of St Anthony ... formerly called Codery ....[48]

Stapleton acquired similar *latifundia* in Nevis, St Kitts and Antigua. He was unable to manage these vast estates personally, so he made use of a system of tenantry. Waterworks was in fact continuously leased until 1737 when, at the height of a recession in the sugar business, it was sold for £2500 to David Fenton, a relative, who bought the estate, which had now grown to 600 acres. William Stapleton himself died in 1685, but his second son (also named William) had inherited Waterworks. In 1810, it was reduced to 160 acres and registered in the name of J. Daley (deceased). Waterworks, unlike most other Montserratian estates, has remained in white hands.

3

Slavery

Development of the trade

Sugar and slavery are twin phenomena, so some aspects of slave society were inevitably treated in the last chapter. This one focuses on the development of the trade, the laws which regulated slavery, and the response of the slaves to their servitude.

There is no evidence of African slaves in Montserrat before about 1650, but it is reasonable to infer that they started arriving in the 1640s. Akenson provides circumstantial evidence including the presence of slaves in St Kitts to support his suspicion that slaves started arriving in the island in the 1930s.[1] In 1651 an Irish trader of the English Guinea Company called at Montserrat, having buried 23 men at sea, including Mr. Dobes, who was a factor.[2] This is the first actual mention of slaves in Montserrat. Four years later, Samuel Waad, Montserrat's premier planter of the earliest period, possessed 50 slaves and only 30 white servants. His outfit was already on its way to being a demographic microcosm of plantation society, with slaves as the largest sector of the population. With the example of Barbados to draw on, slave labour was regarded as the most economical method of providing the labour force needed for sugar.

The emergence of Montserrat as a slave colony coincided with the monopolistic Navigation Act of 1651 and subsequent trade laws with a similar purpose. Slaves to the English colonies in the Caribbean were supplied first by the Guinea Company and eventually by the Royal African Company. The system was fraught with problems, as we indicated previously. The planters turned illegally to private traders when the Company did not meet their needs, but when the private trade capitalized on market forces and raised the price, the planters again complained. However, up to 1708, when the price of a slave averaged between £40 and £60, neither source could supply adequate numbers. Table 3.1 contains data on the island's slave population between 1672 and 1838. (The figure for 1774 reported by English as an estimate, seems suspiciously high.)

Table 3.1 Slave population, 1672–1838

Year	Number	Year	Number
1672	523	1727	5 855
1678	992	1729	5 858
1707	3 580	1774	10 000
1720	3 772	1810	6 880
1724	4 400	1838	6 401

Source: Sundry sources including CO 152/2, 41; The Public Record Office; Higham (1921); English (1930).

To the relief of Montserrat, some British interlopers engaged in a direct trade between the island and the Slave Coast where rum was exchanged for slaves. This helped to accelerate the black population growth in the 1720s, bringing it to 5858 in 1729, just about 1000 fewer perhaps than the peak number for all time, if we query the 10 000 given for 1774. The *Mary and Catherine*, a ship of five tons, left Montserrat for Africa on 25 June 1722, returning on 19 November with 102 slaves. This particular cargo was sold at St Kitts 'at an extraordinary price and did make a very good voiage'. Montserrat seemed to have become for a period an unofficial slave depot in the Leeward Islands where its slaves sold in the highest markets. In 1723 a Bristol ship, the *Joseph and Anna*, under the command of Captain Bird, brought a cargo of 250 to the island, after losing 20 in the crossing.[3] The hunger for slaves led the inhabitants to sidestep official regulations governing colonial trade, biased as these were towards the metropolitan interest.

Planters were not above slave-stealing in a bid to augment their workforce, and a heavy penalty was decreed as a deterrent. A law was passed in 1719 to ensure 'that whatsoever person or persons shall presume to delude any other person's slaves or servants to run away, in his or her plantation, or shall employ the said slave or servant who run or be absent from his master or mistress, shall forfeit and pay the owner or owners'[4] 20 shillings for each day the slave was so retained.

Slave labour was in demand not just for plantation, but for public works. Such services were tantamount to taxes levied on their masters by the administration. Sometimes the order came directly from the Council, as happened in 1695 when certain slaves were required to repair trenches. And in 1738 a law ordered the inhabitants to send their working slaves 'to repair and amend the common road from Nineturn Gutt to Bottomless Gutt and from Nineturn Gutt to Tar River or forfeit 2/6 for the working of each negro'.

In the absence of specific information on the African origin of Montserratian slaves, it has to be assumed that most of the various groups who came to the West Indies were represented here. These included: Mandigoes, Koromantyne, Pawpaws, Mocoes and Eboes.[5] Slave names provide very little clue. Apart from a few recurring names such as Cudjoe, Quashie, Quaco, Eddoe and Bansa, names appear to have been randomly assigned as tags to distinguish one from another, so that plantation demands on them could be better fulfilled. This reflected their nonentity status and the depersonalization inherent in the Caribbean slave-condition. And names like Peter Coone, Cancer, White Wine and Joe Spider may have been intended to ridicule and vilify, and the habit of giving names like Apollo, Caesar and Pompey from classical literature served the same purpose. Sometimes, a slave's estate became a surname. In 1792, for instance, a slave was charged for aiding in the murder of Nancy Water Work. English provides the following schedule of slaves sold in 1764:

Men	£	*Men*	£	*Women*	£
Charles	80	French Quaco	40	Statira	70
Jemmy	85	Simon	120	Clarisa	60
Sam	65	Dick	83	Susannah	65
Quaco Meade	85	London	85	Bridget	55
Jacob	80	Tom	85	Bansa	43
Adam	60	Johnny	95	Esther	63
Ned	60	Quashie	85	Nanny	70
Sharper	90	Pollidore	70	Franky	80
Caesar	75				
Quashy	83				
Peter	70				

A study of this schedule reveals that slaves had appreciated in value and that women fetched on the whole rather less than men. Prices at this time went as high as £175, depending on the skills of the individual. In 1767, Beaunash 'a good tight cooper' of Martin Lynch's estate, was valued at £175; Ned Porker, another cooper, at £120; and Cork, a good barber, was put at £140.

Slaves were unevenly distributed across the island and among households. In the heyday of the plantation economy and right down to emancipation, more than half of the slaves were located in St Peter's and St Anthony's. (In 1770, 50 per cent of the total white population lived in St Anthony's and many slaves would naturally be attached to them.) In St Patrick's, where there were fewer slaves in absolute terms, they were, however, more widely distributed among households. This was due to the presence of many Irish people who could manage only small numbers, going as low as six, three and even two or one.

The St Patrick's community differed in another significant manner from the norm in other parishes and in sugar society generally. Great houses were very few and poor whites and slaves lived in close proximity or in some cases, within the same household. We know, for instance, from the 1677–8 census, that Dennis Tynenan, a free white, lived with a male slave at Palmetto Point in St Patrick's. This may have helped to give rise to the speculation that Irish slave-holders treated their slaves more kindly than did the English, but I have seen no hard evidence to substantiate this claim. Several households, especially in St Patrick's, had no slaves at all; in 1680 only 26 per cent of the free population owned slaves.[6]

Free coloureds also owned slaves. James Welch, Jr, who manumitted a mulatto child in 1748, was himself a mulatto. Slave ownership must have been a symbol of status as well as a means of providing estate sinew. He was just a labourer, but in 1748 Isaac Buntin gave a six-year-old 'wench' to his daughter as a New Year's gift. One does not doubt that in a case like this, a close and cordial relationship may have developed between the daughter and the slave.

We do not have much detailed information on the day-to-day day lives of Montserrat's slaves outside plantation drudgery. There is no reason, however, to think that their lives were markedly different from those of other British West Indian slaves. The laws passed to control them do throw some light on their existence and efforts to survive and even to do well. It is evident, for instance, that some engaged in petty trading and entrepreneurial activity and that many were enterprising farmers with the potential for out-stripping poor whites economically. Many, of course, worked as artisans – masons, carpenters, coopers, smiths – even though they were not paid for it, and some developed craft skills.

Apart from their ration of protein, cereal (corn or rice) and rum occasionally, the slaves had to produce their own foods such as yams, bananas, potatoes and cassava, which reflected both an Amerindian and African heritage. In keeping with the norm, their diet was high in carbohydrates and nutritionally deficient in other respects.[7] Recent archaeological work in Montserrat on the skeletal remains of slaves revealed a high incidence of anaemia; and suggests that these individuals suffered the effects of periodic severe malnutrition, common illnesses and a harsh lifestyle that resulted in the early deaths of plantation males. The average life expectancy for the males was about 40, with women living somewhat longer. The diets were high on fibre but natural sugar, mostly perhaps from cane juice, was high and resulted in many dental caries.[8]

The slaves built their own houses using local materials and kept them in repair. The roofs were made of thatched palm supported by posts driven into the earth and interlined by wattle and daub. The scant furniture and utensils such as the calabash were self-made, and animals such as goats, fowls and pigs were kept in the yard. The slaves obviously brought creativity and resourcefulness to the business of survival in the harsh and inhospitable climate of slavery. Figure 6 gives a hypothetical reconstruction of part of the Galways plantation slave village.

Manumission did take place in Montserrat, but only grudgingly, especially if a slave were particularly profitable. Naturally, it would be the most energetic and industrious slaves who would be able to raise the sum required in the face of all the economic restrictions imposed. In his autobiography the highly literate slave Oulaudah Equiano (Gustavus Vassa), who was a sailor, tells of amassing £470 by buying and selling household and other articles like tumblers and jugs.[9] His Montserratian master Robert King was reluctant to free him in 1766, contrary to his promise, for he did not anticipate that Oulaudah would have raised the freedom price of £40 so soon. The ship's captain had to intervene, pointing out that Equiano had been extremely profitable, having earned for his master over £100 annually.

Slave control

A good working set of the laws generated by Montserratian slave society for the period 1660 to 1740 is available. These include the *Acts of the Assembly of Montserrat* and the *Acts of Montserrat*, located at the Public Record Office in London. Decisions on cases involving slaves are also contained in Council Minutes and some of these are available in local archives based in the Governor's residence. The contents of these laws and court cases provide us with valuable insights into the nature of slave society. The laws betray the economic preoccupation of an exploitative society but, above all, they reflect the mixture of fear, brutality and coercion which was the hallmark of slave society. At the same time, they reflect the value of the human chattel on whom, above all, prosperity rested.

Slaves were important not just for plantation labour and public works. They were, ironically, used in the defence system of the society in which they had no stake. By a 1693 law, 'every twentieth negro' was compelled to work on the construction of a fort at Palmetto Point; and, in November of the same year, an official call for 'two great guns' for Carr's Bay contained an injunction for all negroes in the Middle and Windward Divisions to begin work on a fortification on 4 December and finish on

14 December. The slaves were certainly preferred to the Irish as defence material. Governor Christopher Codrington, for one, preferred to entrust the protection of the island to the small number of English and their black slaves rather than to the Irish. Slaves were even used in offensive assaults, as happened against Martinique in 1761.

The laws reveal the planters' perception of the slave as a potential criminal with socio-economic aspirations. Force in its crudest form was used to repress and keep him subordinate. Some of the laws may not have been explicitly about slave control, but it is easy to see in them subtle limitations on their economic advancement. As we noted in the last chapter, there was concern in Anglo-Catholic Montserrat with proper observance of the Lord's Day, and laws were passed to regulate conduct on Sundays in 1668, 1669, 1683 and 1736. It is true that this concern predated the advent of slaves since a Council Order of 1638 also dealt with the subject. But as a slave society developed, the veneer of religiosity was used to restrict slave movement and their economic activity. If they could not buy and sell on Sundays, they could not accumulate money to buy their freedom and they could not compete with poor whites. Equally important, it was less likely that they would plan an insurrection if their whereabouts and activities were better known on Sundays.

Judging from the laws, the common offences were: petty stealing, estate larceny, running away, arson, damaging estate property (including animals) and murder. It never occurred to the administrators and planters that it was the treatment of slaves and their social deprivation which bred some of these evils.

Whipping and other forms of punishment were used more often than judicial murder in the early years of Montserratian slave society. But this was due more to scarcity of slaves than to humanitarian sentiment. In any case, some of the mutilation and arbitrary punishments were nearly as bad as death; and as the island matured into a full-fledged sugar-and-slave colony, treatment became more heartless and cynical. For stealing cattle, whipping was decreed as a deterrent in 1680. On the other hand, after 1696, stealing stock cattle equipment worth 12 pence carried a death penalty; if it was worth less than 12 pence, the victim was publicly flogged and both ears were cut off. In this period too, it was lawful for 'any person to shoot at and if possible kill any negro' who stole from the provision ground of a poor white. There was no pretence at justice for the slaves in this law. The accuser and executor could be one and the same person and nothing had to be proven beyond doubt.

Dunn asserts that in Antigua and Montserrat, slaves were customarily whipped rather than killed for stealing. This is doubtful, given the number of shocking killings and mutilations on record for stealing. In 1692, Peter

Coone was allegedly caught stealing nine pigs belonging to James Donnelaus and his wife. He was condemned to be cut to pieces, have his bowels burnt and his quarters displayed in the most public places adjoining the town of Plymouth and Kinsale.[10] In 1695, two slaves, one belonging to John Ryan and the other to Richard Forrest, were both accused of stealing a cow belonging to Constant Gollough. After the 'trial', they were ordered to draw lots and the lot fell on Forrest's negro, who was put to death. The other man was severely whipped. Dunn himself cites the 1690 case in which a black man was hanged for stealing two turkeys and five yards of fustian, and another case in which one was hanged, drawn and dismembered for running away. In 1699, Cuffee, owned by William Bedingfield, was convicted of stealing 12 pence, as it 'doth appear', on the strength of the oath of Dennis Mahoomy. He was sentenced to be hanged, his quarters severed from his body and left upon poles in the public place of the island.

What is equally disturbing was the random and irrational nature of some of the judgements handed down to slaves. The *Calendar of State Papers 1696–1697* records the case of a slave-owner who was asked to pay 5000 pounds of sugar for his slave, who was convicted of murdering another slave. Alternatively, he would be executed. Another slave belonging to the same owner was condemned to be hanged for stealing. The only possible logic here is that the murder of a negro was not as heinous a crime as stealing from a white man. And judicial murder almost invariably entailed compensation from the public purse.

Burning to death for stealing was also practised. In 1695 a slave of William Risdon was burnt for stealing a cow belonging to Captain William Frye, the Speaker of Council. He allegedly confessed the theft and the Marshal was ordered to jail him and then 'burn him at the usual place in Plymouth'. (The owner was compensated with 3500 pounds of muscovado sugar from public stock.)

The sensational judicial murders followed by public display were obviously designed to terrorize and deter the slave population from misdemeanours. Arbitrariness, such as the use of lots, was intended to serve the same purpose, while stemming the loss to the valuable servile work force; but one sees little if any trace of humanity in the Montserrat penal system as far as slaves were concerned. Even when a slave was not killed, the mutilation was gruesome. Cutting off the ears and burning on the breast with a hot iron 'intended for the purpose' were common. The instruments of torture and death included the wheel, and the places of execution were given meticulous attention in Montserrat.

The slaves were at the mercy of virtually the entire white population, and mercy was as plentiful in slave society as rivers in a desert. The protection of white persons and property took precedence above every-thing else. Slave society was in a continuous state of emergency. A 1693 law empowered military patrols to beat or stab slaves found outside their estate without the owner's ticket. They were also allowed to disperse any slave gathering by 'pistolling' slaves or killing them if need be. When the island surrendered to France in 1782, Montserratians were allowed to retain whatever arms were necessary for the discipline of their slaves. The French and the English agreed on this particular imperative of slave society – slave control by military arms. In a sense this was a realistic perception, because Caribbean slavery was naked violence.

It was not really until the eighteenth century that increasing costs combined with the scarcity of slaves to reduce the number of death sentences. It was, for instance, decreed that in a gang of slaves apprehended for burglary, arson, murder or maiming cattle, 'only one of them who shall appear to be the greatest criminal shall be put to death'. This measure amply illustrates the mix of expediency, indiscriminateness and unabashed brutality which defined slave-control procedures. It was plantation imperatives and not humanitarian fervour that governed the number to be executed. In 1772, Grace Parson's slave, Tony, was merely sentenced to a severe whipping for breaking into the house of John Potter and stealing a piece of pork, a piece of beef, two knives and a napkin.[11] In 1754, Tom Boy allegedly stole bread from a house, but the fact was only 'partly proved'. Logically, therefore it was not a fact. He was, however, sentenced to be whipped and have both ears lopped off. Accused slaves were obviously deemed guilty and it was up to them, as far as any proper trial was held, to prove themselves innocent. This was a near-impossible task. Mary Hendrick's slave, Mingos, was arraigned for having fresh meat in his house. As he could not prove that he came by it honestly, he was condemned to have his right ear cut off 'close to his head' and to be burnt on his breast with a hot iron.[12] And in 1785 two slaves, the property of Nicholas Hill, were convicted of stealing sundry pieces of wearing-apparel worth 10 shillings. Tom was sentenced to transportation, while Hannah received 39 lashes in the pillory.

There are sentences of whipping on record, but these tended to occur late in the eighteenth century. One can also detect rather more carefulness in the dispensing of justice, with several accused slaves being discharged due to lack of sufficient evidence. The following cases, all described in Council Minutes 1792–5, illustrate both points: Quamina, owned by William Manning, received 39 lashes in the pillory for breaking into his master's cellar. Bridget, the property of Hon. John Nugent, was sentenced to 25 lashes for stealing cotton. For stealing articles valued at 20 shillings, Richard received 39 lashes on each of two occasions; a male slave, Punch, was discharged 'for want of sufficient evidence'. He was charged with stealing cotton from his master valued at £20.8s. and setting fire to another parcel. Apollo, a slave of W. Samuel Lloyd, was accused of breaking open a trunk of dry goods which had been seized by HM Customs, and stealing muslin valued at £100. He was discharged due to insufficient evidence. Two slaves, Quaw and Arnoak, were charged with having stolen two sheep belonging to John and Henry Brinn. They were sentenced to receive 39 lashes each under the gallows. And in a number of cases dealing with absenteeism, theft, aiding and abetting theft and murder, several accused escaped punishment.

Clearly, brutality had not taken flight and, significantly, some beatings took place 'under the gallows', symbolizing the literal and figurative threat of death which hung over the condemned. Sale to the Spaniards and consequential banishment were in evidence, as were the dreaded penal chains. But a new trend is discernible in the attitude of the Council members in the adjudication of cases and the sentencing of convicts. The Spaniards, who needed labour for their relatively new and expanding sugar plantations, were offering good prices and some Montserratian proprietors were attracted to the slave re-sale prospects. This undoubtedly influenced sentencing policy to some degree. In May 1793, Robin, a male slave, the property of the Right Hon. Lord Gray, was valued at £66 when sentenced to be sold to the Spaniards for absenteeism. Less than six months later, when he was sentenced to death for breaking out of jail, he was valued at £55. The selling of slaves, for some persons, seemed a profitable enough traffic to affect the judicial system. One has to be wary of facile generalizations on slave punishments.

Montserrat passed no laws to protect the slaves comparable to the beneficent clauses of the French *Code Noir* of 1685, or even the Barbados code of 1661 which recognized certain 'rights' of slaves. Among other things, the latter aimed at protecting slaves from the wanton cruelty of their masters since the slaves were created even if they were property.[13] The British administration left the inhabitants of the island largely at the mercy of the Assembly, and the Assembly in part left the welfare of the slaves up to the good-will or ill-will of planters and their agents.

Punishment of slaves, however, which was a public spectacle, was not always left up to masters; and usually Justices of the Peace were expected to act on proof. However, very few accused slaves managed to prove innocence, as the system was stacked against them. The Governor-in-Council conducted certain serious cases, but it is not clear whether this was in the interest of justice for slaves or whether it was to ensure that just punishment was meted out publicly and dramatically. Many of the sentences involving mutilation and revolting forms of capital punishment are recorded in the Minutes of Council. Around 1722, Jacko, belonging to Major William White, was brought before the Council for murdering a slave called Jack. He was sentenced to be hanged, head cut off and put on a tree, and his owner was paid £50 (his value) from public funds. The members of Council were themselves planters who were at once plaintiffs, judges and jurors.

In economic terms, slavery was expensive and wasteful. There is general agreement with Adam Smith on this issue. The practice of compensating planters for slaves killed through the penal system added to the cost. A free man made good money in Montserrat as a slave-ranger, as we observed in Chapter 2. The Public Accounts Papers of Governor Stapleton contain entries on sums paid for bringing in the heads of slaves. For the period 1670–80, 3900 pounds of sugar valuing £15.5s. were paid 'for the heads of several negroes brought in'. A white man could earn up to 500 pounds of muscovado sugar for bringing in a slave dead or alive.

Although it was preferable to death, one of the most odious and demeaning punishments was to be sentenced to work in chains for life. In 1796, Nicky, belonging to Peter Dowdy, was so sentenced for stealing cash and various goods amounting in all to £200. The next year, the Assembly moved to abolish the practice and to free all current prisoners, provided they were sold and banished from Montserrat. The Council declined, arguing that because of the terror and ignominy involved, it was a more effective deterrent than public executions. One doubts the genuineness of this argument. These convicts provided a captive public crew which worked on roads and fortifications which the administration was loath to give up. Their contention that they would seem inconsistent if they were to change sentences, and that villains would be encouraged to commit crime, was as vacuous as it was illogical.

The limited forms of diversion and entertainment available to the slaves were circumscribed by law, in the cause of plantation safety. A 1688 law forbade slaves to smoke their pipes in cane-fields, for obvious reasons. Like any white person, they would be censured by the Governor-in-Council. More serious punishment was given to the slave if canes were burnt as a result of his going into the field with a lighted pipe on his own account. This law, however, demonstrates a small measure of humane concern for the slave and some effort to have the sentence suit the crime. The punishment could not be prejudicial to life or limb. A 1736 law not only struck at the cultural arts of music and dance, but also curtailed the pastimes of the slaves. Landlords and their attorneys were compelled to prevent their slaves from beating drums, casks or gourds and from blowing horns, shells or loud instruments for diversion and entertainment. The Africans' propensity for music was to be repressed.

The tendency to restrict the artist for political reasons has a long pedigree in the Caribbean.

It is clear that no thought or effort was spared to establish a tight security and punitive system. The whites knew that their racial policies and oppression of the blacks, who outnumbered them, would provoke retaliation. Their answer to this was more coercion and laws to control what they arrogantly and euphemistically referred to as 'the insolence of slaves'. But the instinct of freedom could not brook restraint forever.

The St Patrick's Day 'rebellion'

Slave-control legislation reveals planter preoccupation with slave resistance in one form or another. Escape by running away was common. And this could be from one plantation to another in search of better treatment, or to another island completely. Several laws were passed to curb slave desertion and to ensure that they had permission to be absent from their estate. They were not only potential criminals to be policed, but puerile wards to be monitored. The Minutes of Council for 1723–4 contain the injunction of the Speaker John Molyneaux to persons owning canoes to secure them in order to prevent slaves from running off in them.[14] In the oppressive administrative climate of Anglo-Irish Montserrat, it was not only the slaves who sought escape in boats. A 1683 law was directed against both bond and free who, if caught, would be returned to the island and prosecuted as felons.

As in all British Caribbean slave colonies, the penalty for striking a white person was death, but we have no evidence that any white was so assaulted in Montserrat. In 1693, however, a slave was convicted for beating his overseer almost to death. The overseer was the agent of oppression and coercion who was in close and continual contact with the slaves. Overseers were usually white, but occasionally black. In the Montserrat context of distrust for the Irish, it is highly unlikely that many poor whites became overseers, so this one was very likely a black man. In any case many overseers were over-zealous and attracted the odium which peonage generated against the white planters whom they represented. Symbolically this slave had struck a white man and, for his pains, he was hung up in chains and starved to death.

References have already been made to the many laws that were passed to regulate the proper observance of Sunday and their economic and social impact on the slaves. No one can deny some genuine religious sentiment, especially in the first two decades of the life of the colony. The 1683 law which dealt with profanation of the 'Sabbath' did not refer to slaves at all, but to the island's inhabitants who had to attend church in their various parishes. If they remained at home, they were to avoid commercial transactions, excessive drinking, gaming and swearing. The appointment and remuneration of clergymen were important matters of state. In 1698 the island was apparently without an ordained minister, but pastoral duties had to be performed. Accordingly the Council appointed James Cruikshank in the interim and paid him a stipend of 2000 pounds of sugar per annum, 'provided he preaches every Sunday, teaches catechisms and reads prayers in the afternoon'.[15] A culture of cruelty was not incompatible with religiosity in slave society.

The proper observance of Sunday as applied to slaves was informed by the need for coercion and control. If they were left to their own devices on Sundays they might plot rebellion. Significantly the 1668 law eschewed 'tumultuous hubbubs' in addition to digging, shooting, hoeing and baking. A complex of motives from which national and personal safety was never absent underpinned the laws governing the behaviour on Sundays of those on the periphery of Montserratian society.

A rebellion was nevertheless planned for 17 March 1768, a day conveniently chosen since the people of the island usually assembled to commemorate it. The Irish Roman Catholics were discriminated against, but the Irish connection was celebrated. The slaves working within Government House were to seize the swords of the gentlemen while those outside were to fire into the house using whatever missiles were at their disposal. They evidently had some arms because the plan was revealed when a white seamstress, noted for drunkenness, heard two of the leaders discussing the disposition of their arms.[16] Her report was at first greeted with disbelief.

On 6 October 1768, Vice-Admiral Pye, Commander-in-Chief of His Majesty's ships in the Leeward Islands, reported to the Governor that the insurrection was totally suppressed. Nine of the ringleaders were brutally executed, and some 30 were imprisoned pending banishment at the earliest opportunity.

The Montserrat planter-lords had cruelly scotched this plot, but it lived on in their memory. In March 1770, there was a false alarm over a slave uprising leading to the arrest of 16 supposed ringleaders and their separate confinement in different ships then in the harbour. The trial proved their innocence and the judges could not be induced 'to put the poor wretches to the torture and therefore I would not suffer it to be done', wrote Governor William Woodley.[17] Perhaps to impress them with his effective administration, he reported to the Lords of Plantations that all was quiet and that the inhabitants were free from fear. And yet some seven months later he wrote again of a petition from Assemblies of St Kitts,

Nevis and Montserrat about the defenceless state of the islands. The whites were anxious, feeling themselves to be in the power of the slaves owing to the numbers of the latter.

The participation in the abortive uprising registered in blood the slaves' love of freedom and unsettled the whites somewhat. It was not until 1985 that the slaves who were involved came to be regarded as national freedom-fighters for their attempt, and Montserratians began to celebrate St Patrick's Day annually as a public holiday. This came about after a few nationalist scholars popularized the event by staging cultural activities around the theme on the date and canvassed John Osborne's government to recognize the day officially.

This author had an occasion recently to warn against incipient distortion in the significance and celebration of the holiday.[18] It was, in his view, beginning to resemble the style in which the Irish diaspora in the United States celebrate St Patrick's Day. The holiday was intended to honour our slave ancestors who bravely essayed to overthrow their oppressive European overlords – and these were English, Scottish and Irish.

The 1770 episode which is associated with Palmetto Point reveals something of the slaves' creative imagination and sense of humour – qualities which undoubtedly helped their sane survival under slavery. It was the custom for slaves on several estates in St Patrick's to meet every Saturday night at Palmetto Point. There they engaged in role-playing and mimicking, re-enacting scenes of slave society and its administration. For instance, they imitated their masters, elected a General, a Lieutenant-General, a Council and Assembly and other officers of government. They usually ended the night with a dance. The creative act gave them psychic satisfaction, provided an outlet for their talents and it may even have kept the flame of freedom burning in their breasts. Ultimately, it was a positive response to slavery in a police state in which the whites had enormous and terrific power over them.

4

Irish and African emancipation

Irish emancipation

There was really no comparison between the horrors of black slavery and the discrimination against Irish Catholics in Montserrat, but both groups in their different ways hankered after freedom. The slaves needed basic personal liberty, while the Irish always struggled for civil and political equality with other whites. The latter achieved their goal six years before emancipation; but this was no more the fruit of human kindness, than was emancipation purely the result of humanitarian action.

Developments of an economic and social nature in the late eighteenth century led to more liberal policies towards Irish Catholics. The sugar industry had declined, due to French raids and natural disasters among other things, and many landlords returned to Britain. Of the small number of whites remaining, some were disqualified from membership in the legislature because of illiteracy. As a result, Protestants without the requisite property qualifications were being appointed as councillors. In 1788, there were only 290 whites in the island and the majority of them were Roman Catholics. Although appeal judges had repealed the 1749 law which imposed civil and political disabilities on Roman Catholics, they were still not allowed to vote, serve as jurors or become legislators. The tendency of whites to concentrate in and around Plymouth worsened the electoral problems for the districts of St Peter's and St George's. To make matters worse yet, the majority of the whites in St George's and St Patrick's were Irish Catholics. It is these electoral problems and not liberal sentiments which led to Irish Catholic enfranchisement.

It was noted in Chapter 1 that some Catholics were willing to compromise on religious conformity for the sake of peace and political advancement. William Stapleton hinted at this in 1676 when he said that in spite of their number, the Roman Catholics gave 'no scandal to the Protestant religion'. As time wore on, this strategy became an art. This is inferred from H. Coleridge's comments on this very phenomenon when he visited in 1826.[1] He deliberately exaggerated the amity which existed between Roman Catholics and Protestants, for he himself criticized Abbé

O'Hannam, the Irish priest, for toasting the health of the Bishop of Jamaica and for generally honouring him. If the relationship was as cordial as he suggests, why did he criticize the priest as being insincere for complimenting the Bishop and even for feasting with Protestants?

Coleridge is on more tenable ground when he suggests that some Catholics were prepared to subordinate religion to politics in order to survive in the illiberal political climate of the island.

> Indeed the faithful Catholic here has anticipated the fruits of emancipation; he considered it highly absurd to suffer himself to be deprived of great political advantages for the sake of a few oaths, when a priest actually resides in the island; and accordingly, having called God to help him as he utterly disbelieves, Transubstantiation, he marches into the House of Assembly, and there gives his vote. Nothing can be easier than this process, and I publish it here for the benefit of all the Irish, English and Scotch Papists, who may not have patience to wait till Parliament opens the doors of legislation to them.

His own Anglican religious bias comes through in the narrative, and he over-dramatizes the ease with which Catholic political aspirants denied central tenets of their faith, but he was correct on the basic issue – the strategic conformity of the Catholic.

By 1828 the climate was right and the Roman Catholics were psychologically ready. Certain enfranchising steps had already been taken before this date. In 1792, for instance, because of the small number of the white population, some propertied Roman Cathics were allowed to serve as jurors; and in 1798 the Leeward Islands Federal Assembly sitting at St Kitts abolished civil restrictions against the Irish and Roman Catholics. After this date, freeholders with a yearly property value of 40 shillings gained the franchise. As a result, all Irishmen of moderate means were in theory able to participate in civil and political life.

In 1826, the Catholics notched another significant milestone. The Assembly granted £100 to the resident Catholic priest towards the building of a church. It was now convinced 'that it would be highly illiberal and unchristian to deny an adequate provision for such purposes, being aware that the portion of inhabitants in this island professing the Roman Catholic religion is both numerous and respectable'.[2] This rationale is moving and high-sounding, but it is more truthful to conclude that the increasing foothold gained by the Catholics in civic life served to make them a more powerful pressure group in the island. It is also likely that a greater premium was placed on white solidarity due to an increase in the

number of free blacks, the exodus of whites and the quickening momentum of the English anti-slavery campaign.

By the 1820s the paucity of whites meant a near-crisis in government.
Some persons held several offices at once, and in 1821 James Masters, the
Slaves Registrar, topped them all, holding 21 positions, most of them unre-
lated. In 1810, Governor Elliot had reported officially on the difficulty of
finding sufficient qualified men to serve in the Council, in the militia, in the
law courts, as jurors and in government departments. The situation deteriorated further to the point where a fine of £5 was imposed on jurors for non-
attendance.[3] Council member and merchant, William Dudley Semper was
suspended in 1816 after he was suspected of colluding with a trader who had
brought goods into the island illegally from Martinique. The Secretary of
State, Lord Bathurst, later reinstated him, although he was in some measure
guilty, because 'in a society so small as that of Montserrat', it was difficult 'to
find proper members of Council who were not more or less engaged in mer-
cantile pursuits'. He nevertheless accepted the principle of the 'impropriety
of merchants being appointed to seats in the Council'. Semper was guilty of
being accessory to a crime linked to conflict of interests, but his services in
Council were virtually indispensable. Montserrat's white ruling elite preferred to compromise the governance of Montserrat by appointing unprin-
cipled men such as Dudley Semper to Council rather than to enfranchise free
coloured freeholders. The only reason why Semper was not a member of the
Assembly is because he had won the election with the help of free coloured
votes in 1813. He was for that reason promptly expelled by the likes of
Henry Hamilton, Thomas Hill, William Shiell and Bernard Gordon.
Nevertheless, flawed as he was, Semper became Chief Justice of Montserrat
in 1826.[4] Indeed because there were so few residents in Montserrat, Antigua
and Barbuda capable of filling official positions, the Governor of the
Leeward Islands, Patrick Ross, suggested a legislative and judicial union of
the three territories. The other aim of such a union would have been to
reduce the power of those few whites who held sway over the islands. The
time was deemed fully propitious for Catholic liberation in Montserrat.

The door to full emancipation finally opened in 1832 when a law
introduced into the Assembly in 1828 to give Roman Catholics civil and
political liberty completed its passage and was published. The preamble to
the law correctly cites expediency as its rationale. The landmark legislation
is reproduced here in some detail:

> Whereas by various Acts of Parliament certain restraints and dis-
> abilities are imposed upon the Roman Catholic subjects of His
> Majesty, to which other subjects are not liable: and whereas it is
> expedient that such restraints and disabilities shall be from hence-

forth discontinued: and whereas by various Acts certain oaths and declarations commonly called the declaration against Transubstantiation, and the invocation of Saints, and the sacrifice of the Mass as practised in the church of Rome, are required by the subjects of His Majesty as qualifications for sitting and voting as Members of either House of Legislature of this island, and for the enjoyment of certain offices, franchises and civil rights: *Be it enacted* by the Governor and Commander in Chief in and over His Majesty's islands of Antigua, Montserrat and Barbuda, and the Council and Assembly of this your Majesty's island of Montserrat, that from and after the publication of this Act, all such parts of the said Acts as require the said declarations or either of them to be made or subscribed by any of His Majesty's subjects as a qualification for sitting and voting in either House of Legislature, or the exercise or enjoyment of any office, franchise, or civil right in this island, be, and the same are hereby, repealed.

And be it enacted by the authority aforesaid, that from and after the publication of this Act, it shall be lawful for any person professing the Roman Catholic religion, who shall, after the publication of this Act, be appointed a member of the Council of this island, or be returned as a member of the House of Assembly, to sit or vote in either House respectively, being in all respects duly qualified to sit and vote there upon taking and subscribing the following oath, instead of the oaths of allegiance, supremacy and adjuration.

This law gave the Catholics not only political freedom, but also religious tolerance. And yet they were not totally trusted. They were required to swear allegiance to the monarch, disclaim the temporal overlordship of the Pope, swear to defend property rights and do nothing to subvert the established church which was, of course, Anglican. The Irish Catholics were willing to comply, at least outwardly, in return for a multi-denominational community and full participation in the social and political life of the island.

The Irish legacy

Much myth and uncertainty surround the abiding legacy of the Irish in Montserrat. While speaking proudly of our supposed Irish roots, a local informant reportedly told Canadian journalist Jane Gyorgy recently that, 'we've lost most of our far roots from Africa'.[5] This can hardly be true when over 90 per cent of the population is black or coloured including the people of the St Patrick's district which had the greatest concentration of

Irish people during plantation times (Table 4.1). The blood of Irishmen still lingers especially in the brown to near-white contingent in the parish of St Peter's, but the number is small and some resulted from African and English as well as Irish miscegenation. As Table 4.1 reveals, 76 per cent of the white men in the St Peter's district were English. The idea of a black Irish enclave in a distant tropical island or, another Emerald Isle with an Irish diaspora, sounds exotic and has prosperous possibilities for tourism, but it has no strong support from the historical evidence available to us.

Table 4.1 Ethnic distribution of the Montserrat population by political district

Constituencies	Percentage of white population	Irish as percentage of white	English as percentage of white	Percentage of slave population
St Peter's	13	24	76	36
St Anthony's	32	60	40	28
St Patrick's	47	72	28	26
St George's	8	56	44	10

Source: Adapted from a table in L. Pulsipher, *The Cultural Landscape of Montserrat in the Seventeenth Century: Early Environmental Consequences of British Colonialism*, Doctoral Thesis, p.66.

It is not that there are no Irish links and social retentions. This would be odd since they were around for over 300 years; but the influence is not nearly as substantial as is supposed either by zealous Irish patriots in search of their roots or by Montserratians, who, mimicking smiling Irish eyes in North American cities, are anxious to regale themselves in green and wave the shamrock on St Patrick's Day.

John Messenger of Ohio State University is a leading apostle of the Irish heritage in Montserrat. In his view, retentions and reinterpretations of Irish forms exist in speech patterns, music, dance, motor pattern, oral art, hospitality, codes of etiquette, the supernatural and a local stew called goat water.[6] There is perhaps a quarter-truth in all of this for it would be difficult for the Irish to have lived in close proximity with the slaves as small slave-owners and indentured servants without some inheritable cultural exchanges. But Messenger bases too much on conjecture and exaggerations and is thin on details. (He himself admits to a certain amount of tentativeness in his conclusions.) He for instance attributes the repetitive phrase 'at all at all' to the 'black' Irish of Montserrat, but this phrase is common throughout the entire island and also in neighbouring Antigua. It is possible that the storied white-skinned mermaid of Chance's Pond has Irish connections, but to say in 1975 that 'every Easter at midnight, hundreds of islanders climb the mountain by torch light to arrive before dawn and surprise the mermaid' is to be basking in the realm of imaginative literature.

Akenson agrees that Messenger's Hibernicist tradition is largely based on fancy and conjecture except for perhaps the mythological reference to the mermaid of Chance's Pool, while recognizing its commercial value. In his balanced way, he also denies claims in the Africanist tradition which he associates with local historians like this author. Happily he recognizes some value for historical myths and traditions including Messenger's which came 'like the crashing of an overloaded cargo airplane on a remote island'.[7] Perhaps Akenson, who in style often comes close to poetry, makes too sharp a distinction between these two supposedly dichotomous traditions in a situation where a cultural amalgam is accepted. This is why Irish historian Higgins suggests that the Irish influence is just one influence and that 'the real issue is what function Irishness fulfils as an ethic, and politics of memory and what it might release in Montserrat and Ireland'.[8] Cultural diversity is a reality, but whatever the mix ethnically, the island is almost totally African and this has to be more than skin-deep even if myths exist.

Montserrat does have an Irish legacy – part of it superficial and part rather more permanent. It is readily pointed out that a wooden shamrock adorns the gable at Government House, but this is only a symbol and one that is not without some irony since Montserrat's colonial administration was never really an Irish one. It is so often said that Montserratians speak with an Irish brogue that though one cannot vouch for it, one is inclined reluctantly to accept that there might be some truth there. And even this bruited brogue is questioned by phoneticists such as professor John Wells of University College, London, who found only one Gaelic word, *minnseach*, in Montserratian creole.[9]

Irish names abound on villages, estates, mountains and shorelines – Farrells, St Patrick's, Rileys, Fogarty, Fergus Mountain, Blakes, Galways, Reids Hill, Banks, Kinsale, Cork Hill, Sweeney's, Ogarro's. And black faces carry Irish names such as Irish, Farrell, O'Brien, Galloway, Ryan, Donoghue, Roach, Tuitt and Osborne. Slaves had no surnames so after emancipation they adopted the names they knew – those of their masters. Some inherited British names through white concubinage and mixed coupling. So in some few cases, names are indices of a deeper genetic legacy. We have already alluded to the presence of the Irish phenotype among the villagers stretching from St Peter's to St John's.

Religion apart, the Irish stamp is not as marked on the local culture as one might have expected. Research is still incomplete, but there is no evidence so far of any Irish influence on agricultural patterns in Montserrat. We may be on surer ground in music, although there is still the problem of isolating what is discretely Irish from what is British or even European.

The *bodhran*, a drum which forms part of the music ensemble for masquerade dance and for other local orchestras, is believed to be an Irish drum (see Chapter 12). A popular 'heel and toe' routine danced to the popular folk song *Bam-chick-a-lay Chiga Foot Myer* is believed to be an Irish dance step. Then there is *goat water*, the national dish, a stew made with kiddy-meat. Some argue that a similar recipe for goat-meat exists in Africa, but John Messenger is certain that it is an Irish stew. In 1965 an aged Connemara housewife allegedly gave Messenger's wife a recipe identical to the delicious Montserrat pottage.

Roman Catholicism came to most of the neighbouring islands through French or Spanish settlement or influence. In Montserrat it is a relic of the Irish, and it is significant that St Patrick's is still the village with the greatest concentration of Roman Catholics on the island. No one is certain when and where exactly the first Roman Catholic church was built, but claim is made for a Catholic church as early as 1678.[10] Following a Fr Morris, Antoine Demets believes that St Anthony's church was originally Catholic, but this is not likely, given the ecclesiastical polity of the time. We now know that the building that he referred to at Galways was a boiling house and not a church. By 1700, there were Catholic cemeteries at Streatham, White River (Andrew Power) and at the site of the former St Mary's school, but these were not necessarily attached to churches. To this day no Roman Catholic church exists in the north of the island, the locale of Messenger's 'Black Irish'.

After emancipation, the Irish started to leave an island of vanishing fortunes in which many of them were not allowed to be masters in the heyday of its wealth. Discrimination had shoved them into St Patrick's, one of the arid corners of the island. A destructive earthquake in 1843 quickened the exodus. It is not surprising that even Catholicism was a restricted legacy never spreading beyond Plymouth and St Patrick's until recently, and that Roman Catholics are outnumbered by Anglicans and Methodists and more recently by Seventh Day Adventists. The Irish as a whole never attained mastery in Montserrat and this is reflected in the leanness of their cultural bequests.

African emancipation

Although the decline thesis put forward by Dr Eric Williams in *Capitalism and Slavery* has come under heavy fire, the role of economic factors in the emancipation process cannot be comfortably discarded. Slavery did arouse moral indignation and 'God's politicians' inveighed against its inhumanity, but by themselves they could not bring the walls of slavery tumbling down at the time they fell.

It is remarkable that Hodge Kirnon, a Montserratian then living in New York, argued eloquently for an economic dimension to the emancipation story 20 years before Dr Williams published his famous thesis in 1945. This is how he penned it:

> Very important factors which were favourable to the cause of emancipation, but which have all this time been overlooked by teachers, writers, and historians, are certain commercial developments which seriously affected the economic life of the West Indies at this time. There was at the beginning of the nineteenth century the development of the beet sugar industry which flooded the English markets and completely swamped the West Indian cane sugar. The market quotations for West Indian cane sugar were the lowest in the history of its market value. It was about this time that India offered excellent prospects for the investments of British capital with highly remunerative dividends, and with hardly any risks. Under such conditions, the sugar industry was at a severe discount and the whole economic structure of the West Indies was on the verge of collapse; thus slave labour became a negligible factor with the decline of the sugar industry and the general financial breakdown. The Abolitionists at this opportune time pulled down the institution of slavery after its economic foundations were loosened by commercial interests powerfully antagonistic to those of the West Indies.

As happened elsewhere in the region, economic forces facilitated emancipation in the island. By the end of the eighteenth century, Montserrat's economy was in decline, due among other things to the trading impact of the American War of Independence, the lack of technical improvements in the sugar industry, natural disasters and French wars and related levies as well as defence costs. It is very likely that some of the many cases of manumission in this period were mainly due not to humanitarian sympathies, but to the falling interests of sugar. In 1782, John Allen willed the freedom of his negro slave Matty after his death, although any children born to her would be bond slaves to his heirs.[11] In 1793, Frances Wyke Brambley freed her female slave Posey for the relatively modest price of £20; and in 1805 a free negro, James Bowler, paid 18 *joes* (about £30) to Thomas Semper for the freedom of Nelly Ogarra. In 1795, the reputed father of Billy and Sally, the children of a mulatto, Sally Morgan, paid £135 to Eliza Lee for their release. Manumission may have been easier for these light-skinned children to achieve, but they benefited from what seemed an improved climate for slave redemption. In 1812, a mulatto slave woman paid only five shillings for her freedom.

The pattern of planter attitude, however, is by no means simple or clear. It seems that, as the reality of the abolition of the slave trade struck home, coupled with the growing momentum of the anti-slavery campaign in Britain, the planters of Montserrat raised the price for manumission. They even seemed less inclined to execute the death sentences in some cases; and it is significant that, among the laws enacted in 1821, was one instituting the trial of slaves by jury. It was at times difficult though, to empanel enough qualified whites to ensure a proper jury. In 1827 when an astute, even if notorious slave, Ned Minna, challenged the jury on the grounds of their qualification, in order to muster enough whites to form another one, the authorities summoned Methodist missionaries who were serving on the island. After some negotiation they were exempted at the expense of using unpropertied whites, contrary to law. The authorities preferred to do this rather this rather than to use coloured freeholders.[12] In 1823, O'Garro was charged £200 for his manumission, which he complained was not executed. The widow of his deceased master received the money, although she did not have the proper legal authority to manumit. A man by the name of Daly also complained that his manumission was being improperly held up. This was reportedly due to the fact that the consent of the mortgagees, and creditors of the estate was needed.[13] Such irritations did not make for harmony, especially at this difficult period.

In that same year, a slave, sentenced to death for stealing a goat, had his sentence commuted to hard labour in the street gang. (This gang, known as the penal gang, worked under the supervision of the police to keep the streets clean.) In commuting the sentence, the President was at pains to point out that stealing anything above the value of 12 pence was still a capital offence. In fact, between 1803 and 1823 only four of the persons convicted of capital offences were executed.[14]

Economics apart, Montserrat experienced the restiveness of slaves and the consequential unease of the whites, which rendered the climate in the British West Indies more favourable for emancipation. The 1768 slave conspiracy was long remembered in the island. In 1770 the local legislature petitioned the king to send two companies of soldiers to the island since the embers of discontent were still smouldering among the slaves.[15] As the number of whites dwindled through emigration, white fear might very well have increased.

We have no evidence of overt slave agitation in the years immediately before emancipation, but other forces were at work upsetting the equilibrium of the white power structure. These were rooted in the efforts of the free coloureds to obtain political and economic rights, including the right to hold jobs reserved for whites. An 1823 official report on the colony indicates that a coloured man was duly appointed as constable by the

British authority. Although he was fully qualified, he was rejected because of his colour. Peters provides us with another revealing episode taken as he says from the old Montserrat records:

> In January, 1805, John Haynes Skerritt, a free man of colour, appointed by the Commander-in-Chief to be Waiter of Customs, was brought before a Board of Inquiry, appointed by the Council. On being interrogated he was sentenced to imprisonment because 'This Board being of the opinion that the appointment of a coloured man to so important a trust, never before committed to any but a white man of character is, in the highest degree alarming and dangerous to the peace and security of the island'.[16]

The President Richard Symmons did not support this position, but he could not overrule an order of the Commander- in-Chief. The Assembly concurred, taking pains to point out that the job was a menial one and the incident could not be regarded as a precedent for giving offices of trust to coloured people.

The coloureds were undaunted, and insisted on voting in the 1813 general election. Concentrated as they were around Plymouth and Kinsale, in the parish of St Anthony's, their votes may have influenced the results of the polls significantly and led, as we have seen, to the election of Dudley Semper. The Assembly overturned the elections on the grounds that there was no law which granted the franchise to the free coloureds. The Governor sympathized with the latter, but compromised with the Assembly. The free coloureds persisted, voting again in 1820 with the same result. But then continual agitation forced the whites to give way and free coloureds in the British islands won political equality with whites before emancipation.[17] The Montserratian free coloureds had played a significant part in this victory. Within two years following the enactment of the law to give full citizenship to the island's free coloureds, in 1832, they occupied four of the 12 elected seats in the Assembly.[18]

With the slave trade abolished in 1807, the lesson of this triumph could hardly have been lost on whites and slaves. As early as 1795, the latter were obviously aware of and responding to the currents of liberty flowing from Europe, especially in the wake of the French Revolution. In that year the Assembly requested an additional company of soldiers to reinforce the internal defence of the island. This was due to 'the very pernicious and dangerous circumstances of the times occasioned by the enthusiastic spirit of liberty which mistaken and impolitic zeal has raised'.[19] Desire for liberty was answered with force and slaves were generally denied justice in the corrupt and incompetent courts.

Montserrat's response to the imperial call for amelioration and a gradual process to emancipation was typical of the British Caribbean. Its plantocrats were not prepared to abandon the flogging of women, the use of whips in the fields, the separation of families through sale for debt and all the customary tools of coercion. The Assembly met and resolved:

> That it is highly expedient at a period like the present, when a certain set of men in England are doing everything in their power to degrade and vilify the West Indies character by spreading malicious reports and bringing forward unfounded charges against them, this island should have a proper person on the spot to support its reputation, when thus attacked by the spirit of 'Bigotry and Fanaticism'.

There is absolutely no evidence that the Montserrat planters were more virtuous than the norm; the lion of oppression had been wounded and was determined to fight back fiercely. The Assembly voted £100 to pay 'Anthony Brown, a British Member of Parliament to represent planter interests at the highest level – in Parliament'.

Writing from England, Brown warned that the best way to stem the tide of emancipation was through the termination of cruel and wanton punishment and an improvement of the domestic conditions of the slaves. The demoralized minds of white slave-owners could not understand the grammar of amelioration or the gravity of the forces of freedom. Late in 1823, the legislature grudgingly conceded the rights of slaves to give evidence under oath. This was done with the aid and agitation of one or two fair-minded and far-seeing individuals such as Peter Wheatland and Richard Dyett, the latter belatedly so. Their failure to carry out further internal reform coupled with the slaves' hostile anxiety over the denial of freedom, brought them defeat. An Act for the abolition of slavery passed by the British Parliament in August 1833 came into force on 1 August 1834.

Apprenticeship and jubilation

A slave census (1810), shortly after abolition of the slave trade, showed that there were 3208 slaves in the parish of St Anthony's, 1483 in St George's, 1682 in St Peter's and 537 in St Patrick's, making a total of 6910. Table 4.2 contains their disposition island-wide. Individuals owned varying numbers, Queely Shiell capping all with 266. In 1838 the British government listed 6401 for compensation purposes. Montserrat's share was worth £103 000.

Table 4.2 Partial distribution of slaves, 1810

209	Farms Estate	
201	Richmond Hill Estate	(Grant Allan)
210	Broderick's Estate	
195	Spring's Estate	(Thomas Hill Jr)
182	Trant's Estate	
179	Hermitage Estate	
173	Farrell's Estate	
168	Branby's Estate	
160	Waterwork's Estate	
152	Edward Parson's Estate	
150	John Gage's Estate	
141	Paradise Estate	
138	Roche's Estate	
132	Clement Kirwan's Estate	
121	Dagenham Estate	

Source: T. S. English, pp. 271–2.

The jubilation of 1834 was muted. In addition to compensating planters at the imperial government's expense for their slaves, the Emancipation Act introduced a clumsy Apprenticeship system in which the slaves were free for roughly a quarter of each week, while they were bound to work for their (former) masters for the other three-quarters. Schooled by missionaries, many attended church services celebrating emancipation on 1 August, but they were disappointed when they realized that they were robbed of the full freedom which they anticipated. On many estates the apprentices refused to work and threatened violence, and many whites abandoned their estates, to take refuge in Plymouth. The authorities responded predictably, declaring a state of emergency and calling out the troops. Even so, the folks on the windward estates refused to be cowed by the threat of military force. With the arrival of Magistrates from England, and the unity of Bible and gun, the island came to peace.[20]

Recognizing that this scheme may not have been as commercially attractive as it seemed, the Montserrat Assembly decided to follow the lead of Antigua, which had narrowly voted to grant their slaves immediate freedom on grounds of expediency. The Council, however, held a different view and apprenticeship was instituted. The slaves were bitterly disappointed, and threatened to revolt, but were quelled by an official show of military might.[21]

Apprenticeship had to be policed. Plans were refined to divide the island into two districts, each one to be supervised by a special Justice or

Stipendiary Magistrate. In each district a well-furnished police compound, complete with a gaol euphemistically called 'a house of correction' was to be erected. Each policeman was to be properly remunerated according to rank, given a colourful uniform annually and be armed with a pair of pistols, swords, and a staff with the word 'Police' written on it. Post-emancipation Montserrat expected reprisals for the violence of slavery and was prepared to pay to combat it with institutional violence. A penal gang comprised of persons sentenced to hard labour was organized to maintain the roads in the vicinity of the police compounds and to cultivate the attached provision ground. As English opines, a sufficient supply of such persons was anticipated.[22]

It is doubtful whether this elaborate plan was fully implemented, due to cost. For certain, only one Stipendiary Magistrate was appointed, and this is one of the reasons why the apprenticeship system was not effective. Another reason, as inferred by Sturge and Harvey, was that neither the Stipendiary Magistrate nor the Special Magistrate was always free from planter influence and interest. This was also true to some extent elsewhere in the region. The particular Magistrate they met on their visit to the island, who had been appointed by the President himself, was an apprentice-holder. He was also appointed Police Sergeant, which meant that he apprehended and judged apprentices as well executed sentences.[23] While this particular situation had potential for conflict of interest, it should not be regarded as the general practice. Sturge's moral zeal and his mission have to be taken into account. Hall, for example, points out that there were conflicts between planter and Magistrate.

Apart from the Magistrates, the apprenticeship system in Montserrat encountered other problems. In their aim to demonstrate the virtues of free labour as opposed to apprenticeship labour, Sturge and Harvey were happy to observe that 'the five estates on which apprentices were liberated are quite as efficiently cultivated by free labour, as they were before'[24] and that else-where the apprentices were content to work for four pence per day (double on Saturdays) and remain attached to the soil and to the estates. However, things did not work as smoothly as is suggested here. The example of neigh-bouring Antigua was not lost on the Montserratian freedmen, who recog-nized their value to the planters and their relative independence. During crop-time, when work had to extend beyond sunset, their services had to be bought. Besides, Montserrat's hilly terrain did not make the land amenable to plough and harrow even if its many usually unprogressive farmers were minded to use them. This made the planters even more dependent on the apprentices. Their provision grounds (the term 'ground' was held over from slavery), the prolific breadfruit and sticks of cane from estates reinforced their independence and put them in a position to bargain for wages. It is not surprising that some estate-owners had taken the initiative to free their workers, as Sturge and Harvey's account indicates.

Some planters and attorneys, on the other hand, reacted angrily and violently to the anticipated loss of consistent labour and the full power of coercion. In February 1834, a Magistrate jailed the son of an 'apprenticed' couple for trespass. They had sent him off the estate to learn carpentry and he was arrested when he came to visit his parents. Soon after this, a woman was evicted from her house for attending church without permission. (Tenant eviction has a long and ugly history in this island.) And a manager vented his rage by ripping off the roof of a house with young children inside while the parents were away. The Stipendiary Magistrate J. C. Collins claimed that he promptly punished the offender, although he did not reveal the nature of the punishment.[25]

If such action presaged what was to happen over the next four years, the outlook was not good. Fortunately, the presence of the Stipendiary Magistrate and the calming effect of religion helped to maintain some order. The Methodist ministers whose diaries and reports provide valuable information on the period were not modest about their effectiveness during apprenticeship and in the general transition to a free society. Generally speaking, the Montserrat managers suffered more from the lack of funds than from the lack of labour. Apprentices needed cash to fund their love for attractive dress and good grooming and were therefore very willing to provide their labour to the estates. They worked avidly in their free time, either at task work or for a daily wage. The itch for cash caused some unfortunate apprentices to be lured on board ships of traders from British Guiana, ending up in indentured servitude. Some disreputable proprietors who were short of money encouraged the shameful traffic and actually sold some of their workers under the guise of manumission.

Apprenticeship only postponed the problems and challenges of establishing a free society. Unfortunately, all of the compensation money went to proprietors, who could hardly be expected to use it to establish a civil society. Health, for example, was neglected. An epidemic of yellow fever and dysentery debilitated and killed many. In 1837 alone, a fever took the lives of 20 of the 600 which it afflicted. The addiction to rum-drinking (naturally remarked on by teetotaller Sturge), aggravated the situation. (Some proprietors took advantage of this weakness, paying in rum instead of cash.) Physician and Speaker Dr Richard Dyett repeatedly blamed the epidemic bouts on the importation of compost by an absentee proprietor. This might not have been the only cause, but it was unwise and unnecessary and tantamount to taking coals to Newcastle.

The education available during apprenticeship was fragmentary and religion-based, as it was delivered by missionaries. The latter needed to win the confidence of the planter-government which was suspicious of education as a liberating factor. Their interest was in sugar rather than school, and they perceived conflict between the two. One gets an uneasy feeling about John Maddock's effort (as reported by G. E. Lawrence) to exculpate the judges and Montserrat planter society for their brutal treatment of slaves by alluding to the cruelty of the English penal system. The authorities tolerated the missionaries who taught subordination and obedience as prime Christian virtues, but they put no money into education. The Methodists started a day school at Tar River, where the children were enthusiastic about schooling but, attracting no government assistance, the school was soon closed. A person like Dr Dyett, the free-coloured Speaker of the Assembly, who solicited money from his friends for education, was the exception. Stipendiary Magistrate J. C. Collins had the enlightened and ambitious idea of establishing a school-house on each estate with a garden attached. These would have been the island's first vocational schools, for 'agriculture and other branches of useful knowledge might, nay ought, in a simple and gradual manner, to be introduced into the general routine of school instruction'.[26]

Many Montserratian apprentices were relatively independent economically, but they realized that their rights were being abridged by planters who were against their social advancement. They regarded managers as stingy, since the usual Christmas extras in food and drink were no longer forthcoming. There was no strong basis for harmony between the new sellers of labour and the planters as employers. Apprenticeship had failed in its main purpose.

The British anti-slavery movement campaigned vigorously to abolish apprenticeship, but again it was practical economic factors relating to the need for a regular supply of labour which proved decisive in effecting the early demise of the system. Besides, it was a compromise of slavery, which is an impossible phenomenon, however laudable was part of the aim. (It was not just a mechanism for adjusting gradually to the life of freedom; it was a means of providing planters and the sugar industry with captive labour.) It was difficult to contain men impatient for freedom. In November 1837 the Montserrat Assembly voted to end the irritation and appointed 1 August 1838 as the date on which all slaves would be emancipated. Slaves who were in prison as runaways were also set free. Nevis, St Kitts and Barbados followed suit between March and May 1838.

In congratulating the Montserrat legislature on its initiative in the early termination of apprenticeship, Sir William Colebrooke, Governor of the Leeward Islands, alluded to their 'enlightened humanity and wisdom'. Wisdom it was for sure, but it was more enlightened self-interest than humanity. The Speaker of the House of Assembly better captured the truth when he referred to the decision as the result of 'mature reflection and consideration'. Some of that consideration doubtless turned on the economic and security advantages of early emancipation. Richard Dyett, the Speaker, was sagacious enough to recognize the need for mutual confidence between 'the proprietors of the soil and the peasantry by whose labour it is rendered productive'.[27] It is a pity that no such consideration was given to the same workers when, though human chattel, they were the backbone of the economy.

5

Establishing a free society

Constitutional arrangements

The pre-emancipation attitudes and perceptions of white Montserrat persisted long after slavery and, to a great extent, the metropolitan government supported this thinking. Whites were leaders and landowners while blacks were labourers. The new constitutional arrangements reflected this position and reinforced the social and economic backwardness of the early decades of the new era. The constitutional developments are themselves an important thread in the skein of the island's story, but they also help to explain the pattern of ensuing positive and negative growth. Neither the old plantocracy, nor Crown paternalism (which was in many respects a modified mode of the former), was psychologically suited to building a civil society from the smouldering cinders of slavery.

As has already been observed, even before emancipation, planter self-government was imperilled by a dwindling and illiterate white population. In 1837, when the estimated population was 7119, there were five electoral districts returning, in all, 15 legislative members. However, the total number of voters was only 144, with 75 having voted at the last election; and, according to an official report, there was no law which defined the qualification of voters.[1] The island operated like an inefficient English rotten pocket borough.

Matters grew worse after 1838. When John Davy visited in 1851, there were only about 150 whites in the island. He found the legislative process and personnel rather comical. 'In reading the speeches of the president administering the government, and the addresses of the council and the house of assembly in reply, and his honour's replies to each of them, in set form, language and length … it is difficult to refrain from a smile, or to avoid the idea that the proceedings are a burlesque.'[2] The prospects did not seem good. Of the 170 persons who paid taxes, 59 were under the age of 16, and only 85 of those over 20 were literate. Antigua, by contrast, had a larger percentage of persons able to read and write. Montserrat's backward and ungenerous attitude towards education now haunted the governmental process.

The legislative bodies were not just unrepresentative and incompetent. They and the minority they represented were corrupt and racially prejudiced. In 1844, following a massive earthquake the previous year, the island negotiated an imperial loan of £23 000 at an interest of 5 per cent to restore public buildings and relieve private individuals on a loan basis. They used £3000 on public buildings and gave five of the 52 applicants a total of £15 000, two receiving £11 000 between them. The few big beneficiaries defaulted and the treasury was saddled with the huge debt. The British reduced the interest by $\frac{1}{2}$ per cent in 1853, but in 1861, the debt was still a millstone around the neck of the island.[3]

Property qualification was in operation but, even so, the legislature continued to be seen as a preserve of whites with some tolerance for coloureds. An effort was made in 1851 to evict Samuel Irish, a coloured Puisne Judge, from his seat in the Council. He complained that he was being denied the rights of English men, including the right to be presumed innocent unless tried and convicted, and that colour factored in the treatment which he received.[4] The episode arose out of problems with the finances of a Friendly Society of which Irish was the secretary. It was not clear who, if anyone, had misappropriated some funds of the short-lived Society. An ex-slave did get elected to the Assembly in 1842, but declined to occupy the position, due allegedly to modesty. He perhaps saw it as a mainly white club, because even if he had only modest gifts, he would have been among like minds.

A dash of colour was coming to the Assembly at a time when it was ceasing to attract traditional white planters. Significantly, three years after the first ex-slave was elected, the plantocrats voted to abolish the Assembly in favour of legislative union with Antigua or St Kitts. Both colonies cold-shouldered the move. Montserrat saw economic advantages in such a union at a time of severe economic downturn, but it was also a strategy to exclude the freed-persons from political power. The desire for dependency and tutelage has a long pedigree in Montserrat.

The first major post-emancipation constitutional change came in 1852. The Council and the Assembly were merged into one legislative body of 12 members – four nominated, and eight elected by the freeholders of the island. The parishes of St Anthony's, St George's and St Peter's each returned two members, and Plymouth and St Patrick's one each. The elected members, who could not make laws 'repugnant to the laws of England', held office for three years. The President and administering officers who presided over this legislature found it a more workable developmental instrument. President Hercules Robinson, in particular, used it to great advantage, passing many acts which benefited the island in his short tenure of three years.[5] By 1852, however, a strong peasantry had not emerged, so the vast majority of the population was outside the pale of electoral power.

Electoral change came again in 1861. Writing to the Duke of Newcastle, the Principal Secretary of State, the Speaker bemoaned the unworkability of the constitution 'for want of a sufficient number of persons qualified by education and respectable by position to discharge sufficiently or adequately to understand the duties of legislators'.[6] This view, coming 23 years after full emancipation, is an adverse comment on the attitudes and policies of the British government and the local Assembly and their attitudes toward the education of ex-slaves. The phrase 'respectable by position' harbours overtones of class-consciousness and even discrimination. In 1861, an Act entitled, 'An Act to fix the number of representatives each parish shall elect to serve in the House of Assembly of the Island and the several qualifications of the electors and candidates and to secure the freedom of elections' was passed. A law to settle the vexed question of extending the franchise was welcomed. Elected members were increased to ten and nominated members to five, all with a tenure of five years. A freehold valued at £25 six months prior to election day or an income of £100 per annum qualified a man for electoral office. The franchise was confined to male taxpayers who owned an acre of land in fee simple with cottage attached, or owned 20 or more acres of cultivation, or persons who obtained a rent of £10 per annum.

This constitution was not as liberal as it may appear, although Council President S. Cockburn glowed in his praises of it. Of those entitled to participate actively in politics many were still apathetic. Nevertheless there was some cause for hope. The number of freeholders had grown to nearly 400[7] and, in spite of unfavourable circumstances, a peasantry was emerging. Commenting on the results of the first election based on the 1861 constitution, the President referred to new faces and anticipated a 'happy equilibrium between experience and youth'. It is not clear whether there was any ex-slave among the new breed, although there probably were one or two. Among the pressing matters awaiting legislative action, Cockburn cited compulsory vaccination, registration of marriages, births and deaths, a Road Act, repairs to the jail and the restoration of churches – a useful social mix.

It can be regarded as somewhat ironical that this constitutional arrangement, hailed by Cockburn as 'an auspicious dawn in the gloom of your political system', was jettisoned in favour of direct Crown rule five years later. But the old guard of proprietors was of the ilk of Edmund Sturge and did not share his enthusiasm for the new faces nor did they kindly contemplate the prospect of being outnumbered and overpowered by an up-and-coming black peasantry whose capacities were not trusted.

In the event of a riot similar to the Morant Bay episode in Jamaica, Montserrat's white oligarchy could better shelter behind the skirts of the mother country. With their parasitic and dependency mentality, they also anticipated receiving largesses from England in times of economic distress such as the recent earthquake, hurricane and drought.

In 1866, the local legislature acted 'responsibly' and voted to surrender legislative power to the Crown. This coincided with the wishes of the Colonial Office and the administering officers who were impatient with the problems arising in the transition from a white oligarchy to popular multi-coloured democracy. The officer representing the Crown, and he alone, was empowered to introduce bills to what was now a fully nominated Council comprised of officials and (though unstated) men of landed substance. The leading proprietors were shrewd enough to realize that under the new dispensation, they would still dominate the corridors of power.[8] The narrow Old Representative system came to an end in Montserrat in 1866, giving way to a more subtly exclusive system as far as the free blacks were concerned. There was only room in Crown autocracy for whites or their wealthy coloured equivalents. The auspices for a balanced and equitable development of the new society were not favourable.

Federating the Leeward Islands

Hopes were placed in a federal structure as one means of achieving administrative efficiency and promoting the development of the Leeward Islands in the last quarter of the nineteenth century. Dogged from the start by insularity, the General Assembly was first summoned by William Stapleton in 1672 and later established by an Act of 1705, but was largely ineffective. It took over 90 years before it met again in 1798 to pass a law to improve the condition of slaves in a bid to stave off abolition. A final attempt was made to revive it in 1837. So the Governor Benjamin Chilly Pine was correct in asserting that the 1871 Leeward Island Federation was a restoration.[9] He himself saw wisdom in the union, but in proposing it he was executing the will of the British Government which expected the federation to bring about more convenient, efficient, economic and rational governance.

Being a Crown colony, Montserrat could do very little about this imperial imposition, and it did not wish to do anything but submit, anyway. It was, of course, known to have requested union with Antigua or St Kitts earlier in the century. Mr Pine and the British government had their way, but not without strong dissenting voices. The British Virgin Islands (BVI) and Antigua, like Montserrat, had no elected Assembly, so the proposal had an easy ride there. St Kitts petitioned against the move: they managed their affairs well, they insisted, and were a prosperous people who preferred to retain their independence of the other islands, fearing that they might be saddled with the financial burden of the weaker economies.[10] Dominica was more sympathetic. It saw some advantage in pooling common interests, but resented the lack of proper consultation and the undue haste with which the resolution establishing the federation was passed.

The Nevisians were even more violent in their opposition and threatened arson and riot. They drew the Secretary of State's attention to Pine's conduct in endeavouring to force a scheme of confederation on them contrary to their wish; and referred to 'their independence won by self-denial and painful privation'. They requested that the issue of a political and administrative union of the Leeward Islands be tested in a general election in Nevis, but this request was not granted. In the present era of feverish discussion on Caribbean integration, one cannot fail to recognize the similarity of the negative arguments to those raised in 1956. Insular interests and failure to recognize the impermanence of boom periods have dominated attitudes to unity in the British Caribbean for a long time.

St Kitts and Nevis were 'not independent' enough to thwart the union, for individual island referenda were not allowed: the British barely stopped short of imposing the union; the Governor used his influence, and the support of nominated and official members was virtually guaranteed. In December 1870, the measure went through. Table 5.1 gives the analysis of the voting. Of some 58 votes cast in favour of federation, at least 43 were by nominated or official members, while only 15 represented the voice of elected persons.

Table 5.1 Analysis of votes on federation

Island	For	Against	Absent	Total
Antigua	22	–	2	24
St Kitts	12	6	2	20
Dominica	9	5	–	14
Nevis	5	0	5	10
Montserrat	5	–	–	5
				1 vacancy
BVI	5	–	–	5
Total	58	11	9	78

Source: CO 7/143, The Leeward Islands Federation. For discrepancies, adjustments and rationalisation, see D. G. Hall, 1971, p.179.

The subjects which came within the competence of the federal council included property and real estate; criminal law and justice; a police force; education; a common convict establishment; telegraphy; currency; audit; weights and measures; the care of mental patients; quarantine; and copyrights and patents. The federation was not a particularly strong one, for island Councils had a veto on any measure placed before the federal legislature and there was no common treasury. It was under this federal constitution that the islands were termed presidencies, and each presidency was administered by an Administrator or Commissioner. (In 1882 Nevis was united with St Kitts and Anguilla into a single presidency.) The information in Table 5.2 shows that, apart from the British Virgin Islands, Montserrat was the least prosperous at the time of the federation.

Table 5.2 Data on the federal Leeward Islands, 1869

Population			Finances		
Islands	*Males*	*Females*	*Total*	*Revenue* £	*Expenditure* £
Antigua – Barbuda	–	–	35 412	40 035	31 810
St Kitts ⎤	11 437	13 003	24 440	29 812	27 584
Anguilla ⎦	–	–	2500	555	553
Dominica	–	–	26 065	15 620	13 947
Nevis	4526	5296	9822	9006	5631
Montserrat	3447	4198	7645	5433	5046
Virgin Islands	–	–	6051	1665	1969
Totals			111 935	102 126	86 540

Note: The figures for Anguilla and the Virgin Islands are given in terms of race – the former had 100 whites and 2400 blacks and coloured, while the latter had 476 whites, 4081 blacks and 1557 coloured.
Source: CO 7/143, History of the Present Scheme of Federation.

Montserrat was not just a Crown colony, it was part of a Crown-imposed federation. In addition, there were as many nominated as elected members in the federal Assembly, which consisted of a President, three ex-officio members, six nominated members and ten members elected by the four elective presidential Councils. Montserrat and the British Virgin Islands were represented by nominated members. Montserrat's first representative was a friend of Pine, W. S. Odlum, who had requested the job of island President. Indeed it was Pine's wish that Antigua, St Kitts, Nevis and Dominica would abandon the elective principle and choose full Crown-colony status like Montserrat and the BVI.

This was obviously a serious preoccupation of the colonial office, for in 1886 the Governor tabled a constitutional amendment in all of the presidencies, calling for the abolition of local legislatures and the transference of their powers and duties to the General Legislative Council of the Leeward Islands. The Council would consist of 22 members – three ex-officio, eight nominated by the Crown, and 11 elected, three of whom would come from Antigua and Barbuda, four from St Kitts-Nevis-Anguilla, two from Dominica and one each from Montserrat and the BVI.[11] These changes were perhaps unacceptable, because they were never implemented.

Montserrat benefited somewhat from the Leeward Islands federation, particularly in the areas of education, the common civil service, and the federal police force. The constitutional arrangements, however, took too little account of the creative capacities and energies of the people of the new emerging society. They were dictated too much by imperial convenience, as Hall suggests, with too little account taken of the needs and aspirations of the ex-slaves.[12] In thwarting their ambitions for self-rule and self-determination, British policy bred and reinforced a sense of inferiority in the black man which militated against real development for many years after. The free coloured who, as we have seen, were anxious to share in the political leadership of the island after the abolition of the slave trade, and who had won the right through struggle, must have been very disappointed at this reversal of their fortunes.

In a rhetorical flourish, Benjamin Pine had promised that federation would take the islands on 'a career of great dignity and importance, attract capital and enterprise to their shores; while their people of every grade and class will be gradually elevated'. This was not realized in Montserrat, where development needs were rather different from those of Antigua and St Kitts which continued to be prospering sugar islands. The federation was too limited in scope and flawed in its conception and design to answer the multiple needs of these several islands. Being a Crown colony and a member of a Crown federation limited the horizons of the new society and slowed down the process of real emancipation.

The emergence of a peasantry

Some of the immediate post-emancipation officials confused the terms 'peasants' and 'labour', using both interchangeably. For instance, in his report for October 1839, the Stipendiary Justice Thomas Shirley Warner used 'labourer', 'negro' and 'peasant' to mean roughly the same thing – wage earners with 'grounds'.[13] By 'peasantry' we shall refer to ex-slaves who owned or controlled land from which they derived at least a partial living. Economic activities such as fishing, animal farming, trading and shopkeeping engaged in independently of estates are also peasant activities and, as Marshall explains, a peasant had control over his time,[14] even if he operated as a part-time labourer and worked for wages. A peasant had control over land and over his labour.

Even though the sugar industry languished (with occasional temporary booms) after emancipation, several factors militated against the rapid development of a peasantry in Montserrat. And this is so in spite of the fact that peasant activity of a kind existed before emancipation, as Berleant-Schiller has argued.[15] In the days of slavery, there were opportunities for free labour in building and maintenance, in the service sector and in domestic work, but these almost always went to white workers. So, although some semblance of continuity can be claimed, pre-emancipation 'peasantry' was different and not perceived as a great threat to the plantation system, as was the case after emancipation. Local officials were conscious of their mission to preserve the *status quo* as far as estate labour was concerned. The Stipendiary Justice Thomas S. Warner reported with satisfaction in 1839 that 'the different classes understand and act on the knowledge of their relative position, and everything promises well'.

'Relative position' included the respective roles as proprietor and labourer. This was in keeping with the general policy enunciated earlier by Secretary of State Glenelg in 1836. He had advised governors to impede land acquisition on the part of the blacks by pricing land out of their reach so that they would be forced to work for estate owners, and so promote the production of sugar.[16] Squatting was also to be stamped out. Montserrat had little or no Crown lands, so any squatting had to be on abandoned estates. There were only two acres of Crown land after emancipation, and none when Davy visited in 1851, or when the Royal Commission of 1882 came. Another method used by managers to stifle the development of a peasantry was low wage-rates. In 1848 wages had dropped from six pence to as low as three pence; and this prevented significant savings, land purchase and independence. When labourers refused to work for such measly sums, managers victimized them by destroying their provision ground, 'pulling from the root young and ripe'. When they complained to the Stipendiary Magistrate, they were told to go back to work. As a result of this kind of harassment, many workers migrated to Guadeloupe and elsewhere.[17]

As long as labour continued to be abundant and fairly cheap, acquisition of land by the new labourers would be difficult. Labour was secured from roaming gangs in search of good wages or from persons who remained on or near estates. Besides, many proprietors resorted to the expedient of tenancy-at-will whereby labourers were allowed to retain their cottages and were allotted some land in return for two or three days of compulsory labour on the estate, mostly for wages that were well below the current average – sometimes as low as two pence a day. These workers cannot be deemed peasants in any meaningful sense, since they had no legal contract and no real control over the land they cultivated. They could be, and frequently were, evicted by the proprietor for not complying with his demands.

In fact, tenancy-at-will contained two vital elements of slavery – coercion and compulsion. It was a means of retaining both regular labour and land, and therefore it forestalled the development of a peasantry which was perceived as inimical to plantation prosperity. But tenancy-at-will proved to be an inefficient source of labour, while at the same time it embittered relationships. The threat and reality of evictions still did not tie some labourers to the estates. Indeed some labourers felt that custom gave them an entitlement to their cottages and grounds.

Métairie was the other infamous Montserratian expedient used by proprietors to keep their lands and have them cultivated by unpaid labour. Especially during periods of depression in the sugar industry, it seemed the perfect solution for impecunious landlords. Details varied, but generally the *metayers* were allowed to cultivate a certain acreage utilizing their own labour up to the stage of the production of the raw material. The crop was then shared equally between the labourer and the proprietor, and in some cases the latter enjoyed two-thirds; the landlord paid no wages and took no risks. The system was open to abuse, as the managers who kept accounts and determined shares were not always honest. Besides, this kind of tenure was doubly insecure, for when price prospects were good, the proprietor terminated the system, leaving the labourer with little option, and the sharecropper could also be evicted, if he displeased the estate manager in any way.

The number of acres cultivated by some estates appears quite small in 1870 when they were put up for sale in the Encumbered Estates court. Weekes (River Head) Estate, which was about 212 acres, had only 16 under *métairie*; but this was still more than the estate itself had under cane-cultivation. A similar pattern existed on some other estate, as Table 5.3 indicates.

Montserrat's sugar output increased to an annual average of 1265 tons between 1866 and 1876, up from 343 in the previous decade. Rented cane-lands were undoubtedly responsible in part for this resuscitation. *Métairie* was certainly being used in an effort to keep these bankrupt estates in sugar. It became such a panacea that it persisted into the twentieth century, assuming even more inequitable and iniquitous proportions on cotton plantations. In Montserrat more than in any other British colony, *métairie* was the big obstacle to peasant development. *Métairie* received strong official backing generally. The only exception was Edward Baynes, the island's President, who criticized it as being unsuitable for the island, but he was overruled by the Acting Governor, Cunningham.[18]

Table 5.3 Some estates for sale using *métairie*

Estates	Total acreage	Peasant proprietors	Cane acreage under Métairie
Weekes (River Head)	212	15	16
Upper Streatham	150	9	$25\frac{1}{2}$
Riley's	110	7	24
Windward's (White's)	223	37	30
Hermitage (Irish's)	706	$22\frac{1}{2}$	30

Source: CO 441/8/2 Information on estates for sale in the Encumbered Estates Court.

However, obstacles, including discriminatory land-taxation policies, did not prevent the painful and slow emergence of a peasantry. Official policy was not consistently antagonistic, especially if estate labour could be guaranteed. In December 1839, the Stipendiary Justice wrote approvingly to Sir William Colebrooke of the first person in the island to grant a lease to a labourer on his estate, pointing out that he was someone who was known to be against leaseholds previously. The lessee was Samuel Daly of St Patrick's who, in 1839, leased two acres from Henry Hamilton, the President of the island, on his Mountain and Sulphur Estate. The land together with the house in which he lived and his provision ground, cost Daly (who was unable to write), £7.10s.0d in current gold and silver money.[19]

Job or task work which guaranteed somewhat reliable labour to estates, while leaving the peasant worker with time to invest in his own pursuits, promoted the development of leaseholds.

This is how a Stipendiary Justice conveyed its advantages:

> The change of mind is deduced by the parties themselves inter-
> ested, from the adoption of job work, which has now forced its
> way into all parts of the island, and which, by at once calling
> forth the utmost efforts of the labourer, and properly renumerat-
> ing them, economises time and industry, and leaves to the perse-
> vering workman a surplus beyond his bare support, that either
> adds to his present comforts, or forms the nucleus of future com-
> parative wealth; even if hoarded, still more if it can be properly,
> that is, beneficially invested.

Quite apart from supporting leaseholds, job work had the potential for otherwise stimulating extra-plantation activities of a peasant kind. Leaseholds grew very slowly, nevertheless, and by 1850 only one other proprietor had followed Hamilton's good example, by Davy's account.

There is, however, an earlier reference to the 'tenants of a resident gentle-man who had rented parcels' to his former apprentices who had previously worked together in a task gang during slavery.[20] As proprietors and their sugar estates became bankrupt, rentals and leaseholds grew. In 1870, when Lower Streathams, owned by Hugh Riley Semper, was put up for sale, $19\frac{1}{2}$ acres were on rent to 12 tenants at a total annual rental of £23.4s.

We have already indicated that there were no Crown lands for squat-ting, but that opportunities existed on the many abandoned estates. Soon after emancipation, fewer than half of the island's 75 estates were produc-ing sugar, and no substantial staple had replaced it. In 1847–48 about 15 of them were sold for tax arrears. Some squatters felt justified in moving into uncultivated lands, especially where proprietors actually owed them wages. Davy reported that one proprietor owed as much as £600 in wages. Squatters contributed significantly to the economy, growing crops like arrowroot, corn and sweet potatoes and rearing livestock; they were granted official recognition in 1860, when they were required to pay taxes.[21] The government later coveted the land and moved to replace them with itself. A resolution brought before the Legislative Council in 1886 asserted that there were many lots occupied by private persons in different parts of the island from which the Government derived no benefit. The resultant law authorized the Governor to ascertain the number and to take steps to acquire them for public benefit.[22] A poor government pitted its legal strength against a land-hungry citizenry.

One reads more of the Montserratian ex-slaves' love of bright-coloured dress and rum than about their thrift, industry and ambition to advance socially. It was these latter qualities that led to the eventual emer-gence of a freehold peasantry in the face of unfavourable circumstances and humbug. A good example is the ex-slave described in 1840 as a yeoman who bought a 'couple' of acres of land on which he lived and which he profitably cultivated with the assistance of his family. His expla-nation for not attracting labourers is instructive. Although he offered a quarter of a dollar per day, 'the people would rather labour upon a sugar estate than for small settlers'. Apart from confirming the existence of small settlers, he points to an attitude which has not totally disappeared – a pref-erence on the part of poor blacks to patronize persons in a higher social class rather than to aid an equal who is attempting to surge ahead. Of course, another explanation could have been that other more profitable job opportunities were open to his neighbours.

This particular peasant was enterprising in other ways. He introduced South American wheat, although the prospect was not good as the site was unsuitable; and on the whole, his cultivation was considered as good as that of an English or Flemish farmer. (The European frame of reference has always been with us.) He at first wanted his son to become a mason, but decided in the end that he should be apprenticed in the farm that he would inherit. Farming, however, did not prevent his son from travelling three miles to Plymouth every afternoon for private tuition.[23] It is this kind of drive, good sense and ambition that underpinned the emergence of a peasantry in an oppressive environment – an environment that included stoppage of wages by grasping managers, and destruction of livestock of the poor by their dogs as happened on Thwaites estate in 1842 when a woman lost as many as eight goats.

Schedules to the frequent Acts imposing taxes on real estate between 1840 and 1855 provide a crude indicator to the slow but constant growth of the peasantry. Taxes ranging from one to one-and-a-quarter per cent of their value were levied on estates and plots of land, and on houses and vacant lots in the towns. Taking £50 and below as the value of small individual or family plots, we discovered an annual growth in the ownership of plots of these values and sizes. They grew from 22 in 1841, to 29 in 1842, to 33 in 1843, to 37 in 1844, to 46 in 1845, to 55 in 1846, to 137 in 1853, to 134 in 1854, to 139 in April 1855 and to 145 in October 1855. This is merely a clue, for a large landowner like Queely Shiell,[24] in the parish of St George's, possessed a few small plots; but it is a useful guide. In St George's the parish with the most landless people right down to the middle of the twentieth century, there was not a single plot valued at £50 or below in 1845 or 1846. By 1853, there were 12, and individuals emerged as rate-payers. This growth was not necessarily a growth of freeholders, but a peasantry was developing.

After the island adopted the Encumbered Estates Act in 1865, several estates were sold. By February 1868, the following properties were put up for sale: White's Upper Streatham, Lower Streatham, Riley's, Hermitage or Irish's, Tar River, Weekes' or River Head, Morris, Upper Cove or Dudley Semper's Cove, Andrew Power's Estate, Bushy Park, Cove or Riley's Cove with land in and around Plymouth, Dowdy's Bay, Martin's Store and Land in Parliament Street owned by Hugh Riley Semper. Everyone did not have the money to buy entire estates, like the Sturges of Birmingham, who bought seven, so some estates were divided into lots for sale to smaller buyers. Joseph Sturge himself sold some small lots, thereby adding to the peasant stock, and his company certainly leased lands to local farmers. One of the plaintiffs in the Encumbered Estates Court in 1868 was a labourer, George Willock, formerly of Morris Estate, who claimed two lots conveyed to him by deeds of lease.

According to Berleant-Schiller, the number of peasants grew from 400 in 1862 to 1628 in 1928, while the 1897 West India Royal Commission cited 1200 smallholdings. This is a picture of steady growth, but some holdings were only one acre; so although these persons lived in thriving villages, many had to do task work on estates in order to survive. A number of peasants were interviewed by the West India Royal Commissioners of 1882, as spokesmen for their various districts. Among these were Charles Tuitt from the North, who was a carpenter; Henry Piper, a storekeeper; and J. S. Meade of St George's who had to labour on the road for four days to obtain needed cash. Some of them were struggling and complained, like the proprietors, of an oppressive horse tax, and a dog tax. Charles Tuitt found it necessary to ply his trade in Redonda, where he earned 2s. 6d. per day. The fact that they were interviewed bears testimony to their social significance, and the recognition was of psychological value. They staunchly represented the cause of labourers who were hurting from a high rum tax (rum was their only liquor) and a high import duty on tobacco.

Mr Hollings, a planter of Richmond Estate, was critical of the peasant cultivators for poor agricultural practices, but he was not unbiased and the standard of farming in the country on the whole was not high. What was needed was agricultural education for all, to remedy the defects that were undoubtedly present.

Alternatives to sugar as the staple commodity will be studied in the next chapter, but it is useful to note briefly the element of diversification which the peasants brought to the economy. By 1651, new exports included 628 cords of firewood, 321 cords of timber, 107 barrels and 11 boxes of arrowroot, 201 bushels of Indian corn and 18 bales of cotton, yielding a total revenue of £800. In addition, cassava and ground provisions which had a profitable market in Antigua, were produced in addition to the usual livestock. It is difficult, if not impossible, to determine how much of these were produced by labour hired by estates, and how much by peasant farmers; but it is clear that the latter contributed, since their smallholdings of from two to five acres or even more were amenable to the small cash crops. By 1860, the year when sugar exports hit an all-time low, the list of possible peasant produce expanded to include: cedar logs, cocoa, logwood, peas, beans, sweet potatoes, tamarind, fish, shells, dried fruits and hides. Export duties were imposed on some of these commodities for the first time in 1862.[25]

The new export crops resulted in new trading relationships within the region. So instead of a purely vertical trade and connection with the mother country, a horizontal one emerged to embrace Antigua, Barbados, Tortola, Bermuda, Guadeloupe and even the United States. A number of boats were built locally to facilitate this trade, a tradition which is still alive today, although the nature of the trade has changed.

The establishment of villages is a well-known off-shoot of peasant development. Freehold peasantry grew slowly in Montserrat, and so did village settlements. Berleant-Schiller cites an 1870 map with two villages between estate boundaries on the windward side of the island. One was Long Ground, wedged between Tar River and Hermitage estates. Land was most likely bought from Tar River estate by a few families who pooled their resources. It was deemed 'undivided property' and registered in a single name. The tax had to be collected from house to house and paid in by one person.

Two decades after the Methodists had established themselves and built a school in that corner of the island, it was located on Tar River estate, then described as a 'wretched place'. We can conjecture that by the time the Long Ground (Tar River) village was born, there were others in other parts of the island. As early as 1822, the diary of Rev. Janion speaks of 'a little settlement called Two Rivers' as distinct from Blake's and Barzey's estates. By 1846, there were 108 persons living in villages formed after emancipation. In 1897, the Royal Commissioners alluded to many thriving villages.

Village life generated new service occupations such as shopkeeping, and an increase in handicrafts such as earthenware and bark-ropes. The peasants were among the members who joined the Friendly Society established by Anglican clergyman Rev. J. C. Collins. It collapsed in 1846 due to misman-agement and, perhaps, chicanery after Collins died. Mismanagement by persons in high places caused many to lose their savings.

Social life

By social life, we mean here selected elements which contribute to civil society, such as law and order, care of the sick and disadvantaged, educa-tion, and the general well-being of the people.

For a people who suffered such oppression and indignities under slavery, free Montserrat settled into orderliness rather quickly. There was ample provocation to violence as some managers 'hired' labour without paying wages and others arbitrarily 'stopped pay' – that is, robbed the employee of one or more day's pay, or simply reduced his overall entitle-ment. Methodist missionaries can justly claim some credit for black docil-ity. In their bid to cultivate official support, they were at pains to emphasize their loyalty and the harmlessness of their gospel as far as the *status quo* was concerned. 'Actuated by sentiments of esteem and venera-tion for so illustrious and dignified a personage', John Maddock had in 1820 written to the Governor Sir Benjamin D'Urban assuring him that he would teach the slaves their duty in that state of life in which it had pleased God to call them.[26] His epistle and its exaggerated tone sounded more like a politician's than a parson's. The example set by Maddock was followed by his successors, and was in keeping with Charles Wesley's philosophy of education: to teach 'humanity, gentleness, long-suffering and contentedness in every condition'. The gospel may not have been the opium of the people, but it was certainly a sedative.

Rum-drinking, a sedative of another kind, seemed to have been rife, but the planter-merchants had a vested interest in exploiting this tendency. (The English poet Lord Byron once wrote: 'There's naught so much the spirit calms/As rum and true religion'.) It was sold in the estate's provision shop. When an ordinance to regulate the sale of spirituous liquor was introduced in 1869, the powerful voices of Hubert Burke, Joseph Allen, George Wyke, Hugh Semper and William Wilkin were raised against it. The intention was to restrict sales to 12 hours from 6.00 a.m. to 6.00 p.m. The opponents argued that labourers and mechanics received their wages late in the day and could not get to the shops until 8.00 p.m.; and the proprietors were not, of course, prepared to separate the rum from the provisions.

One of the vexing problems was the persistence of slave laws into the era of freedom. Larceny, for instance, continued to be punishable by death. In 1842, Stephen and Edward Frith were tried for larceny and sentenced to death 'in conformity with the existing law'. President Edward Baynes had the good sense to commute the sentence to imprisonment, but needed formal authority to suspend capital punishment. In his petition to the Governor, he observed that the law was framed in the most oppressive period of slavery.[27] The very poor woman who lost her goats near Thwaites estate in 1842 could receive no redress for the malicious injury due to legal niceties. In his Report for February and March 1842, Stipendiary Justice Marten Nanton noted with satisfaction that no one was ejected from his grounds by force of 'colonial law'.

What was needed was an urgent programme of law reform. Some useful laws were passed which guaranteed personal protection and contributed to social civility. Rape, the ultimate invasion of personal privacy, for example, was severely, indeed cruelly dealt with by an 1842 law. When perpetrated against a child below the age of 10, the penalty was death. The humanity of a President like Baynes and the sense of justice of most magistrates were vital for harmony in the society. Managers like John Lavincourt and Anthony Dowdy felt the force of the law for 'stoppage' of pay. The settlement was said to be amicable and the compensation ample.[28] There was of course, the exception like John Osborne, a Stipendiary Justice, a salaried man, who was also a barrister and attorney at law and who was reportedly retained by almost all proprietors on the island. The poor labourers were the victims of his corruption and this cruel conflict of interest.[29]

In situations like these, it is perhaps not surprising that violence flared up from time to time, especially in Plymouth. Angry gangs stoned the houses of authority figures. Magistrate Harris, for one, feared for his life and had to be removed. Since the level of violence expected immediately after emancipation did not ensue, the police force was allowed to disintegrate, but it had to be re-established in the 1840s. The tendency of white Montserrat was to call for troops to deal with an emergency instead of creating a proper force to prevent crimes. At the end of his tenure in 1852, President Baynes boasted of an empty jail. Even allowing for Baynes' need to varnish his regime, which had run into trouble and criticism to the extent that the leading citizens petitioned for his removal, this says something for the general peace of the island.

President Edward Baynes described the 11-year period during which he held office as one of unparalleled depression of commercial and agricultural interests. It was a difficult decade even though the gloom was not without periods of relief. And reporting on the first Christmas in freedom, the President Henry Hamilton, described a well-dressed peasantry, crowded churches and a nearly empty jail. What really aggravated the situation was the earthquake of 1843, and a smallpox epidemic of 1849–50, followed by a drought. The result was poverty and disease which reinforced each other at a time when health care hardly existed. The epidemic took 200 lives and assistance in the form of money and food had to be obtained from Antigua. The 1841 Plymouth landing of men from the ship *Megara*, on which yellow fever was raging, caused panic, for there was no vaccination against the disease.

Responses to this wretchedness were varied, characterized on the one hand by a parsimonious proprietor class and on the other by fitful acts of humane concern. One of the aims of the Friendly Society established by Rev. J. C. Collins was to give a daily meal to the indigent, but this, as we have seen, folded up rapidly. The Legislature addressed the problem by voting £400 annually for outdoor poor relief to be dispensed by a committee of the Council and Assembly. This was typical; the plantocracy sought to control all avenues of patronage and charity, linked to public funds. The grant rose to £1000 in 1843.

Later on, indoor relief was established, but the indigent shared premises with the physically and mentally ill. (The harsh term 'lunatic asylum' was used to describe the home of the mentally ill.) In 1847 a law was passed to rationalize arrangements for the support and maintenance of the destitute. A Board of 18 guardians, at least five of whom had to be members of the Council and the Assembly, was instituted. They were empowered to manage the lists and apportion aid, and encouraged to provide food and lodging rather than monetary handouts. This is what led to the lease of premises to house the very indigent. The resolution to purchase the premises was officially adopted in 1876. However, there was a budget shortfall in 1897, expenditure on relief was reduced, and some inmates were discharged and given outdoor relief, which cost the government less. Montserratian inmates at Skerritts in Antigua were discharged due to the budget squeeze. This was a home for delinquent boys, euphemistically called 'the Industrial School', because some practical instruction in farming was given.

Apart from the individual effort of the occasional Anglican bishop to teach the catechism in or near Plymouth, education was virtually non-existent before 1800. In the early nineteenth century, a sprinkling of persons became barely literate through Sunday Schools established by Methodist missionaries, who used their church buildings 'for school as well as Praise'. Education was regarded as socially disruptive, irrelevant and even inimical to slave society, and only 'harmless' religious teaching was tolerated. The emergence of formal education had to wait until after emancipation, and unfortunately the same thinking and prejudices persisted into the new era.

Education was conceived as competing with sugar for labour, and the politico-economic leaders were unwilling to spend money in that way. In 1836 Joseph Sturge remarked on the need for teachers and school buildings; and in 1850, Davy compared the opportunities for education unfavourably with Antigua. Stipendiary Magistrate T. S. Warner spoke of the desire to establish on each estate, which was virtually a little village, a school building with a garden so that agriculture and other branches of useful knowledge might be taught. Funds, however, were lacking. Sir Thomas Neave donated £10 per annum for education on each of his estates, hoping in vain that other proprietors would follow his example.

By 1840, Methodist day schools for both sexes covered most of the island and provided education for about 490 children, as Table 5.4 indicates. Rev. Lawrence, the Methodist chronicler, suggests that there may have been as many as 12 (including one at Blakes and one at Friths since the 1830s) at an earlier date. The curriculum of these schools was linked more with the hereafter than with the here-and-now imperatives of a livelihood and self-direction.

This contrasted with the programme of practical instruction conceived by T. S. Warner, the Magistrate. Children memorized and recited hymns, and copious scripture verses with little understanding; and because the meagre salary of about £10 a year could not attract competent teachers, many of those used 'were extremely ignorant, unable to give explanations'.[30] Spelling and ciphering were later added to the curriculum.

The Anglicans, who could not afford to be outdone by the Methodists, soldiered on. Schools were a means of ensuring a continuing and growing flock. Established earlier and being the state church, the Anglicans drew larger grants. In 1842, when the Wesleyans received a grant of £42, the

Table 5.4 Methodist and Anglican day schools, 1840 and 1837

Methodist day schools, 1840		Anglican day Schools, 1837
Location	*Enrolment*	*Location*
Plymouth	143	Frye's
Salem	50	Flemmings
Brodericks	56	Brodericks
Carty's	59	Riley's
Bethel	68	White's
Tar River	42	Roache's
Cavalla Hill	72	St Peter's
		Gerrald's

Source: G. E. Lawrence, *Montserrat and its Methodism*; C.O. 318/138, 1837 Report on Negro Education

Rev. J. C. Collins of St Anthony's received a whopping £500, although some of this was intended to cover ecclesiastical expenses other than education.[31]

Very few buildings were erected solely for school purposes in the first half of the century. The Methodists had a school-room and a teacher's cottage at Friths estate before 1839. In that year they obtained a national grant of £60 to rebuild it after a fire destroyed it; and when in 1855, they built a church building of stone at Cavalla Hill, the wooden building was turned into a school. The first non-denominational school building sprang up in 1870 when the Sturges of the Montserrat Company built one at Olveston to cater mainly to the children of their workers. In 1875, a Leeward Islands Act recognized state responsibility for education and regularized grants to denominational schools. This boosted the development of education. In 1881, the Methodists built a school-room in Plymouth; and when the 1899 hurricane demolished both church and school, a decision was made to rebuild the school first.

The Anglicans also stepped up their building activities in the 1880s. Hitherto they used mainly church buildings or parsonages. A list of their schools around emancipation is given in Table 5.4. Rev. J. C. Collins built the St Mary's school-chapel in 1883, and this later became a full-blown school. In 1890 a similar building was established at St Patrick's. St George's had a school-building before 1888 for, in that year, it was rebuilt at a cost of £90, with the government providing about two-thirds of the money.[32]

Beleaguered by the Protestants, the Roman Catholics, who saw education as a prime instrument of religious propagation, also taught in their churches. They opened a parish school in 1860, and by 1875, they had erected a building of stone in the church grounds in Plymouth.

Prior to the 1875 Education Act, primary education developed in a piecemeal and uncoordinated manner under the aegis of mainly religious bodies, with fitful grants from the Government. These schools provided simple instruction in the three Rs, grammar, poetry-memorization, and religious indoctrination. The curriculum bred submission and docility rather than independent thinking and personal autonomy. With the passing of the Federal Elementary Education Act in 1890, Montserrat became an Education District of the Leeward Islands, and education became compulsory for children between the ages of five and nine. This meant that learning was not allowed to compete with labour. Poor performance, aggravated by a flood in 1896, led to a suspension of compulsory education, abolition of the position of District Education Officer, and a reduction of grant-in-aid by £100. It would be the twentieth century before the state took full responsibility for education.

A start had been made by the churches; but education not only reflected denominational ideology, it also reflected educational patterns in England from whence the missionaries came. The problems of relating education to indigenous developmental imperatives is a continuing one. Intellectual dependency has a long history in colonial Montserrat. At the end of the century, Thomas S. Warner's 1839 hope that provision 'for the education of the labourers' children will be looked upon as the duty of the capitalist and of the landowners' was still far from being realized.

The establishment of a public library was another useful step in the direction of an enlightened society. With an initial government grant of £20, and an annual subvention of £25, Francis Burke, a leading citizen, formed a Library Institute and started a library in 1868.[33] Theoretically it was open to all persons but, in reality, location and lack of money robbed the majority of its use. Users were required to pay a small annual subscription. It nevertheless had a great symbolic value for the entire society. Located at 'the Grove', it was really an initiative of the Montserrat Company which played such a significant part in the post-emancipation development of Montserrat.

Government took over the library around 1890, having voted an annual grant of £50 for its maintenance in 1889. By then, it was sited in downtown Plymouth, and subscribers paid eight shillings annually, while readers paid a penny weekly. Due to financial problems, government found it difficult to maintain the library which again had to depend on private support. By 1907 Government was again giving a grant of £50 which was increased later to £75, but private subscriptions were still vital to its survival. In 1923, in addition to an entrance fee of five shillings, first- and second-class subscribers paid 24 and 15 shillings annually; third-class subscribers, who paid no entrance fee, paid six shillings annually. There was a total of 43 subscribers in 1923.[34] These naturally had extensive privileges in a library which was out of reach of the majority, physically and financially.

By the end of the nineteenth century there were many encouraging signs of social and economic transformation, but it was and would be a slow and painful evolutionary process, with reverses on the way. Constitutionally, the island had taken a backward step, and economically, the smell of slavery still lingered in the cane-piece and the mountain grounds; but one of the encouraging signs was an ambitious peasantry, some of whom were prepared to purchase private education for their children.

The officers who administered the colony for the British government were important as co-architects of development along with the people. They became even more crucial after 1866, when they became the mediators of Crown autocracy. Development would have been even slower in Montserrat in the first quarter of the century after emancipation, were it not for caring presidents such as Henry Hamilton, who preached and practised alternatives to servile wage labour and offered creative ideas on alternatives to sugar; and a committed and energetic, though enigmatic, Edward D. Baynes who did not manage his financial affairs well, and became too intimately involved in personal squabbles (as Douglas Hall suggests). Indeed, he himself confessed to occasional errors. With better cooperation from his superiors in the colonial administration, Baynes might have done a better job. He saw and dared to criticize the evils of *métairie* from the labourers' viewpoint and the same local leaders whose damning report precipitated his recall, later gave him a positive testimonial. They admitted that he ruled well, alleviated evils and maintained harmony in the different branches of the legislature in a period of unparalleled economic depression.[35] It is perhaps significant that the Crown trusted Montserrat to two of his descendants – Edward Baynes in 1889 and T. E. P. Baynes in 1932.

The former had his problems, and his dignity was bruised in the incident known as the Fox Riot of 1 May 1898. It grew out of an attempt by the police to arrest the Fox family of Friths for illicit rum-distillation. Three police from the Salem station first attempted the raid, but were driven off. Due to hostile sentiment against the Government at the time, the crowd sympathized with the Foxes and aided and abetted the resistance. Reinforcement came from Plymouth, accompanied by the Inspector-General of the Leeward Islands Police Force, who happened to be visiting the island, and Commissioner Edward Baynes. The angry crowd greeted this posse with a shower of stones and sticks and completely overwhelmed the police, who fled panic-stricken, most of them ignoring the order to fire. Pressed by the crowd, one of the police fired, wounding six persons with buckshot. The Commissioner and Inspector, who were left to the mercy of the crowd, were both wounded, Baynes seriously. It took the arrival of HMS *Intrepid* with reinforcements from Antigua to restore normalcy. The 40 persons who were arrested and tried in Antigua were eventually freed due to the astute advocacy of lawyer Moore.[36]

This was a costly riot and the lessons, including the show of black solidarity, were not lost on Edward Baynes. Among other expenses, the owners of the SS *Spheroid*, which the Commissioner sent to Antigua for assistance, were paid £53.14s.3d.;[37] and £27.16s.6d. was paid to the navy for expenses which it had incurred with the riots. The riots cost the Montserratian Treasury a total sum of £871.15s.2d. Seven weeks after the riot, a motion was passed in Council to establish a Defence Force. The force was fitted out and equipped (complete with musical instruments) at public expense and could be summoned in the event of war, invasion and any internal emergency which threatened the security of life or property. If the Salemites and other Montserratians did not respect Baynes's position, they were expected to respect the military power at his disposal. Order was a priority in the new colonial society, and the Montserratians had to foot the bill.

6

Alternatives to sugar:
Cotton becomes King

Sugar dethroned

The sugar industry was described by the 1897 West India Royal Commission as being in imminent danger of extinction. Although some 6000 acres, or three-fifths, of all the cultivated lands were growing canes, and muscovado sugar and molasses accounted to 81.69 per cent of the island's exports, the industry was not profitable. Only one rum distillery was in operation producing for local consumption; and additional rum of better quality was being imported from Demerara and St Kitts to satisfy local demand. The fact that Farrell's, Riley's, Amersham, Broderick's and Webb's had absentee owners and were the subject of litigation did not help the industry. In fact, the only reason why sugar was still the main export was because there was no major alternative export to replace it.

Edward Baynes, the Commissioner, told the Commission that the depressed state of sugar was not principally due to inferior equipment and manufacturing process. This was a useful argument in his bid to persuade the commissioners that capital was needed for new industries, but the state of sugar technology was an important contributing factor to the state of the industry. True, the topography of the land, with its numerous hills and ravines, could not readily accommodate central factories, especially without the coercive cheap and brutish facility of slave labour but, up to 1883, the farmer Mr Lloyd, in an interview with a Royal Commission, gloated over the fact that 'we have no steam engines or any of that botheration here'.[1] In 1897, only 12 of the 26 estates in the island employed steam power.

About the only technological initiative taken was the introduction of a German steel hoe, which was lighter than the British iron hoe, did faster work and therefore economized somewhat on human labour. The suggestion came from Francis Burke, an enterprising proprietor who played a prominent role in the economic and political affairs of the island. In commending the idea of the new hoe, the Stipendiary Magistrate T. S. Warner lamented that the upper classes were not interested in small but valuable changes or in ameliorative devices for the workers.[2] There is little evidence that they were interested in any modernization of the industry. They did not, as happened elsewhere in the sub-region, attempt to produce vacuum-pan or centrifugal sugar; these would have produced more and a better quality of sugar from a given quantity of cane. And even allowing for the hilly and uneven terrain, it is surprising that only one estate was using the plough by about 1850. A combination of primarily attitudinal and secondarily environmental factors prevented that modernization of the sugar industry which alone might have meant its successful survival after emancipation. In 1848, the Governor of the Leeward Islands found Montserrat to be the most backward of all. He observed that neither the plough nor any other modern equipment was in use.[3] By the end of the century there was little change in this verdict, and the British Government did precious little to assist.

Table 6.1 gives export figures for sugar between 1882 and 1896. In 1896 only 530 gallons of molasses were exported, a recovery from 35 in 1895.

Table 6.1　Exports of sugar production, 1882–96

	United Kingdom		United States		Canada		Other		Total	Total
	Quantity	Value £	Quantity	Value £	Quantity	Value £	Quantity	Value £	Quantity	Value £
1882	–	27 381	–	961	–	–	–	394	–	28 736
1883	–	16 997	–	2 592	–	–	–	1 153	–	28 742
1884	230	2 889	1 466	16 578	–	–	49	452	1 745	19 919
1885	203	2 250	1 103	9 841	–	–	63	568	1 369	12 659
1886	25	246	1 026	9 120	–	–	4	31	1 055	9 397
1887	1	5	1 601	13 125	–	–	16	131	1 618	13 261
1888	81	721	1 800	15 103	9	84	4	35	1 894	15 943
1889	270	2 213	1 182	13 197	–	–	73	839	1 525	16 249
1890	13	109	1 395	11 667	–	–	11	82	1 419	11 858
1891	–	–	1 030	9 741	–	–	42	407	1 072	10 148
1892	535	4 397	1 732	14 282	215	1 742	42	332	2 524	20 753
1893	7	55	1 298	14 311	350	3 821	93	1 037	1 748	19 224
1894	–	–	1 617	14 487	61	507	123	936	1 801	15 930
1895	199	1 542	381	2 877	44	261	81	571	705	5 251
1896	–	–	1 197	10 543	349	3 129	98	765	1 644	14 437

Source: West India Royal Commission Report, 1897, p.117.

Diversifying the economy

While sugar was undoubtedly dominant, Montserrat's agricultural economy was more diversified than that of most other West Indian colonies. In Chapter 5 we observed that a variety of crops was associated with the peasant population. In the second half of the nineteenth century, the menu of minor cash crops grew, and some formed a significant segment of the export economy. Limes, coffee, cocoa, arrowroot, vanilla, tobacco, ginger, nutmegs, kola-nuts, ground nuts and a mix of fruits were considered important enough to be listed as alternative industries by the 1897 Royal Commission. Table 6.2 gives the value of exports other than sugar and lime juice. In 1893, 134 869 gallons of raw lime juice and 6265 gallons of concentrated juice were exported, carrying a total value of £8843; and in the 1940s, livestock, potatoes, tamarinds, charcoal and volcanic rock were on the export list.[4]

Table 6.2 Alternative export industries, 1892–6

Year	*Arrowroot* £	*Cocoa* £	*Coffee* £	*Bay oil* £	*Papaine* £	*Total* £
1892	333	8	2		40	383
1893	906	76	31		133	1146
1894	663	125	379		149	1316
1895	391	98	112	162	393	1156
1896	669	62	789	461	501	2482

Source: Report of the West India Royal Commission, 1897, p.128 (C.8655).

Some estates, but particularly those belonging to the Montserrat Company, were at the moving edge of the diversification process. The Company took particular interest in coffee, cocoa and ginger, in addition to limes, which we shall treat separately below. It was a Mr Hamilton, of the Montserrat Company, and a local proprietor, W. H. Wilkin, who rein-troduced coffee in the economy. A former Ceylon planter, Hamilton brought skilled management, practical experience and improved varieties to the industry. Papain, a preparation from the unripe fruit of the papaya, was used as a meat-tenderizer, and as medicine. It was a small industry with a limited market, but was an important peasant crop. Bay oil from the cinnamon leaf also offered an opportunity for the small farmer at the primary production level.

The establishment of a Botanic Station south-west of Plymouth in 1890, gave a fillip to the multi-cultural economy, and to the fruit and veg-etable trade in particular. The station cultivated and distributed a number of economic plants, including Blue Mountain coffee and bananas from Jamaica, Liberian coffee, pineapple suckers and grapevines. In 1902, an onion industry was formally approved. The brakes on the fruit and veg-etable trade were the lack of suitable facilities for shipping. Unfortunately, the Botanic Station was short-lived due ironically 'to the straitened cir-cumstances of the island'.[5] An institution which should have been a key part of the infrastructure in an agricultural environment felt the sharp edge of the financial axe. Some years later, the Botanic Station was reintroduced.

A Peasant Information Bureau established in 1928 performed some of the duties of the Botanic Station, adding marketing advice. It distributed new plants and seeds from nurseries established island-wide at the Groves, Gages, Amersham, Sweeney's, Carr's Bay, Whites and Tar River. Breadfruit, budded limes, coffee, cocoa, onions and tomatoes received special attention, and onions and cotton survived into the cotton era to preserve the element of diversification. Tomatoes did particularly well and penetrated the Canadian market (see Table 6.3); and onions, as Commissioner Major H. W. Peebles observed in an address to the Legislative Council in 1929, deserve more than a passing glance. From an export value of £919 in 1921, exported onions fetched £6000 in 1927 stemming from 447 000 pounds. An experimental canning outfit set up to utilize rejected tomatoes which could amount to as much as 20 per cent, was late for the 1929–30 season. However, pineapples, guavas and mangoes were canned and sold in neighbouring markets. This innovation is particularly interesting in view of the failure of a tomato-canning factory that was established in 1960 and in the light of perennial talks and sterile efforts to establish a fruit-canning factory in contemporary times.

Table 6.3 Tomato exports, 1929–30

Markets	Crates	Gross receipts	Price per pound
Canada	3111	£1003.6s.5d.	$4\frac{1}{2}d.$
Barbados	116	£33.9s.5d.	$2\frac{1}{2}d.$
Antigua	18	£5.9s.4d.	$1\frac{3}{4}d.$

Source: CO 177/36, Report on the Peasant Bureau.

The search for alternatives to sugar led to the novel experiment in the growing of silk-worms and the establishment of a silk industry at a time when there was a demand for the commodity in the United States of America. The enterprising investor was Francis Burke of Dyers estate, whose name is linked with other pioneering ventures in the economic life of the island. Mulberry groves were planted, *coconières* built and eggs imported from France and Italy; and for a while there were promising results with small yields of white and yellow reeled silk. Wine from the mulberry fruits was also anticipated as a by-product of the silk industry. Problems of a technical nature, however, dogged the industry. Ova had to be shipped at exactly the right temperature, and the long transatlantic journey made this difficult. But even when Burke visited Martinique and Guadeloupe, which were also experimenting with the industry and procured a quantity of eggs in 1841, the problems were not solved.[6] The mulberry and the cocoons all needed very careful culture and the *coconières* had to be constructed according to certain specifications. Add to this the problem of an alien climate, and it is not surprising that the worms developed diseases and the experiment languished after about six years. The technical and management skills available locally were not adequate, although Burke and his *coconière* director were keen and enthusiastic and the Secretary of State was supportive. The Foreign Office proposed sending skilled French advisers to the island, but this did not materialize.[7] More capital for on-the-spot research and experimentation might well have saved the venture.

Limes

Francis Burke was again associated with a new agricultural venture, but this time with resounding success. He started to grow limes commercially on Woodlands in 1852, in collaboration with his financier, Edmund Sturge, a Quaker. When the Sturge's Montserrat Company was formed in 1869, it took over the industry and held a virtual monopoly over lime-culture and lime-products on the island. In 1878 the Montserrat Company had 600 acres growing 120 000 trees. By 1897, the acreage had more than doubled to 1247, with 250 000 trees; at the same time other sugar estates and small properties had only 153 acres of limes.[8] By the end of the century lime-growing had spread to more or less the entire island, but the Montserrat Company was still the giant producer. The lime industry requires large acreage, so it was easier for the Company, with its many *latifundia*, to lead the industry than smaller proprietors and peasants, whose few acres had to be more diversified for total survival. The failure of the lemon-crop of Sicily in 1853 gave Montserratian lime the opportunity to dominate the British market.

A. Aspinall has provided us with interesting details of the island's lime-culture. Transplanting of limes took place from June to December, when the seedlings were 12 months old. The tree

> flowers from February until June, and the main crop season extends from June to December, but the period varies according to the weather. The yield per acre is also variable, but where cultivation is good, it should amount to as much as 150 or 160 barrels of fruit per acre annually. A barrel of limes gives $7\frac{1}{2}$ to 8 gallons of juice and the yield of citric acid varies from 12 ounces where there is high rainfall to 14 ounces where it is low.[9]

Apart from its economic value, lime-juice production for use in beverages appealed to the abstemious temper of the Quaker Company.

Another reason why the lime industry flourished was the relatively simple and cheap technology required, compared to sugar. The processing of lime oil, for instance was simple, but interesting. Young limes were bruised by hand in a saucer-shaped vessel called an ecueller, fitted with sharp projections. The oil cells in the rind were punctured by these spikes, and the oil collected at the bottom of the vessel; it was then filtered and bottled for shipment. Lime oil was used in the perfume and soap industries.

Writing in 1912, Aspinall found that the latest available figures showed that the lime products from Montserrat were worth £9403 and this was second only to Dominica to which the industry had spread from this island. Montserrat, however, had better lime years, as Tables 6.4 and 6.5 reveal. There are discrepancies in the two sets of figures, but it is evident that the industry reached its zenith in the mid-1880s. Thereafter there were fluctuations and declines as disease, flood and hurricane took their toll. The hurricanes of 1899 and 1928 were particularly ruinous, and the diseases wither-tip and blossom-blight hit Salem and the leeward districts particularly hard. These setbacks did not kill the industry. In 1933 the island reported 4841 crates and 1319 barrels of green limes and 48 691 gallons of raw lime juice; and in 1929 a decision was taken by the Montserrat Company to set up a lime-crushing plant in Trinidad which was less hurricane-prone than Montserrat. Montserrat had become the operation's base for a regional industry. The industry did not regain nineteenth-century levels, but continued to feature in the export economy down to the second half of the twentieth century.

Table 6.4 Montserrat Company's lime products, 1882–6

Products	1882	1883	1884	1885	1886
Lime juice (raw gallons)	44 880	132 840	133 139	16 275	145 440
Concentrated (gallons)	9 540	9 940	13 966	1 000	7 080
Lime essence (cases)	5	37	26	4	26
Pickled limes (boxes)	150	50		47	80
Fresh limes (boxes)	216	144	953	822	2 051

Source: Government House Archives. Correspondence with the Colonial Secretary, 1884–90.

Table 6.5 Lime juice exported from Montserrat, 1884–96 (gallons)

Year	Raw	Concen-trated	Value (£)	Year	Raw	Concen-trated	Value (£)
1884	133 139	13 975	10 300	1 891	119 493	10 145	9 419
1885	12 900	2 000	810	1 892	72 590	5 190	4 859
1886	121 250	5 875	8 554	1 893	134 869	6 265	8 843
1887	107 500	10 574	6 995	1 894	8 280	2 100	729
1888	5 275	12 736	8 340	1 895	130 245	2 272	6 802
1889	66 800	13 950	6 711	1 896	65 260	6 663	4 261
1890	68 503	15 451	7 063				

Source: Adapted from West India Royal Commission Report, 1897, p.148.

By 1900 Montserrat's lime juice had become famous in the British world and had placed this somewhat undistinguished sugar colony on the map. 'Montserrat Lime Juice' was splashed across several English newspapers and periodicals in lavish advertisements. Among these were *The Wine Trade Review, Pictorial World, Agricultural Journal, The Grocers' Journal, Church of England Temperance Chronicle, The Globe* and *The Baptist. The India Planters' Gazette* of 3 November 1885 contained this item:

> The *Lancet* says, 'We counsel the public to drink their Lime Juice … either, alone or sweetened to taste and mixed with Water or Soda and a little Ice if obtainable … but care should be taken that Montserrat Lime Fruit is only used, as it has the delicate aroma and flavour peculiar to the Lime Fruit and found in no other Lime Juice'.[10]

One can perhapes take this with a grain of salt. It was certainly popular with British sailors, known as *limeys*, as a shield against scurvy.

Limes linked Montserrat's name with the famous Schweppes Company. From 1928, Schweppes Limited of Australia and New Zealand, with an office at Connaught Place, London were the main customers for Montserrat Company lime juice. Renewable contracts of five years were signed, making Schweppes the sole consignees and bottlers of Montserrat lime juice and users of the 'Montserrat' Lime Juice trade mark. The quality of the juice – its flavour, acidity and specific gravity – were all specified. The exclusiveness of the trade was entrenched in this clause:

> The Licensees shall not market in Australia and New Zealand as 'Montserrat' Lime Juice or Schweppes Lime Juice Cordial and Lime

Juice other than that which they have obtained from the Company, prepared solely from Montserrat Lime Fruit Juice or market any 'Montserrat' Lime Juice under any other name or description.

The Company, on the other hand,

undertook to use their best endeavours to supply the quantity of lime juice ordered from limes grown on their own plantations in the Island Montserrat. Should they, however, be unable to do so in any year they shall be at liberty to substitute juice as nearly as possible of equal quality produced under their supervision in the West Indies.

In limes Montserrat found something distinguishing and something to be finicky about apart from a dubious Irishness, and she was. Table 6.6 shows the quantities of lime juice supplied to Schweppes between 1928 and 1933.

Table 6.6 Lime juice supplied to Messrs Schweppes Ltd, Australia

	Puncheons	*Mont's Juice*	*Puncheons*	*West Indian*
1928	35	3 887 gallons	12	1 334 gallons
1929	61	6 525	nil	nil
1930	75	7 947	"	"
1931	7	764	"	"
1932	25	2 932	"	"

Source: Sturge Family Papers seen at Waterworks, Montserrat.

But limes could not make up for the fallen fortunes of sugar. It was most profitable when it covered a large acreage and was therefore more attractive to the Montserrat Company with its many estates than to lesser proprietors and to the peasants who needed to diversify production on their holdings. The island as a whole benefited from the industry in direct and indirect ways. The Company hired workers and were good corporate citizens, as we shall demonstrate below, but the lime industry was essentially a monopoly venture. It was to cotton that the island turned to occupy the wasted throne of sugar.

King Cotton

When Montserrat embarked on the serious cultivation of cotton in the twentieth century, it was a reintroduction and not an innovation. When the island was captured by the French in 1782, cotton was already being exported. Act 214 of 1782, passed under the administration of M. de Goullon, placed a tax 'on all sugar, rum and cotton already shipped and now in the road of Plymouth'.

In 1902, having hardly recovered from the 1899 hurricane, the island found itself still in straitened circumstances, with the majority of people facing unemployment. In that year, the preamble to a request to Queen Victoria's government requesting urgent assistance, read: 'Whereas it has been notified that the majority of the sugar estates still in cultivation in this island will after the present crop, be abandoned and whereas a large proportion of the labouring class and mechanicals will thus be thrown out of employment ...'. Fortunately, there was a shortage of cotton due partly to an interruption in production in the United States of America caused by the American Civil War. In the West Indies, and in Montserrat in particular, cotton started to take root at this opportune marketing moment.

Experimentation in sea-island cotton began in 1901 with a sample of seed received from J. R. Borrell, the Superintendent of Agriculture in Barbados, and lasted for about 10 years.

> A small plot of cotton was planted with the seed received in the Experimentation Station at Montserrat in the year 1909, and from the outset the plants showed marked vigour. The selection of individual plants was undertaken later in the year, and after analysis of the factors of each, Nos. 8 and 9 were considered to be the best, and were grown on the breeding plot in 1910.[11]

Further experimentation led to the adoption of Heaton 9 and its offspring (the seeds came originally from an English firm of spinners, Messrs William Heaton and Sons) as the most profitable strain for the Montserrat conditions. It is instructive to note that experimentation and some research had begun to inform agricultural practices.

Pre-empting the result of the experiments, the industry had taken off since 1909 with the help of 'Hurricane' loans from the imperial treasury. Indeed, cotton was partly responsible for the island's improved finances in 1910 when the revenue was £10 611 and the expenditure for that fiscal year (1909–10), was £7806. The surplus of £2805 was described by the Governor as the second largest in the island's history. By 1912, the 'latest figures available' showed that there had been 2000 acres under cotton with a yield of 402 000 pounds of lint for export. The scope of cultivation equalled that of St Vincent and was second only to Barbados with 4000 acres of cotton. Table 6.7 provides production details (1911–38).

Table 6.7 Cotton production, 1911–38

Year	Acres planted			Lint produced			Selling price
	Estate	Peasants	Share	Total	Total	Per acre	per lb
1911				2700	244 753	128	
1912				2063	292 181	141	
1913				2200	293 167	133	
1914				2350	380 923	162	
1915				1953	279 595	143	
1916				1997	313 322	156	
1917				2608	409 855	156	
1918				3167	438 222	157	
1919				3200	548 334	171	
1920				3200	395 035	123	
1921				2070	367 536	178	2s.3d.
1922				2023	464 082	229	2s.3d.
1923				2600	517 893	199	2s.4d.
1924				3500	228 845	65	2s.6d.
1925				2500	282 759	113	2s.1d.
1926				2800	600 127	214	2s.
1927				2900	668 301	230	2s.3d.
1928				2600	600 472	231	2s.
1929				3200	726 129	226	1s.10d.
1930				4079	737 719	181	1s. to 1s.5d.
1931				3425	400 389	117	1s. to 1s.1d.
1932				1500	187 131	125	1s. to 1s.1d.
1933				2182	477 097	219	10d. to 1s.
1934	455	1143	1508	3106	881 595	283	1s.2d. to 1s.3d.
1935	760	1796	1882	4438	1 016 387	229	1s.2½d. to 1s.7d.
1936				4550	457 000	101	1s.6d. to 1s.7½d.
1937	859	2063	1458	4380	641 000	146	1s.6d. to 1s.7d.
1938	1049	1895	1509	4453	500 000*	112*	Mostly unsold

Note: * = Estimated.
Source: CO 950/545, Submission to the Moyne Commission.

Cotton continued to strive during the second decade of the century, increasing in acreage from 2050 in 1911 to 3200 in 1921. By 1930, it had definitely become the main staple crop and the mainstay of the economy; the crop produced 4079 pounds of lint at an average of 181 pounds per acre. Estates bought cotton from peasants at a penny per pound. Cotton was king. The peak year was 1941 when 5395 acres produced a record of

1 175 935 pounds of lint. Food shortages aggravated by the Second World War led an 'observer' to suggest in 1942 that for 10 acres of cotton planted, estates should be required to grow one acre of ground provisions.[12] A similar law was passed in the heyday of sugar.

The cotton was ginned on the island and the seeds produced two valuable by-products. One was the rich cooking oil and the other was an animal feed known as 'cattle cake'. In 1939, there were seven gins on the island. Cotton remained, nevertheless, a primary industry with the raw material shipped to Liverpool and later to Manchester in the United Kingdom for manufacturing in classic colonial fashion. It was not until the 1970s that a tepid effort was made to create a fully integrated cotton industry, to include the manufacture of fabrics, garments and other household articles. Ironically, the industry was by then a mere shadow of its former glory with fewer than 100 acres under cultivation.

The reign of cotton was not one of unbroken success or tranquillity; some problems were natural and some were social. The crop was susceptible both to drought and to wetness if the two phenomena did not occur at the correct stage of the industry. When the bolls were at an advanced stage of ripening, for instance, heavy rains could ruin the crop. After a record export of 1 016 000 pounds of lint in 1935, a bad drought followed early in 1936 and an abnormally wet season followed upon that. The result was a fall in production to only 450 000 pounds of lint.[13] Table 6.8 gives the lint production for 1938.

Finding a fixed season for cotton planting became a problem in an island with an erratic seasonal rainfall. In an effort to capitalize on the elusive rainy season, the planting had variously been June to September, April to May, and February to March, by 1912. In 1936 there was yet another change. A 1953 British Commission of Inquiry recommended October as the general planting season. Apart from the unpunctual and unpredictable tropical showers, the industry had enemies in the cotton-stainer, an insect pest. In a bid to control, if not eradicate the stainer, silk cotton, mahoe trees, wild cotton and

Table 6.8 Cotton lint exported in 1938

	Cleaned cotton		*Stained cotton*	
	Weight (lb)	*Value (£)*	*Weight (lb)*	*Value (£)*
January to Nov.	320 346	19 875	12 825	321
December	191 950	11 975	31 542	778
Total	512 296	31 850	44 367	1099

Source: CO, 950/561 Evidence given to the West India Royal Commission by Commissioner T. E. P. Baynes.

other uneconomical malvaceous trees had to be statutorily destroyed, along with the cotton plants themselves at the end of the season.

In some years, market prices fluctuated or remained static while cost of production rose. Montserrat Company records show that part of the stock of Montserratian cotton remained unsold in Liverpool in 1926. The labourers and peasants, of course, bore the brunt of the downturns of the industry. In 1936, the Montserrat Cotton Growers' Association was formed, presumably to cooperate to improve production as well as to safeguard their interests in the face of demands for higher wages. This incorporated body, which made its own rules, proved a formidable barrier in the path of the poor majority who were mostly estate workers, in their bid to subsist. Many of their members, among whom were names such as H. R. Howes, Charles Griffin, H. F. Pencheon, H. S. Osborne and W. W. Duke, were members of the Legislative Council, and were in fact the direct heirs of the planter oligarchy which wielded near-absolute power delegated to them by the Colonial Office in the days of slavery.

Meanwhile the poor labourers groaned under the weight of the cotton industry driven by the unfair share-cropping system. The landlords provided cotton seeds and in some cases credit, but the 'peasant' workers provided the labour and took all the risks. At harvest time, the estate managers or their attorneys or agents used dubious expedients to ensure that they obtained the bigger half. For example, when the cotton was weighed in, apart from downright (or is it *down wrong?*) cooking the weight, 10 pounds or more were subtracted for 'shrinkage'. In some cases the grower was asked to clean up the cotton to the satisfaction of the estate before it could be weighed. Even credit could prove a perennial millstone around the neck of the grower, who was ever-indebted to the landlords' grocery and cloth stores. Payments were deducted before the disbursement for the cotton. Invariably the grower began the planting year in the red. The labourers' mountain grounds felt the grabbing hand of *métairie*, in that estate authorities felt entitled to reap a portion of the food crops, and did. Some 'good labourers' were allowed to rent mountain grounds, but had very little time to cultivate them since they had to be in their master's fields every day. Pink and yellow cotton blossoms disguised an ugly servitude in Montserrat cotton fields.

Cotton brought a measure of prosperity to peasants with sizeable acreages, but most labourers were unable to improve their lot beyond subsistence level. Their circumstances became worse after 1941, when yields decreased sharply. Acreages of 4000 produced just about 600 000 pounds of lint in 1942 and 1943, and by 1953, when an official inquiry into the industry was commissioned, production had further declined to 325 000 pounds. There were also years, as in 1937 and 1938, when the price dropped to unremunerative levels due to competition from sea-island cotton grown in the United States and imported into Liverpool on the same basis as Montserratian cotton.[14]

With the birth of unionization and popular political consciousness in the late 1940s and early 1950s, labourers, through their leaders, began to demand fairer wages in the industry and achieved some success. By then, cotton had seen its best days. Mass exodus to England in the late 1950s and the 1960s pulled the rug from under the industry as able-bodied labourers left in droves. In his February 1969 Budget speech, Chief Minister W. H. Bramble observed that 'cotton is losing its significance as an economic factor in these parts'. Cotton too had fallen.

Postscript on sugar

Cotton occupied the economic throne between 1910 and 1960, but never reigned as supremely as did sugar. There were periods when tomatoes had to come to its rescue, as in 1936, when there was a severe drought and a bad crop, and up to the 1920s, limes made the kingdom a duumvirate.

Sugar, however, did not completely disappear and in the years when cotton languished, efforts were made to resuscitate it. As muscovado sugar was locally used, a few estates, such as Farrell's and Broderick's, continued to produce it up to the late 1940s; they also produced rum from local molasses. Children of the author's generation were treated on Empire Day to buns and lemonade from muscovado or 'black' sugar. (No pun was intended in those days of innocence.) Muscovado sugar fetched an uneconomical price as an export commodity, and in 1933 'A Report from the Department of Agriculture' observed that production was at a standstill. The local demand too was low and confined to the very poor and to children's imperial treat. Grey crystals and refined white sugar were capturing local taste.

Farrell's, with its less forbidding terrain, continued to grow cane and even to seek to improve the yield. A sugar-cane experiment was actually carried out there in 1935. This was guided by the realization that the island was losing some £5000 annually by importing 1 000 000 pounds for local consumption. Accordingly the Moyne commissioners were told of a plan to put 600 acres under cane and to establish a small factory to manufacture about 1000 tons of sugar annually.[15] Alternatively, loan funds could be sought to purchase and install a centrifugal plant. Montserrat was at last ready, in conception at least, to introduce more efficient sugar technology, after sugar had lost its pivotal place in the economy.

The proposed revival of the industry in the Farrell's-Riley's area had a number of aims other than import substitution. It was intended to contribute to livestock raising, improve soil conditions and provide an additional means of livelihood for the 2000 peasants and labourers of that area who, finding the soil unsuitable for cotton, had continued to grow canes. Local molasses was also needed to support the small rum industry. These grand plans never materialized, but they illustrate the abiding influence of sugar even after its glory had departed.

The strong taste for sugar demanded action again as recently as 1953. In conference with the Montserrat Development Association, the Governor, K. W. Blackburne, spoke of the Government's intention to repair and operate a small mill at the Otway Land Settlement. The aims were similar to those which led to the plans for Farrell's in the 1930s – the need to reduce the quantity of imported sugar which retailed at 12 cents per pound, agricultural diversification and soil conservation. The Government's overall plan was to encourage private enterprise to establish two or three muscovado-mills to produce the 600 tons of sugar needed annually for local consumption.[16] Again the plans perished at the conception stage.

About 200 acres of sugar cane were grown in 1953 producing 20 barrels of muscovado sugar. In 1954, production dropped to 150 acres and only six barrels of sugar. The bulk of the cane was used for making rum; 1900 gallons valued at EC$3900 were produced in 1953, and 51 529 gallons at a value of $9625 in 1954.[17]

Effectively, sugar ended with slavery in Montserrat. Producing a small quantity for local consumption seemed sensible and the idea attracted successive administrations. However, the viability of the proposed small factories was doubtful; and, in any case, short-sighted or not, the grand-children of slavery wanted a better sugar than the one they were being asked to produce.

The Montserrat Company

The Montserrat Company, a Birmingham-based conglomerate, played such a commanding role in the island's post-emancipation history, that its study requires an essay on that role and some analysis of the giant company's con-tribution to a tiny island. It was the direct result of the humanitarian tour to a number of West Indian islands by the famous philanthropist Joseph Sturge in 1836. His mission to Montserrat, engendered by Quaker piety and liberal sentiment, gave rise to a commercial connection which was destined to bring wealth to the Sturge family and their associates, and give them the oppor-tunity to influence the affairs of the island.

Sturge, who had supported the causes of amelioration and emancipation from England, came on the site to promote the advancement of the newly emancipated. He purchased his first estate in 1857, about a mile from

Plymouth and named it Elberton, after his birthplace in Gloucestershire. Apart from finding work for recently freed slaves, his avowed aim was to demonstrate 'that by fair and just treatment of the native labourers, sugar could be profitably produced without the aid of the servile labour of Indian coolies'. He was to be the model capitalist and humanist rolled into one, the pursuer of gold and godliness, and Montserrat was the laboratory for the experiment. As Alex Tyrrell, his biographer, observes, there was nothing shamefaced about his notion of a humanely managed capitalist enterprise.[18] Sturge had however, started this project too late and before his death, he regretted not starting it earlier and reiterated his belief that 'he would thereby have advanced the object he had at heart in the West Indies, more than by much labour and expenditure in other directions'.[19]

Edmund Sturge took up his brother's torch when he bought and named an estate Olveston in 1857, thereby giving island-immortality to the village of their early life. He added Woodlands the same year and several other estates by 1869, when the Montserrat Lime Juice Company was formed. Montserrat lime-juice was essentially a legacy of the Sturges' company. In 1875, the Company was reconstituted as the Montserrat Company and by 1916, it possessed estates or property at Olveston, Woodlands, The Grove including Richmond and Fryes, Isles Bay, Elberton, Fogathy's, Brades, Ogarro's and Tar River. There was nothing modest about this liberal company which gobbled up about half of the arable land in the island. Table 6.9 shows that Company's profit between 1917 and 1927. (Although only lime exports are shown, the accounts reflect cotton and other pursuits.)

Table 6.9 Montserrat Company's profit, 1917–27

Year	No. of barrels	Company's profits
		£
1917	17 844	3997
1918	17 913	1813
1919	15 677	2924.19s.3d.
1920	13 647	6407.15s.8d.
1921	11 187	1861.13s.5d.
1922	6 947	1065.0s.0d.
1923	8 437	1039.6s.6d.
1924	5 406	1451.0s.0d.
1925	2 090	3186.0s.0d.
1926	2 670	3010.13s.1d.
1927	3 800	1812.0s.4d.

Source: Complled from printed annual reports of the Company in the possession of Joseph Sturge, a grand-nephew of the founder.

The distribution of land in Montserrat in 1953 is instructive. Of the total of 16 300 acres, companies or individuals in England owned 5900, the inhabitants owned 9200 and the Government 1200.[20] The largest company was, of course, the Montserrat Company. Land needed for special use by the partly-dispossessed inhabitants had to be sought from it – for example, for the Botanic Station at the Grove and for a public recreation ground in 1936. The idea of the public park surfaced in 1894 when the Government spoke of approaching the Company to purchase land 'at a Moderate rate'. It is not clear why it took so long, but it was not until the hundredth anniversary of Joseph Sturge's missionary excursion to Montserrat that the purpose was realized. Five acres of land were donated 'in commemoration of the association with Montserrat of Joseph Sturge the elder, and of the late Joseph Sturge ... for use in perpetuity as a public open space to be called "Sturge Park"'. The land was given at a strategic time to immortalize the founders of the Company and its fortunes, including an agreement not to sell alcoholic beverages on the premises. The proviso was observed with sabbatarian rigour up until recent times. Through the Company the spirit of Quaker Sturge had a controlling influence on the island.

The Montserrat Company's relationship with the island was obviously not altruistic, but the enlightened and liberal attitude of the founder continued to be in evidence. The Company tended to be more progressive in its farming practices than other landowners and to offer leadership in farming. As we have already observed, they led in the search for alternatives to sugar, and where other estates chose to exploit the servile system of *métairie*, it encouraged a wider distribution of land and the development of a peasantry by renting and selling; the Company made no use of *métairie*. It seemed to have recognized that the concentration of so much land in a corporate proprietor was incompatible with the development of the people.

From their strong economic base, Company personnel felt confident to criticize the administration of the island, and their opinions were highly valued by Westminster. One official observed that the Company 'contributes no doubt quite properly under the law, very little to the revenue of Government'.[21] He was probably referring to the fact that profits were repatriated after only a relatively small tax of two shillings in the £100 was levied. The Company was one of two companies based in England with operations in Montserrat; the other was Wade Plantations. In 1938, Sir Walter Citrine of the West India Commission suggested, through a question to the Montserrat Taxpayers Association, that the English shareholders of these Companies might benefit from paying a higher tax in Montserrat and obtain a corresponding relief in England where company tax was as high as 13s.9d. in the pound. H. S. Shand, who was chief spokesman for the Association and the Company's attorney, rushed the information to Birmingham, whence T. A. Twyman, the Managing Director, promptly provided Mr T. I. K. Lloyd of the Commission with a response. He did not mind having all the tax paid into the revenue of Montserrat, if the English Treasury would approve.[22] The Company was conscious of its influence, but tended to marry, where it could, the interests of Montserrat with those of its shareholders.

But Sturgean magnanimity did not always win through. When Twyman visited Montserrat in 1950, at the height of an industrial conflict, he rejected an opportunity to be generous to the labouring class. Requested to sign a wages agreement, he refused, calling for penalty claims for non-observance on both sides.[23]

While criticizing the tax paid by the Company, the official referred to above admitted that 'it has always been very well disposed to the interests of the labouring classes and the maintenance of this Company in the island must surely have been of considerable benefit to it'.[24] The benefits went beyond economic to social concerns. The Company invested in education, particularly the education of the children of workers on their major estates. This is why it established a school in Olveston in 1870, 'long ere the Government realized its responsibilities in educating the masses'. The school was operated through the contributions of individual shareholders until 1932, when it was handed over to the Government, who rented the grounds and the teacher's quarters for £20 and £6 per annum respectively. The school boasted 'proficient' supplies and an excellent teaching staff who received higher salaries than those who taught in denominational schools.

The Company's enlightened attitude to education stood out in sharp contrast to that of other managers and attorneys. Visiting the island in 1891, the second Joseph Sturge pointed out the need for some form of technical education. A school was in fact established subsequently even though the curriculum was restricted to apprenticeships in simple trades. In an island where such education as there was was entirely bookish, this must have filled a crying need. In 1893, an Act was passed authorizing a loan 'of the sum not exceeding £1000 for establishment of an engineer's workshop in connection with the technical school'. The school did not survive the century, but its brief existence must have been a continual reminder to successive administrations of the need for technical-vocational training. The Company also contributed to education by providing an annual scholarship to the secondary school although it tended to be confined to children of their workers. Children belonging to parents who worked for the Montserrat Company enjoyed a distinct advantage.

Another social area in which the Company led was housing. In 1940, it built three experimental labourers' cottages to demonstrate the type of housing that the Government might provide.

To appreciate the influence of the Company, one has to recognize that, like many estate owners, it combined political power with economic power. It is, however, to its credit that it did so with some benevolence. As early as 1867, two years before the Montserrat Lime Juice Company was formed, John Edmund Sturge took the oath as a member of the Legislative Council. The Sturges had moved from philanthropy through property to power politics. A councillor in 1922, H. S. Shand, the Company's attorney, led the unofficial members in vigorously opposing a clause in the new Masters and Servants Ordinance, which required that estate workers be paid at the customary rate where there was no agreement, and that overtime be paid. His plan intended that it should apply to all workers, but it was planter-interest he was championing rather than the principle of egalitarianism. Although official members were in the majority in Council, the Acting Commissioner, H. Peebles, postponed forcing the legislation through.

When a new constitution brought an element of representative government to the island in 1936, Shand topped the polls in 1937. This was a symbol of the pinnacle of power and influence that the Company had attained in Montserrat. When his death, supposedly by suicide, occurred in 1943, the Company lost political power, although not political and social influence. When the Producers Association attempted to repudiate an agreement made with the Trades and Labour Union in 1954, it was the Manager of the Montserrat Company (also a signatory to the document) who insisted that it was binding. On his initiative the workers benefited from new rates. To the end the Montserrat Company was able to harmonize the profit motive with benevolence and humanitarianism. Its operation in a progressive and businesslike manner aided this progress. (The Company manufactured cooking oil and cattle-cake, both from the cotton fruit.) This is one of the happier stories of an expatriate business in a Caribbean territory. The Montserrat Company was not all sweetness, but it was outstanding, amidst the meanness of other estate proprietors.

In 1961, the Company assumed a new profile under new owners when it became the Montserrat Real Estate Company (MORECO). To an extent, MORECO kept alive something of the spirit of its predecessor in that it sometimes donated land for public purposes. The spirit of Sturge lived on.

7

Trade unions and politics

The birth of a union

The mobilization of the working class for industrial relations and political action had a late start in Montserrat. The regional labour storms of the 1930s, which raged as near as St Kitts in 1935, blew past this island, although social and economic conditions were worse here than in St Kitts or Antigua. (The only riots the island experienced in this period were the Toby Hill riots at St Patrick's in 1942, and these were due more to smuggling and insensitive policing than to prevailing social conditions.) Government hourly wage rates for unskilled men and women in 1947 were 7.1 and 3.9 cents respectively. The corresponding figures were 16.4 and 7.0 for Antigua and 8.62 and 6.47 for St Kitts. The Cost of Living Index in December 1947 was 196 in Antigua, 196 in St Kitts, 180 in the British Virgin Islands and 205 in Montserrat.[1]

An official report described workers in the cotton field at Whites in 1945 as 'underfed, dressed in strings, haven't had soap for weeks'.[2] The eastern area was the island's great ghetto. It was there that *métairie* in its worst form was resurrected in the second decade of the twentieth century. The description of this labour system by J. H. A. Meade of the Montserrat Taxpayers Association (MTA) in his appearance before the Moyne Commission in 1938, is worth repeating here:

> The great objection to the system is that the tenant pays £5.00 or £6.00 rent. If he gets 400 pounds per acre, 200 pounds of it belongs to the land owner. The tenant benefits if it is a good season, but if it is a bad season he loses and in any case, the landlord stands to benefit no matter what happens because the tenant supplies his labour and the landlord stands to lose nothing.[3]

This analysis reveals the oppressive and unjust nature of the system. But, in addition, some landlords gave the tenant a third rather than a half of the harvest and others manipulated weights and payments to the disadvantage and distress of the worker. For instance, a hundredweight was counted as

100 pounds and since many tenants were illiterate, they were unaware of the deceit. The limited rights of the tenants were raped in a system that was already inherently abusive.

By 1953, when Professor Beasley headed a commission of inquiry into the cotton industry, the depressing social conditions had not changed:

> The fact is that Montserrat with its decaying economy exhibits what have been called the pathological symptoms of peasant farming – tiny and fragmented farmholdings, malnutrition, illiteracy and backwardness among peasants; misuse of land; primitive and insanitary dwellings; land hunger; and the elevation of mendicancy almost to the status of a social philosophy.[4]

Beasley could easily have been describing conditions of the late 1930s. Add to this sordid milieu the tyrannic regimes of landlords and their attorneys – starvation wages, the impounding of animals, harvesting of provision grounds and at times feeding the loot to estate animals, vindictive tenante-victions – and you have an explosive situation which needed only a spark of leadership.

Leadership was precisely what was lacking. In 1938 some 2000 labourers depended on wages, but they were disorganized and unprotected. A Minimum Wage Act was on the statute books, but it remained unimplemented. Government by the administering authority in association with a merchant-planter legislature had failed the people. A Federal Labour Officer based in Antigua did not serve Montserrat well, and achieved little against an elite of wealth and power; and while Antigua and St Kitts had Labour Advisory Boards, no such machinery existed in Montserrat. Interviewed on the desirability of a trades union, A. H. Allen of the MPA saw no reason why there shouldn't be one 'if they are able to keep it together'. The problem was one of organization and leadership and the initiative was not likely to come from among the workers themselves.

An intellectual and ideological backwater except for a small, oppressive elite, the island lacked a pool of persons to champion the cause of peasants and labourers over whose lives estate authorities held sway. In the very depressed eastern areas at Wade and Tar River plantations, some labourers lived in hovels owned sometimes by the estate itself. Slavery had been abolished, but a cruel feudalism without the protective role of the lord had replaced it. In a sense, the estates owned the workers. By 1940, however, both Antigua and St Kitts had registered trade unions under a 1939 Trade Unions Act, and Montserrat could not remain isolated from the trade-union currents which were blowing from Antigua in particular.

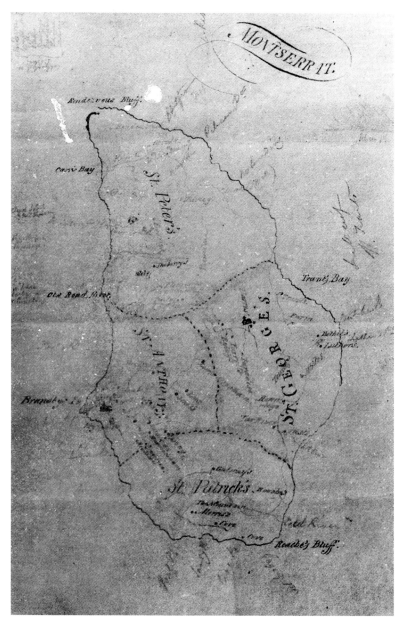

Fig. 1 Early nineteenth-century map of Montserrat

Fig. 2 Ameridian artifact

Fig. 3 Perimeter map of Montserrat, 1673

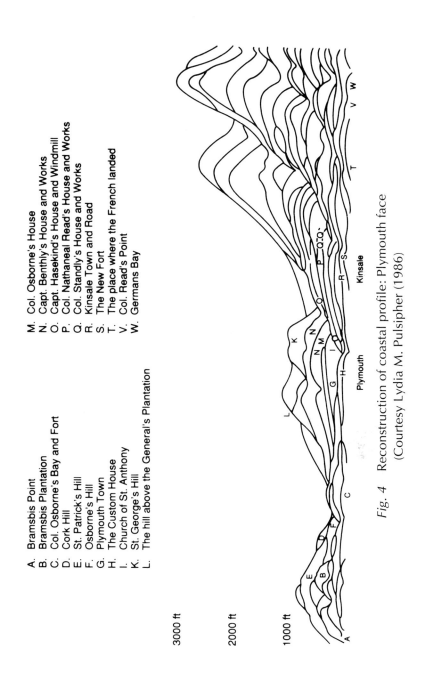

A. Bramsbis Point
B. Bramsbis Plantation
C. Col. Osborne's Bay and Fort
D. Cork Hill
E. St. Patrick's Hill
F. Osborne's Hill
G. Plymouth Town
H. The Custom House
I. Church of St. Anthony
K. St. George's Hill
L. The hill above the General's Plantation
M. Col. Osborne's House
N. Capt. Benthly's House and Works
O. Capt. Hasekind's House and Windmill
P. Col. Nathaneal Read's House and Works
Q. Col. Standly's House and Works
R. Kinsale Town and Road
S. The New Fort
T. The place where the French landed
V. Col. Read's Point
W. Germans Bay

3000 ft

2000 ft

1000 ft

Plymouth

Kinsale

Fig. 4 Reconstruction of coastal profile: Plymouth face
(Courtesy Lydia M. Pulsipher (1986)

Fig. 5   Reconstruction of part of Galway's plantation
(Original by Barbara Tipson, courtesy of Mac Goodwin)

Fig. 6   Grinding cassava, early twentieth century

Fig. 7   Grove Botanic Station, c.1908

Fig. 8   Oxen cart, early twentieth century

Fig. 9   Robert W. Griffith

Fig. 10   W. H. Bramble

Fig. 11   P. Austin Bramble, Chief Minister 1970–78

Fig. 12   J. A. Osborne, Chief Minister 1978–91

Fig. 13   Reuben Meade, Chief Minister 1991–96

Fig. 14   Bertrand B. Osborne, Chief Minister 1996–97

Fig. 15   David S. Brandt, Chief Minister 1997–2001

Fig. 16 Hurricane damage, 1928

Fig. 17 Hurricane damage, 1989

Fig. 18   Volcanic activity, August 1995
(Courtesy of Mitch Lewis Enterprises)

Fig. 19   Volcanic eruption, October 1997
(Courtesy of Stanford Kelly)

Fig. 20   Montserrat masquerade

THE MONTSERRAT HERALD.

VOL. 1. No 13.]   PLYMOUTH MARCH 26, 1898.   [THREE PENCE

THE MONTSERRAT HERALD is Edited and Published by J. T. Allen and James R. Peters every other Saturday in
PLYMOUTH,
and printed by W. H. Humphrey at
KINSALE,
At Five Shillings per Annum.
Postage extra.
Payable quarterly or half yearly in advance. Three months notice to discontinue must be given in writing.

ADVERTISING TERMS.

Twelve lines or under,   } £0 3 0
3 insertions............ }
Every additional line 0 0 1
For every subsequent insrt. 0 0 2
For a single column 0 8 0
Special arrangements will be made to Subscribers or Foreign Advertisers at cheap rates.

BIRTHS & MARRIAGES each 1/-
DEATHS 3 lines Free.

All literary communications must be addressed to J. R. Peters, or J. T. Allen, not later than Tuesday, the week in which the paper is issued.

AGENTS:

Mr. W. H. Meade Plymouth
" W. H. Tracy "
" J. M. Gambs Harris Village
" Samuel Hunter, St. Peters
" Joseph Lambert, Olveston.
" W. H. Fenton Antigua.

James T. Allen,

GOLD & SILVER SMITH
WATCH CLOCK & MACHINE
—REPAIRER—
AND TUNER OF
MUSICAL INSTRUMENTS
—ALSO—
GENERAL COMMISSION
—AGENT—
PLYMOUTH, MONTSERRAT.

Leeward Islands,

PRESIDENCY OF MONTSERRAT.

PUBLIC NOTICE.

COURT OF ESCHEAT.

NOTICE is hereby given that a Court of ESCHEAT will be held at the Court House in the Town of Plymouth, on Saturday the 9th day of July, 1898, at 11 o'clock in the forenoon to take an Inquisition touching certain land situate at VICTORIA VILLAGE in the Parish of St. Anthony in the said Presidency, late the property of Louise Dyett, deceased—to which Our Sovereign Lady the Queen has become entitled by way of Escheat as is alleged.

EDWARD BAYNES,
Escheator General.

Montserrat, 18th March, 1898.

FOR SALE

THE BEAUTIFUL & HEALTHY

RESIDENCE

AT
KINSALE,
known as St. LUKE'S COTTAGE

Please apply to W. Humphrey
or S. D. Palmer

FOR SALE

A COMFORTABLE FAMILY RESIDENCE,
with 17 bearing Cocoa nut trees in George Street,
The sole property of
FLORENCE E. E. BURKE.
TERMS MADE EASY.

Please apply to her Agent

PATRICK RURKE Esq.

NOTHING BETTER THAN A JOLLY GOOD RIDE.

I once heard a song "There is nothing so good as a laugh;" but in my opinion, there is nothing better than a JOLLY GOOD RIDE! as there is more likelihood of realising those external objects which act upon the senses to produce pleasure; and where there is pleasure there will be laughter. For, nothing pleases the townsfolks more than when a public assemblage in the country is to take place,—Tea-meeting, Soiree, Concert, Laying of Corner-Stone, or what not, even an apology for an entertainment—so long as there is an opportunity for a ride, it does not matter whether one possesses the necessary outfit, as nine out of every ten persons, as a rule, would be able to find a soul kind-hearted enough to put his beast at his or her disposal for the occasion. Accordingly, the public having been notified in the HERALD that a stone was to be laid at Bethel, I took in my head to break the monotony of the town life for a little country scenery and its refreshing breeze, and therefore bestirred myself to fish for a horse.

About 1.20 two companies mounted their ponies, one of which was put under my charge, and as six of the number were of the fair sex, I felt no little proud of my responsibility. We started off at full canter; and I soon found out that the fair sex were the fairest and most fearless riders of my party, and were better able to take care of their guard. If I were even desirous to make a display of my authority, and compel them to repress their youthful intrepidity and buoyancy of Spirit by commanding them to rein in, there rose such a cloud of dust in my face and so much thrown in my eyes, I had to pride myself with the thought that the best place for a commander was far back in the rear. We, however, soon learnt that a little mishap had befallen one in the party who was coming behind us, and although it was nothing of a serious nature, we thought it prudent to be mindful of ourselves.

When we reached Gages, we found the wind-mill tower which was damaged by the earthquake on the 15th ulto. was repaired, and the mill in the wind. I also observed that most of the labourers' dwellings were removed over to Hart, which I thought speaks much for the owner, Mr. Willie Wilkin, for the interest he takes to make his labourers safe and comfortable.

As we proceeded at a slow pace to enable those who were coming behind to overtake us, we were able to enjoy to the full the pleasure of our ride. The sky was clear, and we could have seen Low field, Redonda sparkling like a gem in the midst of the "blue sea," and there was the lofty mountain-peak of little Nevis like a mist in the horizon of the West, while, as we went further up, we beheld the more extensive land of Antigua, as it were, laying on the crest of the wave in the east. Although

Fig. 22 Alphonsus Cassell, 'Arrow'

Documentary material on the origin of the Montserrat Trades and Labour Union (MTLU) is limited, but several collaborative oral sources exist, although they tend to differ on details. The impetus came from abroad and from Antigua in particular, and the name of the Montserratian inter-island trafficker William Brade is closely identified with the genesis of the movement. Apart from the leading figures, the other names linked with the formation of the Union include Arthur Riley, the first secretary; Ellen Peters also a secretary; Alma Ryan, B. W. Edwards, S. A. Dyett, W. F. Graham and Walter Neale, a Nevisian by birth. William Brade traded not only in vegetables and groceries, but in ideas of workers' organizations. Neale, a First World War veteran, brought his own experience and vision to bear on the emergence of the movement.

Typically Caribbean, the Montserrat trade union movement relied on middle-class persons to lead it, most of whom were not themselves cotton-growers. With the assistance of Vere Cornwall Bird and a Mr Vannier of Antigua, Robert W. Griffith organized the MTLU in April 1946[5] and registered it the following month with an estimated membership of 600. By December 1947, it reported a membership of 1858, but of these only 237 were financial contributors. The Moyne Commission had recommended a revision of the 1939 Trade Union Act, so the new Union enjoyed some immunity from court action. Unemployment plagued the Union since the unemployed could not be *bona fide* members. Furthermore, the benefits of unionization were not readily apparent to a rural people who survived through the combination of share-cropping, provision ground and pasturage on estate lands; and the employers were reluctant to recognize the Union and its leaders. It took several years before it gained 'the respect of the other side at the conference table'.[6]

A lay Methodist preacher, Robert Griffith was the son of a manager on Weekes estate. He was middle class, with material means and social influence. Having won a place in the Legislative Council in 1943, he brought some political clout to his unionism. He had made a breach into the citadel of the elite ruling class. Griffith was an enigmatic mixture of vision and vanity. In 1951, he reportedly prefaced his call for a demonstration by observing that 'Montserrat never featured in the newspapers and that it was time that action was taken which would place it in the forefront'.[7] He established a union to fight the cause of the poor against a group with whom his father was sympathetic; he delighted in meeting royal persons, but he reserved his fiercest attacks for imperialism and its local agents.

The early years were difficult for the Union and for Griffith; he was himself well aware that he had undertaken a position that called for experience, courage and tenacity and pledged that where he was limited in these, he would rely on 'his sincerity of purpose'.[8] Anticipating a workers' organization, the employers had formed a Producers' Association in 1943 to protect their interest and also to relate to the Federal Labour Officer. Even after the establishment of the Union, some industrial relations matters were settled by the Commissioner and the Council. Two recorded labour disputes in 1947 involved Public Works employees working on Fort Ghaut; one, which had to do with the dismissal of a labourer, was settled by the Commissioner and Council, who upheld the dismissal (in other words, the employers were both defence and judge). In the other, a mason was reinstated, but it was the Assistant Federal Labour Officer who conducted the negotiations.[9] A third case leads one to the view that the locally based British administration was hostile to the Union. When some jetty workers struck for a higher daily wage in 1946, the Superintendent of Works callously fired them, hired a new work gang, and paid them the just wages that were demanded in the first place.[10]

In 1950, the Union had only 434 members, 184 of whom were in arrears with dues. It was described by the Governor as a 'weak and poorly organised body' which suffered from the fact that many of the working people had a stake in the land. His evaluation was not totally correct. Many of them had no land-tenure choice, and some could not be effective union members since they could not afford the entry fee of 2s. 6d. and the weekly subscription of three pence. The fact that the Commissioner was hostile to Griffith, as can be inferred from relevant dispatches sent to the Governor and ultimately to England, also impacted adversely on the Union.

Griffith did not hesitate to use the strike weapon. Between 1948 and 1950 minor strikes occurred, which brought some benefits to the workers. Cotton workers struck on 17 March 1950, but the dispute was satisfactorily settled by 27 March. Later, however, waterfront workers refused to unload a ship from Antigua in solidarity with their Antiguan colleagues. Griffith did not always use the strike responsibly. In February 1950, he called out Montserrat Company workers on Richmond estate, after the attorney had agreed to pay increased wages even though the Company's wages far exceeded current rates.[11] Griffith probably fancied that a showdown with the mighty Montserrat Company would be a red feather in his political cap.

The major strike of August 1950 was justified. Instead of a penny for picking two pounds of cotton, Griffith demanded $1\frac{1}{2}$ pence which was still less than was paid in Antigua where pickers were receiving a cent per pound. His approach was, however, unorthodox. Without the decision or sanction of the Union's executive, he called the strike and intimidated and harassed those who refused to leave the fields. Policemen were assaulted in their effort to arrest the activists, who were armed with stones and cutlasses and accompanied by a steel band. This was industrial relations action, Griffith-style. Predictably the administration responded by calling out the Defence Force and calling in HMS *Bigbury* to restore calm. Some 29 persons, including Griffith, were prosecuted, and he was fined $10.00 or 30 days in prison. With a cutting sense of humour the people dubbed the *Bigbury* the 'penny-hapenny' warship.

Griffith was harshly denounced by the British Commissioner as being hungry for notoriety: 'A generally vainglorious attitude, an overweening desire for the limelight, and occasional displays of personal vanity mask his unawareness of his limitations'. [12] While there is some truth in the assessment, Griffith never enjoyed the support of the British administrators, who feared and even loathed him. Their reports, which were always negative, have to be read in this light. Robert Griffith was a flamboyant demagogue reminiscent of Alexander Bustamente of Jamaica, and his methods were unorthodox. His red tie and red cape and his use of music (especially steelband, bugle and drums) at his meetings drew crowds. This creative strategy, together with his racy socialist rhetoric, added to his appeal and influence.

By lacing his speeches with snippets of scripture, Griffith heightened their emotional appeal and his messianic aura. 'Is it not time for Pharaoh to let his people go? The voice of the man of God says it is time, and all obstacles and hindrances will be clear. God says again, "Let my people go" ... The cries of the poor people have gone up to God and retribution and distribution will eventually come from on high.'[13] What was never in doubt was his genuine compassion for the poor and the underdog. What Griffith lacked was a coherent programme on which to focus his energy and attention. In 1950 the *Montserrat Observer*, in a pointed reference to Griffith, observed that 'leadership means much more than to attempt every now and then to tickle the people's fancy with some sort of jocular fairy tale or some personal affair'; and in June 1951 he was said to have temporarily retired into seclusion.[14] If he had had a consistent developmental work plan, he might have been better equipped to stave off the challenge offered by W. H. Bramble for the leadership of the Union. It was he who nevertheless laid the foundations of the MTLU and should be regarded as the father of the working-class movement in Montserrat. He merits the national recognition which he has received, including the avuncular title of 'Mass Bob'.

The leadership struggle

Like Griffith, William Henry Bramble was a churchman (a Seventh Day Adventist). A carpenter and cotton cultivator, he shared Griffith's concern for the plight of the poor and joined the Union in 1951, the year when a new constitution which would introduce universal adult suffrage and a Council with an elected majority, was enacted. He saw the Union as a ladder to political power, and there is nothing unusual about this either in Caribbean or Montserratian history. It is significant that his 1952 manifesto asserted rather ruefully that in 1936 he lacked the property qualification for membership in Council when a change in the constitution reintroduced representative government. What is evident is that deliverance from post-emancipation neo-slavery was always on his agenda in both unionism and politics. By 1952, he had won his first election and he assumed the presidency of the Union in 1954.

To date no adequate explanation has been offered for Bramble's supplanting of Griffith. In a previous work, I suggested that Griffith found himself 'on the wrong side of the political fence in an issue such as the *métairie* system with its potential for mass appeal' and that Bramble's radical platform, with its socialist overtone, seemed more attractive to the rank and file of the Union.[15] This is only partially true. Although he did not follow through with any strategy for their abolition, Griffith condemned both *métairie* and tenant eviction in 1949 in a major statement.[16] And his employment of a term like 'distribution' imparted a socialist tone to his platform. In his 1946 campaign he stated clearly the intention of himself and his union colleagues to better the social and economic conditions of the people.

How then did Bramble obtain the mastery? There were fissures in the Union executive even before Bramble joined it. According to official reports, Griffith's idiosyncratic style and seemingly erratic attacks on certain authority-figures alienated some members. With reference to his dealings with the influential Montserrat Company, the Union Secretary and Treasurer were described as 'men of moderate views who do not support Mr Griffith and his agitation'. One of these men was his brother-in-law, W. F. Graham, whose reappointment as an official member of Council he protested. Indeed, there was speculation that Antigua-born B. W. Edwards, a drug-store owner, would oust Griffith from the presidency of the Union.[17] In January 1953, Edwards, supported by Ellen Peters, held a public meeting in which he condemned Griffith for opposing a settlement made by the Executive Committee, relating to cotton labourers' wages.[18] When Griffith demanded a higher wage, he brought the division out into the open. His methods and attitudes led to disaffection among the Union leaders. In 1951, when Griffith led a massive demonstration to demand the recall of Commissioner Charlesworth Ross and his 'deputy', Agricultural Superintendent Bassett, he did not have the support of the Union executive.

The Montserrat government, headed by the Commissioner, recognized Griffith's vulnerable position and encouraged its exploitation. An element of divide-and-rule was at work. The Commissioner described him in 1950 as 'a bit of a snob' and the Governor of the Leeward Islands reported with dubious accuracy that 'he does not appear to be taken very seriously even by members of the Union'. He also vilified Griffith as a probably mentally unbalanced person who had the support of the lowest type of people in the Plymouth area.

For his part, Bramble was conscious of his endorsement by the Governor and Commissioner with whom he shared his political aspirations. Writing to Walter Wallace (not the current official of the same name) at the Colonial Office, the Governor considered that it would be an excellent thing if Bramble replaced Griffith.[19]

Bramble saw political power as a mechanism for fulfilling his social agenda, and the union power base as a means of insuring that power. Compared to Griffith, who was something of a political dilettante, Bramble was a serious and aggressive politician with a consistent purpose and a coherent plan. Official views of Griffith may have been flawed but, significantly, the Commissioner described him as having no lust for power beyond being a legislative councillor. Not only did Griffith have powerful enemies within and without the Union, but his lack of a profound vision of development was perhaps his worst enemy. With the introduction of the committee system in government, the fact that he would sometime assume the rotating chairmanship of the Federal Economic Committee was viewed with alarm. He tended to evaluate the success of his overseas trips in terms of the royal personalities he spoke to, rather than in terms of critical contacts of benefit to the island.

Given the general perception of Griffith as being ineffective in the matter of social transformation, it was easy for Bramble to replace him. Bramble saw him as a barrier to his personal and national development ambitions. They were said to disagree on every major issue of policy.[20] The rivalry between the two men was early in the open and, although Bramble moved to replace Griffith while the latter was attending the London Federation conference in 1953, he had made no secret of his intention to oust him. In fact, Bramble wanted him removed from the Executive Council through a Resolution. With key Union officials like Edwards and Ellen Peters on his side, Bramble needed only to erode Griffith's popularity with the masses. One expedient he resorted to was to upstage Griffith by attempting to propose popular projects and increased wages. The Commissioner complained in 1953 that Bramble bypassed the Union and raised the question of increased wages for all daily paid Government employees and compounded the 'error' by promising them increased wages. Griffith supported the Commissioner in defeating the proposal 'because he did not want Bramble to get the credit from the workers'.[21] The workers were made pawns in a serious game for personal power.

Apart from the support of powerful unionists, the 1953 Beasley Commission, forced by deadlocked negotiations over wages in the cotton industry, gave Bramble an opportunity to emerge as the true champion of the people. it was he who ensured that the vexatious issue of *métairie* was included in its remit and it was he who represented the working class before the Commission. Griffith did not speak to the Commission at all. It was Bramble who in a welcome address summarized the case of the Union. It was intended to demonstrate that:

(1) wages in the cotton industry are far from being adequate to meet the present high cost of living.
(2) share-cropping is iniquitous and is disadvantageous to those who are forced to work under that system.
(3) the great monopoly of arable land by a few is a serious handicap to the existence of the majority of the inhabitants of the Presidency.

Bramble possessed the capacity to lend an epic quality to his purpose by his eloquence and messianic accent. 'It may well be that you have come to shape the destiny of a people, who for more than one hundred years were made free in words, but are anxiously longing to be free indeed', [22] he told the Beasley team. This was more Bramble's own life's goal rather than the object of Beasley. He was complimented in the Report for having presented the Union's case 'with sincerity and conviction', and for his 'indefatigable efforts and co-operation' in ensuring that the commissioners received first-hand knowledge of people, places and peasant holdings throughout the island. Griffith's only role was to join with Bramble to ensure that wages were excluded from the Beasley remit, contrary to the wishes of the Commissioner and the employers. The Governor, on the other hand, agreed that the wages were a matter for negotiation between the Union and the employers. Bramble had become the spokesman of the people and the guiding genius of the Union even though he had to wait until the following year to becomes its President.

The Beasley and Malone Commissions

The Beasley Commission is something of a landmark in the development of industrial relations in Montserrat. The Report blamed both the Union and the employers for the bargaining problems and consequently, at least in part, for the state of the cotton industry. It criticized the power struggle within the Union and its sabotaging tactics, which reduced production while raising its costs. Although this somewhat strengthened Bramble's political armoury, Beasley did not recommend the abolition of *métairie*; the Report, however,

condemned it in its present form. The mutual recognition which is so fundamental to the proper functioning of trade unions was lacking, the Report
concluded. For this, a large share of the blame falls on the estate owners and
managers. Their attitude was one of aloofness, suspicion and even contempt.
They perceived the struggle partly in personal terms: boys of secondary or
higher education versus elementary school boys; the propertied against poor
peasants; Anglo-Caribbean against Afro-Caribbean; guardians of the socio-
economic colonial heritage against upstart demagogues. In the Commission's
words, 'there appears to be an unwillingness on the part of estate owners to
concede recognition in the Montserrat of today of the normal trade union
developments, and an equal unwillingness to form themselves into the usual
employers' associations which would complete the essential machinery for
mutual recognition'. Some of the negative and destructive actions of trade
union leaders and their adherents must be seen as a reaction triggered by
frustrations sustained through bigoted employers. Five years later, when the
Malone Commission reported, attitudes had not changed. It attributed
strained relations partly to the fact that 'several employers are still reluctant
to come down from their ivory tower to consult union officials or to
negotiate with them'.

The Beasley Commission recommended the temporary appointment of
a Labour Commissioner whose immediate task would be to develop an effective trade union and a strong employers' federation. The latter was quickly
established and brought signs of improvement in industrial relations, in the
view of government officials, who felt that a Labour Commission was no
longer necessary. Union officials thought otherwise and demanded the
appointment. As it turned out, only after the Malone Commission of 1958
endorsed the recommendation was an appointment made.

Little wonder then that industrial relations deteriorated in the post-
Beasley years. In 1954, E. Grell, the Labour Officer of St Kitts-Nevis-
Anguilla, succeeded in drawing up an Agreement of Procedure for the
Settlement of Disputes with the collaboration of the Union and the
Producers' Association who signed it. The wages agreed on were:

Men	$1.02 per day
Women	$0.66 per day
Farming	$2.40 per day
Picking	$0.02 per $\frac{1}{2}$ pound
Cleaning	$0.66 per 85 pounds
Pulling	$1.80 per acre

But some members of the Producers' Association, with characteristic cynicism, treated the agreement with scant regard. The Manager of Wade

Plantations repudiated it on the grounds that he had authorized no one to sign on their behalf; his colleague W. S. R. Howes, who signed the agreement on behalf of the Association, denied its legality since, he argued, his delegation only had authority to negotiate. It is this kind of duplicity, together with the intransigence of some union officials, which bedevilled industrial relations.

The Montserrat Company acted differently. It contended that the document was signed in good faith and, therefore, binding on all. On the Manager's suggestion, new rates were fixed to conciliate certain categories of workers who were not done justice by the earlier rates.

By 1957, Bramble was not only the leader of the MTLU, but also the political champion of the working class. Having completed his first term in the legislature, he was now ready for re-election. He was criticized by the planters and subsequently by the Malone Commission for using the 1957 strikes as a vehicle to political power. This was true to an extent, but is by itself too facile an explanation for the unsettling disputes for which no single person was culpable. A man worked for £1.14 and a woman 78 cents daily, and many families lived at poverty level. The Producers' Association chose a bad time to refuse to negotiate claims to higher wages in the cotton industry. Following a poor crop in 1956 due to drought, and an anticipated change in the planting season, large acreages were put under cotton in 1957. Estate owners were very vulnerable when the strikes occurred, for the season was well advanced.

The October strike was due to another example of bad faith. After protracted negotiations, Trants Estate agreed to lease to the Government 40 acres to be rented to peasant farmers. The owners then suddenly reneged and announced a sale to the Farrell's Estate syndicate at £18.00 an acre. In November the Union struck when the producers virtually ignored the Union's claim to higher wages. Work ceased on several estates, especially in the east of the island. Unionized or not, workers who failed to cooperate with the Union were intimidated. Condemning the strike, Plymouth merchant and political hopeful Eric Kelsick published details of atrocities wreaked on individuals and damages done on estates during the strike in the weekly *Observer*. Animals were mutilated and a *bagasse* house burnt on Farrell's estate. Bramble's response was reasoned, polite and cutting, as he articulated the social realities of the time:

> but there are atrocities which conveniently escaped Mr. Kelsick's view. For instance, in the cane-field at Farrell's Estate one could see a poor frail woman with her little child of school age who is unable to spell dog, but who has his hoe in hand trying to help his mother to work for 72 cents. On the Windward Estates there are little boys caring for sheep, also of school age, but don't know the

first letter of the alphabet. Because of poverty they must grow up into illiterate men to be ashamed of themselves. Are those not atrocities? Look them up and expose them Mr. Kelsick.[23]

These newspaper repartees became a significant aspect of the struggle and served to harden positions. Besides, each side twisted facts and presented half-truths. For instance, the producers blamed the Union for the fall in production from 1200 acres in 1952 to 600 in 1957, when factors like weather and a change in the planting season were partly responsible. The Union in computing its claims, on the other hand, used figures for a particular estate for a particular year and omitted overhead expenses. Bramble was accused of making share-cropping a political football, but his weapon had always been aimed at that evil and in assessing this charge, which was made by Kelsick and his ilk, one has to remember that they themselves were politically motivated. One has to agree with Bramble's critics that there was a marked correlation between his political rise, his constituency and the strike zone; but then intense union activity tended to coincide with hard times and times were hardest and working conditions worst in the windward area.

To break the 1957 deadlock, the Government invited the Labour Commissioner of St Kitts, Mr R. P. Parris, at the request of the Union. Representatives of the employers were reluctant to meet with the Union and stipulated a return to work as a condition. All that was agreed upon was the need for a Board of Inquiry. Pending this, work resumed due to the intervention of church leaders. A Commission, consisting of Sir Clement Malone, William H. Hagley and Frank L. Walcott, was appointed to examine the cause and circumstances of the dispute and to make recommendations for the establishment of effective machinery for the proper settlement of future disputes in the agricultural industry. The Commission was also required to make recommendations for a settlement of the present dispute. Basing its judgement on the price of cotton, the increased production per acre, and the promising outlook in the cotton industry, the Commission recommended increased wages as follows:

Men	$1.30 per day
Women	$0.90 per day
Picking	$0.03 per lb.
Farming	$4.00 per acre
Other work	$0.15 per cent increase.

The increase in the four-year period was not that spectacular, but it represented a victory for the Union. Malone went further than Beasley and recommended the permanent appointment of a Labour Commissioner. In addition, there was to be a joint Industrial Council for the cotton industry, comprised of representatives of both employers and workers and presided over by a chairman appointed by the Governor.

With the recommendations of the Malone Commission, the MTLU reached the zenith of its achievement, and thereafter it ceased to be a great force in the social and economic life of the island. In fact, the Industrial Council was never established, partly because of the waning of the Union as a social force. This was due to the decline in the cotton industry, which gave way to real estate development and home construction, the mass exodus of agricultural workers to England, and Bramble's rise to the pinnacle of political power. Not only were peasant proprietors increasing in number, but the Government was fast becoming the biggest employer. In addition to the Otway Settlement, which it had been operating for several years, it leased Galways in 1957 for sub-letting to workers. In the following year the Government bought and managed Trants as a rental land settlement. In all, 510 tenants and 590 acres were involved.

Landless workers turned to rental as share-cropping died out, and as the old employers of labour were replaced, union activity, which had thrived on economic maltreatment, died. The MTLU had left a legacy of successful social and political agitation and provided Bramble with a springboard to political power. It had fulfilled the important if limited aim of providing a pressure group which operated against the plantocracy and paved the way for politicians with a paternal benevolence. In that sense, it harboured the elements of its own demise. A new union would have to be differently conceived with broader aims.

Bramble is King

By 1954 Bramble combined union leadership with political leadership of the Montserrat Labour Party, a practice which, though common in the Caribbean at the time, was frowned on by the 1958 Malone Commission. And yet there is no evidence that the Union sponsored politicians on the belief that political advancement in the form of increasing self-government was a panacea for economic ills. That perhaps explains why union agitation tended to be localized, intermittent and short-lived. Constitutional changes came to Montserrat because of agitation in other Caribbean territories and in accordance with the British Government's plan for gradual reform. Bramble himself was no avid advocate of constitutional reform. In 1957 the Administrator was surprised that Bramble agreed with him that the island was not eligible for the next stage of constitutional advance. This was in response to Matthew Gairy of Grenada, who was at the time arguing for greater self-government in the smaller islands.[24]

Bramble led Montserrat from 1952 to 1970, except for a brief hiatus between 1958 and 1961 when he represented the island in the failed Federal Parliament. Even then his MLP was the dominating force. In 1952 he became Chairman of the Social Services and Public Works Committee, and, following the introduction of a new constitution, he became the island's first Chief Minister in 1961. Both developments constituted a significant shift of power away from the merchant-planter oligarchy, although the Governor saw the role of the chairman of a Committee as one of merely providing 'stimulation and advice'. Defeating merchant-planter R. E. D. Osborne in successive elections on his way to being Chief Minister, Bramble used his unbroken tenure of 18 years to emancipate his people and ameliorate their social and economic conditions.

As Committee Chairman, he used the semi-ministerial system to good advantage. In 1953 the Governor, Kenneth Blackburne, in a dispatch to Walter Wallace at the Colonial Office, observed: 'Bramble has done an admirable job, with remarkably few mistakes as Chairman of the Public Works and Social Services Committee; and he has done more than anyone else to make the new constitution work in Montserrat'.[25] One of his first projects was housing. He did not initiate the project, but where it had stalled due to the tyranny and meanness of A. W. Griffin and Wades Plantations, he threw in his energy and influence and achieved results. This was the acquisition of land at Tuitts for an aided self-help housing scheme. With some assistance from Commissioner Charlesworth Ross and nominated member M. S. Osborne, the village which now bears the name of Bramble was established as a model in cooperative self-help activity. By 1958 a similar scheme, comprising 14 houses, was completed at St Patrick's and two others were started at Salem and Cork Hill. He started in his constituency, but his vision was island-wide. On a housing-related matter it was Bramble who, in his role as the island's representative in the Federal Legislative Council, tabled a motion in Antigua which had the effect of abolishing the law which authorized tenancy-at-will.

A few months after his inauguration in 1952, he moved a resolution against *métairie*, only to be defeated by a combination of merchants, planters and officials, although there was some modification. From their predictably biased perspectives, M. S. Osborne and A. W. Griffin saw it as the best system, while for Walkinshaw it was 'a severe social injustice' – a view later echoed by Robert Brandshaw of St Kitts when he addressed a mass meeting in Plymouth on 5 December 1957. For him, it was a legacy of feudalism. By 1960 it vanished as cotton dwindled and emigration and real estate took over.

With the support of a ministerial colleague, B. W. Edwards, Bramble showed marked interest in the education and plight of poor children. In 1953 he placed his car at the disposal of school children at Kinsale to take them to the hospital for medical treatment from time to time.[26] The initiative to establish a senior school in 1955 came from the British Government, but he enthusiastically grasped the opportunity to give post-primary education to more children, although this school did not have parity of esteem with the grammar-school wing. The decision, however, to establish an Island Scholarship in 1962 was his government's.

Bramble was approaching his zenith in power when cotton and agriculture were at their nadir. Push-and-pull migration (linked with hard times at home and unskilled labour opportunities in England) was fed by the decline in cotton, but also fuelled that decline. Bramble's policy of peasant farming on a rental basis did not quite pay off, since the land became too fragmented and the lots uneconomical. After this had failed, he welcomed emigration as another means by which the working class would escape post-emancipation slavery. 'They are leaving our beautiful sunshine to fight adverse weather, bitter winter and the like, but they are fleeing from share-cropping, from feudal landlords and economic pressure.'[27] Bramble was more correct than the lecturer, S. B. Philpot, who attributed emigration, in addition to the decline of cotton, to the establishment of a universally elected governmental system and the growth of trade unionism.[28] Between 1955 and 1961 some 3835 Montserratians arrived in England. On the one hand it seemed a loss of vital manpower but, on the other hand, remittances from the United Kingdom became a major source of revenue for the island.

Bramble's real answer to agricultural decline was real estate development and residential tourism, beginning in 1961. Large stretches of land were cleared in Olveston, Old Road, Woodlands, Richmond and Spanish Point, and expatriates came in to build or buy houses. Local revenue increased more than 25 per cent in 1965 over the 1964 figures and the total value of imports was $4 887 839 (an increase of $868 000 over 1964).[29] Administrator Donald Wiles spoke of a 'break-through' in the early 1960s and his successor Dennis Gibbs, who allied with Bramble in the new thrust, detected a turning point in the economic life of the country. Bramble himself claimed to have encouraged private enterprise and the importation of foreign capital. Consciously or not, he had adopted the Puerto Rican model of development by invitation, but it was for real-estate development, not industrialization. By 1966 a boom was evident, and several hundreds were employed in the building industry, which was linked to the descent of North Americans on winter-home sites in a tropical paradise. A tourist trade accompanied home and villa construction and the island's first luxury hotel was built in 1961. The number of stop-over visitors rose from 1592 in 1962 to 2700 in 1964.[30] Table 7.1 gives information on the building boom between 1966 and 1972.

Table 7.1 Houses built or under construction in residential tourist areas, 1966–72

Area	1966	1967	1968	1969	1970	1971	1972
Olveston Woodlands Old Town	64	75	91	106	114	127	134
Spanish Pointe	10	13	16	21	25	28	31
Richmond Hill	17	31	36	38	43	49	53
Isles Bay	1	6	6	6	7	8	9
Elberton Foxes Bay	1	9	9	13	15	16	19
Total	93	134	158	184	204	228	246

Source: J. H. Momsen, 'Report on Food Production and the Tourist Industry in Montserrat', University of Calgary, Canada, 1973 (cyclo).

In 1966, with the economic wind at his back, Bramble was powerful enough to introduce his son, P. Austin Bramble, to the prestigious Plymouth constituency, where he defeated Robert Griffith in his final bid for a seat in Council. Bramble's power was unrivalled until 1970, when he was removed by a palace revolt.

Although Bramble's real-estate policy brought palpable economic growth, it drew criticism from some quarters for alienating agricultural land. His own son and Social Services Minister, P. A. Bramble, felt that wanton traffic in real estate was inadvisable, for it incurred the distrust of the expatriate community. Montserratian intellectual Dr James Irish charged that the real estate policy placed locals at the inflationary mercy of powerful capitalists. Illustrating his claim, he pointed out that a piece of land bought for EC$1000 was sold within a year for EC$8000.[31] Political aspirant J. N. Edwards also raised doubts about the wisdom of selling off the lands. And when premier calypsonian Arrow (Alphonsus Cassell) sang:

> Hold on to your property I am warning you my friend
> Hold on to your property and will it to your children.

it was the same issue to which he was alluding.

These criticisms seemed insightful at the time, and certainly the rapid rise in the price of land did affect local persons. The issue of land alienation does not seem so controversial with hindsight. There has never been any lack of land for farming on Montserrat and no economic transformation has since been undertaken by any government with a focus on agriculture. The economy still turns largely on the building industry born of Bramble's real estate vision. Besides, the venture brought jobs, generated the development of critical infrastructure such as island-wide electrification and road-building, and led to an improvement in the quality of housing for the entire population.

Two things, however, were disturbing about the new orientation of the economy. One was the mendicant and fawning approach to investors. The blandishment is evident in this spread of the red carpet in the island's weekly newspaper:

> There are private clubs to which visitors have access merely on the introduction of a member, and it is not rare for the members of these clubs to entertain visitors and friends alike. Here people mingle with due respect for individual freedom and without constriction of dislike.

These clubs were in fact very private and exclusive, and local membership was based on a rigid and ridiculously discriminatory screening process. This welcoming society came 'complete with maids, cooks, gardeners and baby sitter', as *Travel Holiday*[32] advertised it. The racial stereotype which linked the black and poor with lowly jobs was reinforced.

The response to any local critical reaction to all this was also disturbing. The merchant-planter editor of the *Montserrat Mirror* was angry at the ideas of J. N. Edwards. He also apologized to the island's visitor-investors for Dr Irish's critical comments, which he associated with 'cheap popularity or sensational journalism'. Raymond Philips, the absentee president of the Montserrat Company and Montserrat Estates, joined in the lists from Canada. His Company had not alienated agricultural land, he contended, but had developed and improved properties by investing hundreds of thousands of dollars. Mr Philip was right to some extent and his Company had demonstrated that it had corporate conscience, but his tone was unsettling. How dare these local boys ruffle the tranquillity of the strangers' paradise? After all, insisted Philips, 'we have arranged for this land to be improved to attract people, their capital and their income', as if it were mainly an altruistic venture, as if the natural and social endowments of the island were not inducing assets.

The negative social fall-out from a policy of establishing expatriate palatial 'ghettoes' on a poor black island was not as great as feared. This is because locals used their enhanced income to improve their own housing quality and the new residents sought useful avenues of integration through service clubs. The establishment of a museum is a monument to their efforts. I poetically attacked an attempt to form a cinema club in Montserrat's only cinema to show 'quality' films during the normal working hours. Karate genre pictures were to be reserved for the evenings and the plebeians. A verse from the poem ran,

> Take it easy stranger man
> In your imperious drive
> To build an ivory wall
> In my black sand.

This alarmed the expatriate community and locals with special vested interest in the welcoming society. Independent thinkers were treated as deviants and their nuisance value went unrecognized. Irish's comments on real estate development would at least have signalled to Philips that there were Montserratians who were prepared to take a critical look at the real estate traffic, Montserratians who were not prepared to give the foreign investor a blank cheque. Such locals helped to give the society a modicum of self-respect.

The other economic activity associated with Bramble was an experiment in an agro-industry based on tomatoes. A Canadian-based Leeward Islands Company was authorized to establish a tomato-paste factory in 1960. The event was greeted with euphoria as the first step in the modern industrial development of Montserrat. In one year the factory was a fiasco. Farmers who retailed their second- and third-grade tomatoes on the local market for 24 cents per pound were paid one cent per pound by the Company. With such a low price and the attractive emigration route to England, the factory operated just three or four hours daily and eventually closed. In his understandable haste to embrace foreign capital and support an industry with inter-sectoral linkage, the champion of the workers had settled with his investors for too low a price. The project was not feasible and it took its toll on Bramble's popularity.

Bramble did make another serious effort at agriculture; it was to grow bananas on a commercial scale. In 1961, 1000 bunches were shipped to the UK via the Windward Islands. The industry continued to expand but the lack of feeder-roads and the high winds severely affected it. Exports to Britain were valued at $24 972 in 1963 and $19 666 in 1964. The producers formed themselves into a Banana Growers' Association in 1965, but hurricane Inez destroyed about 80 per cent of the crop in 1966, and after that the industry virtually disappeared. This is one of several instances in the history of the island when a promising initiative in agriculture was not vigorously sustained.

Along with his economic policy, Bramble's regime was criticized as being authoritarian and class ridden. Claude E. Browne, his political enemy, who constantly peddled this idea, dubbed him 'the dictator'. Browne admitted that he had 'proved by his experiences as a councillor and associations with others outside this island his worth as a member of our present legislature',[33] but nevertheless wanted him removed, presumably because in Browne's prejudiced view he was not a man of culture. Bramble is charged with opportunism for drafting Rose Kelsick, of merchant stock, into his Labour Party for the 1958 general elections, and there may have been an element of truth in this. Browne, however, saw it as a recognition by Bramble that men and women of culture, ability and education were needed in politics. Supposedly possessing these attributes, Browne and persons like Eric Kelsick were offering themselves for office.

The fielding of Rose Kelsick against Griffith in 1958 may not illustrate the point, but by then Bramble was shifting from a purely labour and union-oriented Government. He retained the service of M. S. Osborne, a leading merchant and the brother of his rival R. E. D. Osborne, as a nominated member. He seemingly recognized the need to utilize all the human resources available and favourable to him for economic reconstruction in the 1960s. M. S. Osborne's luxury hotel, built in 1961, dovetailed well with his resident-tourism and real estate policy.

In the 1960s Bramble was powerful enough to take on all opposition with great self-confidence. His role as the champion of the poor gave him a moral basis which barely prevented his response from merging into arrogance. Replying to a political meeting by Eric Kelsick and E. Laurel Meade, he wrote:

> In my view, it is entirely too early to begin to campaign for the coming elections, but some political infants have begun disturbing the waters, and as a watch-dog of the people, I must begin to bark with an intention to bite at the slightest attempt by an intruder to approach the people's camp.[34]

He was the guardian and only those he favoured would be admitted to political power. The one attack he could not stave off was that of his son, P. Austin Bramble.

Young Bramble echoed and gave some credibility to Claude E. Browne's criticism of his father as being autocratic, although he blamed this partly on his Cabinet colleagues who were yes-men. He further attacked him in the very area of his success, real estate development, accusing him of alienating agricultural land in his policy of accommodating 'resident' tourists from North America. He respected his father as a man and acknowledged his achievements for the country, but his father's blunders were grave enough to outweigh kinship ties and justify an internecine political war. With assistance from John Osborne, Austin Bramble defeated his father at the polls in 1970, bringing an end to the first illustrious chapter of the Montserrat working-class movement.

Only his son could have defeated William Bramble at the time. Bramble fell because the mass exodus of agricultural workers to England had robbed the island of the beneficiaries of his liberating work; the rallying-cry of labour had a less appealing resonance to the new generation. In denouncing his father's weaknesses, Austin struck home and, with his better formal education, his words weighed heavily with the younger generation. The island took his courage and sincerity at face value and allowed him to snatch the mantle from his father in the unnatural conflict.

Trade unions after 1960

A Montserrat Seamen and Waterfront Workers' Union (MSWWU) emerged in 1961, led by a young lawyer, Kenneth Allen. He preserved the link between unionism and politics when the same year, he led the United Workers' Movement (UWM) into the general election and personally lost to Rose Kelsick. Allen demitted union office the following year due, claims J. A. Irish, to his antipathy to the dishonest practices which were entrenched in the docks.[35] He also abandoned his efforts to secure electoral office, and the UWM, which had included other prominent unionists, including the General Secretary, became defunct.

The MSWWU functions as a private club, with leaders using the closed-shop mechanism to exert a heavy hand on the processes and activities of the organization. The leaders tend to maintain a cordial relationship with the shipping agents (mostly merchants) so that any semblance of militancy is readily muted. The union has succeeded as a social club which fostered fellowship and camaraderle among dock-workers, but scored no gains in participative democracy. It had limited aims, served a small group and could not lay the foundation for the establishment of modern industrial relations. It attracted only that quality of leadership which correlated with its narrow and non-democratic aims.

The Montserrat Allied Workers' Union (MAWU) was differently conceived from the UWM, but shared with it and the MTLU the nexus with politics, as it turned out. It was founded in 1973 by University of the West Indies lecturer, Dr J. A. Irish, who combined militancy with political activism. In 1978 Irish actually took to the platform in support of John Osborne and his bourgeois-backed People's Liberation Movement (PLM) after securing an agreement from Osborne to support certain union demands and programmes. Osborne's victory cannot be attributed to Irish (Osborne defeated Irish in 1983), but Irish made the PLM victory a more resounding one and helped to brighten Osborne's populist image. Part of Irish's motivation for supporting Osborne was the defeat of Austin Bramble whose regime he has consistently castigated as being anti-union.

In a sense, then, the MAWU became as politically oriented as the MTLU, so it was not surprising that in 1983 Irish used the union as the platform for his United National Front (UNF) whose candidates were all trade unionists. The MAWU failed dismally at electoral politics, but suc-ceeded markedly at labour relations, worker education and at raising the self-image of many an otherwise ordinary worker. Vereen Thomas (Woolcock), for instance, who started out as a part-time office employee, rose to become General Secretary, electoral hopeful and committee member in many international worker organizations.

The establishment of the MAWU coincided with a growth in the service industries sector, a development of infrastructure and essential ser-vices and continued buoyancy in the building industry. There was, there-fore, a strong basis for a membership since the level of employment was high, and some non-established government workers also joined the union. In spite of its comprehensive outreach, the MAWU did not seem to attract sufficient financial members to subsist and implement its ambitious education programmes. Like other small unions in the region, it depended on regional and international labour organizations for aid.

Open hostility to the MAWU was not comparable to that faced by the MTLU at the hands of the plantocrats of the 1940s and 1950s, but it cer-tainly was not embraced as a partner in social and economic development. The government of the day regarded it as a threat to its 'development by invitation' economic regime, which tried to woo investors who unreason-ably sought conditions which would not obtain in their country of origin. This kind of attitude reinforces the mendicant approach to development in these small, vulnerable economies. The MAWU has been generally con-structive and has been able to maintain cordial relationships in the labour arena for two decades. Its construction of a headquarters in 1982 symbol-ized the deepening of its stakes in the country, and the establishment of the Montserrat Trades Union Congress (MONTUC) in 1990, spearheaded by the MAWU, is another landmark achievement. It is to the credit of the leadership of its founder, J. A. Irish, and its education programme, that the union has survived his migration to the USA in 1987, and continues to be effective. With revitalized management, the union will be well poised to make a contribution of even greater quality to the development of the island, not as a political force in the conventional sense, but as a critical social partner.

The Montserrat Teachers' Union, registered in 1977, is a beneficiary of the progressive trade union climate created by MAWU. It is a direct descendant of a Montserrat Teachers' Association formed in 1920 under the presidency of Mr T. T. Adams. That Association was an affiliate of the Antigua Teachers' Association, which was itself part of a larger body covering British Guiana and the West Indies. One of the proposals made to the Moyne Commission by a four-man delegation consisting of F. E. Peters, C. Edwards, R. Mason and Mr Barton was that schools be graded by size for the purposes of salary, so that whereas the head of the school of 100 would receive £20, the head of one of 200 would receive £40. This somewhat illogical request was not granted.

The teachers' associations have always suffered from the snobbery and division which have characterized relationships between primary and secondary teachers. Secondary school teachers regarded themselves and were regarded as being superior to those operating at the primary level. This has robbed the association and union of numerical, intellectual and moral strength. Some change was evident in the mid-1970s, so the MUT properly represents both groups. Membership of the Teachers' Association has never been overwhelming, but this has improved, as the presence of secondary school teachers is an incentive for attracting primary teachers.

The Teachers' Association was not particularly effective. In chronicling its achievement, Irish describes it as making history 'by holding out a threat of strike action' in 1960 against W. H. Bramble's Labour government. Its other high points were a protest march 'with the Civil Service Association'[36] and a sick-out in 1980 again with the CSA. This is typical. The Teachers' Association attains some prominence at salary negotiation times when attendance at meetings belies real participative membership. It has, with external assistance, also sponsored a few in-service training programmes in addition to those organized by the Government. Its membership in MONTUC, its affiliation with the Caribbean Union of Teachers and its membership in the World Confederation of the Teaching Profession should have given it greater authority as a union and a more stimulating professional presence. As more secondary school teachers become active members, one expects to see the union take and articulate reasoned and professional positions on critical issues in education, as befits a sector in which a very large slice of the education and training budget has been invested. If the teachers demonstrate responsible intellectual leadership, they should become partners with government in policymaking. The bargaining process for improved conditions of service should then be more harmonious.

Although the Civil Service Association registered as a trade union in 1977, members are (like the MUT) governed by the statutory General Orders. They can and do bargain effectively, but are not allowed to participate actively in politics, in accordance with the Westminster administration model. As I have written elsewhere, 'in theory, they are supposedly neutral, although in practice many surreptitiously support parties in positive and effective ways. One frequent method is to take confidential information to opposition politicians.' Another way is to give damaging information to hostile newspapers.[37] With their insider knowledge and the difficulty of securing confidentiality in this mini-society with a close kinship network, civil servants are a political force to reckon with. They can also stymie policy which will present a government to which they are opposed in a bad light. This reportedly happened when PLM restructured the education system to abolish the eleven-plus examination and the elitist secondary education system which it created. (It was by this examination that fewer than 10 per cent of the primary-school population were selected for secondary education.)

On the whole a stable industrial relations climate exists, and the trade unions, on the whole, act with a high degree of responsibility.

8

Education in the twentieth century

Primary education

At the beginning of the twentieth century, primary education was in theory compulsory for children between the ages of five and nine, but attendance was not enforced or enforceable. Administrative officials and legislators bemoaned the irregular attendance and alluded to the legal provision and the need to prosecute delinquent parents, but ignored the real cause of the problem. As late as 1935, in a memorandum to the Moyne Commission, the Commissioner referred to the increasing number of stray and vagabond children in the island and linked the problem with the increasing number of crimes and young criminals. Irregular attendance, which had hitherto always plagued schooling, was due largely to poor socio-economic conditions. Children were required to assist their parents in the fields in the interest of survival, and for most of the first half of the century, school space was, in any case, inadequate to accommodate all the children. Besides, some parents who could not provide the requisites such as books and slates kept their children at home.

In 1918, there were 13 primary schools in the island with rolls ranging from 18 at Roches to 194 at St Mary's. As Table 8.1 shows, the total enrolment was 2802, but the average attendance was only 1331. Apart from one private school, all were state-aided. The schools were jointly managed by a Board established by Government under the 1925 Education Act (Cap. 86) of the Federal Acts of the Leeward Islands, and by managers who were generally ministers of religion. Government's financial contribution was £779.10s.4d. and voluntary contributions were £113.6s.9d. But, although the Government contributed the lion's share, it was really a paltry sum. Just over six shillings were provided annually for each child on the roll. Restriction of expenditure on education appeared to be a deliberate policy. When the Marriot–Mayhew Commission was appointed in 1932 it was only allowed to visit the Leeward Islands Colony, 'on the understanding that we recommend no immediate increase in expenditure'.[1]

Finance apart, dual management posed its own problems. The Board of Education made regulations which had to be observed by the managers who owned the school buildings and hired the teachers. As a result, the

Table 8.1 Primary school enrolment, 1918–19

		Scholars on roll			Average attendance		
		Boys	Girls	Total	Boys	Girls	Total
1	St Mary's Anglican	194	193	387	101	96	197
2	Kinsale Anglican	124	101	225	57	52	109
3	St Patrick's Anglican	41	28	69	18	14	32
4	St George's Hill Anglican	28	29	57	11	12	23
5	St George's Anglican	168	152	320	88	76	164
6	St John's Anglican	112	95	207	46	40	86
7	St Peter's Anglican	92	92	184	43	44	87
8	Bethel Wesleyan	179	147	326	92	67	159
9	Cavalla Hill Wesleyan	137	153	290	66	71	137
10	Plymouth Wesleyan	123	101	224	55	47	102
11	Plymouth RC	124	128	252	55	50	105
12	Olveston	120	105	225	59	52	111
13	Roaches Anglican	18	18	36	11	8	19
Totals		1460	1342	2802	702	629	1331

Source: Adapted from C.O. 157/32 Blue Book 1918–19. T6.

clergymen made denominational membership a necessary condition for teaching and this meant that the best-qualified persons were not always employed. As we observed in Chapter 6, propagation and perpetuation of a particular brand of the Christian faith was a critical aim of education. Because of this, potentially qualified teachers from other denominations were rejected. Denominational schools also affected some children adversely since they were forced to bypass the neighbourhood schools and travel long distances on foot in order to attend the school of their parents' religious persuasion.[2] A District Education Officer supervised the schools, but visits were sparse, for he sometimes held the position of Clerk to the Commissioner and Registrar of the High Court all at the same time. In 1936, he visited Cavalla Hill twice, six schools once each, and some schools including Kinsale and St George's, not even once. The Federal Inspector of Schools came periodically mainly to inspect and conduct examinations.[3]

Even when the government recognized certain problems, it was reluctant to interfere, because the schools belonged to the churches, and it could not marshal the resources to take them over. In 1928, the Commissioner, Major H. W. Peebles, recognized that space and equipment were inadequate and that overcrowded schools posed a grave danger to the prosperity of the island. However, he felt that the system rendered it difficult for Government to interfere 'except with a view to take over'.

By 1929, the Government sought to play a more direct role in the development of education. When the Montserrat Company surrendered its Olveston school, Government accepted it and paid rent for the building. The Wesleyans, however, opposed the establishment of a Government school in Salem and threatened to close all of their schools if they were not allowed to inherit the Company's school. In the event they won,[4] but the Commissioner, T. E. P. Baynes, recommended the building of another school in Salem. A school was also planned for Cork Hill, following the closing of the small Church of England school at St George's Hill.

The joint administration of Government and denominational schools generated a problem of another kind. There was a disparity in conditions of service between the two types of schools, and a teacher lost pension when he or she was transferred from one to the other. This is in spite of the fact that a pension scheme was established for denominational teachers in 1930. Throughout the first quarter of the century the whole business of remuneration for teachers was dealt with in an *ad hoc* and unsystematic way. Disparity existed not only within the island, but between one presidency and another. As a result Montserrat could not attract good teachers from other Leeward Islands. In 1926, a deputation of Head Teachers petitioned the Board of Education for the abolition of 'payment by results', a practice long discarded in England, whence it was copied. This was an expedient whereby the remuneration received by teachers was based on the success of their schools as determined by examination results. The inefficient functioning of the Board of Education, which was seldom meeting by 1935 and even so acted merely in an advisory capacity, did not improve administrative efficiency. This problem persisted until 1945, when Government assumed full responsibility for all schools, with the exception of the Roman Catholic school, which continued to be grant-aided.

The debate over relevant curriculum and the need for practical subjects has a long and recurrent history in this island. The Education Board Minutes (1925–36) reveal that reading, hygiene, elementary science, geography, history and needlework (for girls) were made compulsory in 1925. A law of 1930, however, made it clear that a teacher did not mean a 'sewing mistress'. The rather progressive Montserrat Company seemed to have always intended to provide technical training in subjects like agriculture and carpentry at their Olveston school. Wesleyan chronicler Rev. Lawrence suggested that the aim was not fulfilled, possibly because 'it may have been found that ordinary subjects were bound to come first'.[5] He thus introduced an unwarranted dichotomy between practical and 'ordinary' subjects into the curriculum dialogue. (In fact, the Company did establish a technical school to provide apprenticeship in certain trades and crafts.)

In his memorandum on education in 1938, the Commissioner argued that the happiness of the people would depend on the intimate association of agriculture and education as the basis of a sound rural economy. Two years before this, the Teachers' Association had objected to the suggestion that teachers be given an intensive course in agricultural science. They were purist products of a bookish educational culture. When the Moyne Commission visited, the curriculum consisted of the three Rs, hygiene, geography, history, occasional botany, and some agriculture. One can imagine how little and what quality of agriculture was taught, given the teachers' lack of enthusiasm for the subject. It was evident too, that these subjects were not integrated to reflect any coherent concept of an educated person for the particular society. Commenting to the Commission on the widespread practice of smuggling, particularly in the north of the island where the smuggling chiefs 'fear neither God, man, nor beast, nor police', the Anglican priest Fr Morris blamed the situation in part on lack of training for citizenship in the schools. It was felt that an association incorporating teachers, school authorities and parents could serve to ensure such meaningful teaching.

The debate was taken up in a comprehensive policy statement on education for the Leeward Islands in the immediate post-Moyne years. Education was criticized as being too academic and verbal rather than 'real', cutting off the living interest of the child. As a corrective, it suggested practical instructors for senior pupils and even on-the-job attachments. Although such recommendations were but partially implemented, they made sense in Montserrat, for at this stage primary schools had become all-age schools taking children up to age 14 *de jure* and to age 16 *de facto*. The authors of the statement recognized the need for balance in the introduction of a practical bias to the curriculum. They placed the emphasis on general pre-vocational training rather than a narrow specialist training,[6] an emphasis that is still applicable in a country whose economy has a shifting and unstable base.

It was not until 1953 that a comprehensive policy statement which sought to link the primary education curriculum to the needs of the community emerged. The policy was directed towards:

(a) the extension of facilities for more practical work in such subjects as husbandry and school gardening, woodwork, light handicrafts and home economics; (b) teaching children how and where to get information both for profit and pleasure; (c) training children to read fluently and with understanding; (d) teaching children to write clearly and to express their thoughts concisely and accurately; to think clearly and reckon accurately; (e) training in intellectual honesty and the cultivation of an inquiring mind; ... (f) and the selection and training of teachers.[7]

These somewhat rational and relevant-sounding intentions were not matched by concrete action and adequate funding. Efforts were made to teach handicrafts and home economics by peripatetic teachers, but with very little realistic relationship to consumer needs or the job market. The high point, which was the school exhibition, was an end in itself.

Untrained teachers constituted a major obstacle to the advancement of primary education in the early decades of the century. In fact as early as the 1840s, the Stipendiary Magistrate voiced his anxiety over the lack of enough competent teachers in face of parental keenness for the education of their children. At that time they looked to Nevis, whence a Mr Miller, the Superintendent of the school, promised to send teachers who were already trained.[8] Except for a very short period in the early 1970s, Montserrat has always looked outside for the professional training of its teachers. Rumours of a community college with a teacher training section may break this external dependency in the twenty-first century.

In 1931, when the entire Leeward Islands colony was training only seven teachers annually, Montserrat's quota could not have been more than one. Men were trained either at the Rawle training institute in Barbados or the Mico College in Jamaica, while women were trained at the Moravian Training Institute at Spring Gardens in Antigua, which dated back to 1840. Not only were the numbers inadequate, but the quality of the training offered in Barbados and Antigua was criticized for its inferiority by the Marriot–Mayhew Commission. Neither the two full-time members of staff nor the part-time member of the Antigua college possessed the requisite qualification of a teachers' college. They had neither mastered the techniques of teaching nor understood the relationship of the primary school to communal needs.[9] As qualifications correlated somewhat with status, it was difficult to attract persons of the right calibre to the profession.

To address the training problem, Marriot–Mayhew proposed that all the teachers be trained at a Central Training Institute in Trinidad. The institution would be organized in such a manner as to ensure that the discipline and moral influence which the women enjoyed (presumably) at the Moravian college would still obtain. A small number of Montserratian teachers were trained in Trinidad, but when Barbados established an improved teachers' college at Erdiston, the island turned to that institution and later to the Leeward Islands Teacher Training College which was established at Golden Grove in Antigua in 1960. This replaced the Spring Gardens College, which was closed in 1958.

In spite of the availability of these institutions, the proportion of trained to untrained teachers remained low. Attrition and the small annual output ensured this. The British were not too generous with scholarships to the institutions, and the local treasury could not fund overseas training. Of five teachers in three colleges in 1954, only two completed their course in that year;[10] and because there was no proper arrangement for in-service training, the percentage of trained teachers remained low perennially. In 1968 only 45 out of 93, or 48 per cent, were trained. In fact as recently as 1981 of the island's 91 primary school teachers, 43 were untrained.

In-service training of a kind existed in the pupil-teacher system whereby Head Teachers inducted graduated of the all-age primary school in the methodology of teaching and rudimentary principles of education. Having passed through three stages – the first-, second- and third-year examinations – they were admissible to training colleges and to further examinations which gave qualified but uncertificated status. It needs to be noted that this training occurred at the end of a hard-working day for both the Head and the pupil teacher. Though a valuable stop-gap measure under the circumstances, the system led to a kind of inbreeding which reinforced the rote and recitative methods which were so prevalent at the time.

Primary education was driven by this cheap system of training and con-sequently low remuneration right up to 1960. With so many deficiencies – unqualified teachers, over-crowded classrooms, inadequate provisions, including too few blackboards and books, unrealistic curricula and reliance on rote learning – it is a wonder that some students achieved so much. That they did is a tribute to the dedication of some teachers, the pupils' native ability, and their own and their parents' enthusiasm for learning. With 76 per cent, Montserrat had the highest school-attendance in the entire Eastern Caribbean including Barbados (70 per cent) at the time of the Marriott–Mayhew investigation. Table 8.2 contains information on the grades of teach-ers over a six-year period. It is clear that in 1950 some 69 per cent of the

Table 8.2 Grades of teachers, 1945–50

	Certificated teachers		*Uncertificated teachers*	*Pupil teachers*	*Total*
	Class 1	*Class 2*			
1945	8	16	16	36	76
1946	12	14	22	35	83
1947	12	14	24	42	92
1948	12	15	25	53	105
1949	13	19	26	45	103
1950	14	19	28	46	107

Source: Hammond Report IV, 1952, p.41.

teaching force were untrained and the overwhelming majority of these (62 per cent) were pupil teachers.

The Teachers' Association drew the attention of the Moyne Commission to the weakness of the system, especially where an inexperienced pupil teacher was in charge of a class of 40 to 60 pupils. The commissioners did recommend that all teachers obtain adequate training at some properly organized training college, but this was obviously not done. The 1950 figures speak for themselves. S. A. Hammond did precious little to relieve the situation beyond saying that teachers be encouraged to qualify. Even then, he took care to stipulate that they would not necessarily gain admission to the pensionable establishment. He was either very shortsighted or cared little for the education of the grandchildren of British slaves.

With such a high incidence of untrained teachers, adequate professional supervision in the schools was crucial. We have already observed how sparse educative and monitoring visits were in the first quarter of the century. To improve the situation the Marriott–Mayhew Commission recommended a Commissioner of Education to replace the Federal Inspector, and an Island Inspector. However, it spelt out no new description to accompany the new designation. In any case, these recommendations were not implemented. Island Inspectors were not introduced until 1956 with the break-up of the Leeward Island Federation. What Hammond met in 1952 was a Supervisor of School for primary education with the island's Commissioner as the coordinator of both primary and secondary education.

The unimaginative Hammond re-established the Board of Education, but wanted the administration of education in the hands of the representative of the British Government, since he saw no justification for a Department of Education. The Education Board was to be re-established and the Commissioner empowered to appoint officers to supervise and staff the schools. Thankfully, his proposals were not fully endorsed. The leading teachers were themselves acutely aware of the need for the close supervision of pupil teachers. This is why they requested an increase in the establishment to free Head Teachers for this in-service on-the-job training function. But Hammond, whose parsimonious mandate was governed by the need to effect savings, completely missed the point. He responded with a simplistic metaphor about 'the swelling trunk starving the branches and the fruit'[11] which betrayed his insensitivity and lack of understanding of the role of education in development. Primary education was the root, not the trunk. It was another two decades before improved arrangements were made for periodic in-service training and teacher supervision.

Secondary education

A Government grammar school for boys was established in 1928, the year of a disastrous hurricane. Several efforts, however, were made before this time to provide secondary education for a few. The first such effort was made in 1891 when government gave £60 to the rector of St Anthony's, Rev. William Evered, to provide a master. Educational partnership of church and state already existed in the primary sector, but N. Dyett, a member of Council, criticized the decision to place the management of the school under the Anglicans to the exclusion of the other two denominations. This school was shortlived, but its establishment and the consequent criticism focused attention on the need for a Government secondary school; finance was the problem.

Another effort was made in 1909, this time by the Government, which appointed a Board to advise and to raise funds for some of the initial expenses. It folded up in 1914 due, it was said, to lack of support, meaning presumably insufficient fee-paying students. As a result, J. Wall, a member of Council, suggested to the Governor that £100 per annum be granted to a suitably qualified male teacher to open a high school for a minimum of 10 boys. This did not materialize, but his persistent suggestion that Government grant four scholarships – two for boys and two for girls at the Antigua Grammar School and the Antigua Girls High School respectively – was eventually adopted in part. These were to be valued at £25 each and were to be enforced for a period of 'say three years'. In practice, this meant that a tiny few from wealthy homes would be educated at public expense. But ever since the 1891 experiment failed, rich Montserratians had been educating their children at secondary schools in Antigua, St Kitts and Barbados. One such boy was Charles Norman Griffin, son of the Manager of Paradise plantation, the first Montserratian to win the prestigious Leeward Islands Scholarship in 1917, although the Government had to supplement his award with £50.

The early debate on secondary education betrays a decidedly male bias, but girls were not totally neglected. An English woman, Miss K. L. Gray, opened a girls' high school around 1926, and attracted a grant of £100 in 1928. The school shared some of the teaching facilities of the boys' school in return for Miss Gray's service in teaching drawing to the boys. Her school was shortlived, in spite of an effort to extend its life under a Miss Griffin,[12] for the Marriott–Mayhew Commission found no secondary education provision for girls in 1931–2. Yet another girls' school was established by another Briton, Mrs A. G. Horner in 1932, and this lasted until 1938 when it amalgamated with the boys' grammar school.

The Montserrat Grammar School was opened in 1928, with 26 boys. Five of these were already working as pupil teachers in elementary schools in the colony, while another four had already been attending the Antigua Grammar School under the tuition of the Headmaster, Mr H. G. Carrington. In a sense, one reason for establishing the school was to bring these well-to-do children home. It was a 'classical' school intended to train boys for the Cambridge Local Examinations and 'to provide an education suitable for boys who might be capable of competing for the Leeward Island University Scholarship'. The curriculum was as narrow as the aim; it started with a small range of arts, and elementary science was added in 1930, with general science planned for the following year. The 1931 Ordinance which formally established the school laid down the subjects to be taught – 'bible study (undenominational) mathematics, English, Latin, French, Geography, History, natural science (elementary physics, chemistry, botany, agricultural science) and such other branches as may seem advisable'. Drawing, handwork or handcrafts and gardening were to be added, but there were neither the teachers available nor the inclination to teach subjects which detracted from the English model of the classical curriculum.

The Marriott–Mayhew Commission criticized the social irrelevance of the curriculum and proposed a conversion of the school to a Modern school for both sexes. In such a school, which would draw suitable students from Antigua and St Kitts, practical subjects related to life, livelihood and local concerns would be taught. Visiting in 1934, Mr Marriott also criticized the relatively large sum that was spent on a very small elite in a programme geared towards preparing students for the learned professions. The 44 students in the two secondary schools consumed 30 per cent of the public funds voted for education, leaving 70 per cent for 2960 elementary children. Mr Marriott told the management committee that this situation would have provoked a storm of protest if the island had a Labour Party.[13] The children of the poor were short-changed.

Stimulated by Marriott's views, Mercer and Shand, two members of the Education Board, lent support to the few who were condemning the lack of any utilitarian content in the curriculum. In this, they differed sharply from the two clergymen on the Board. It is just possible that Shand and Mercer, who represented planter and business interests, saw the modern school as serving their concerns better, but even so their needs and concerns were more consonant with community interests than was the training in the traditional grammar school. It has to be remembered too that Shand belonged to the Montserrat Company which had consistently sought to promote the vocational training needs of the island.

Some curriculum changes, including more emphasis on science and agricultural science, were made in the post-Marriott years, but the basic philosophy did not change. Citing the number of passes, the Headmaster, Mr H. G. Carrington, defended the *status quo*, and in rhetorical language that missed the real issue, argued that the school should continue as a classical school. To change the orientation 'would have a parlous effect on the tone of the school and would undoubtedly wreck, or render unstable, the structure that has been so carefully built up during the past seven years'.[14] After upwards of 50 years, this kind of biased and shortsighted argument still has a disturbingly modern resonance in some quarters of Monserratian society.

The truth is that the school reflected and reinforced the class divisions of the society. A study of the surnames of the 24 students on the roll in 1934 is very revealing sociologically. Seven boys belonged to a single family group, four to another family and at least 17 stemmed from merchant and planter houses. None came from the labouring classes, whose sweat and toil sustained the school. In 1935 each boy cost the Government £21 annually (with each girl costing rather less – £7. 11s.0d)[15] Secondary education was not just elitist, it was parasitic. The geographical catchment reinforced the class-based nature of the school; the boys came from in and around Plymouth, or from great houses. Indeed, geographic distance reflected social distance, for a poor child from the country would have incurred additional expenses since he would have to pay for weekly accommodation in Plymouth, in order to attend the school. Although their parents were financially able, strenuous efforts were made by the Headmaster to relieve the boys of the road tax which they were required to pay. The curriculum they followed suggested an education for social alienation, but they received very special treatment with the resources of the society.

It was not just the term fees of £4 which put secondary education beyond the reach of ordinary children (there were reductions for extra brothers). The culturally-biased entry tests based on standard English and borrowed from elsewhere, as well as an interview of the parents, served to debar the rural poor. Commenting on the small number of children who wrote the scholarship examination to the grammar school, Mr Marriott suggested that the school should cease to require students to wear expensive clothing and that stockings and socks might be discarded. Not a chance: the 'dignity' and social status of the school must prevail against liberalization. There were two or three Government scholarships, but primary school Headmasters tended to christen their own children first and then coach others from 'respectable' homes.

The management of the grammar school further demonstrated its elite character and set it well apart from the primary schools. Producing candidates for the Leeward Islands Scholarship and ultimately the learned professions of law and medicine in particular, the school was first managed by the

Executive Council. It thus benefited from its closeness to the source of power. Even when this arrangement ceased, the management committee was headed by the President of the Council and consisted mostly of representatives of the landed sector and the church. H. S. Shand of the Montserrat Company, however, who sat on the Education Board, under whose purview secondary education eventually came, exerted a progressive influence on the school. In 1936 he expressed his dissatisfaction with the small numbers who were competing for the available scholarships to the school.

True to its mission, by 1952 when the school had grown to about 120, it had produced seven Leeward Island Scholars and several scores of Cambridge Certificates. Carrington's claim in 1934 that the school had contributed to the development of sports is tenable, but his claim that it had exerted an immense influence on the community and on citizenship betrayed a misguided understanding of that concept. There were those who were moved by the glaring injustice of spending so many resources on so few and argued that Leeward Island scholarship winners should be bonded to serve the island for about five years after training.[16] This was not however considered a practical thing to do.

The school was renamed the Montserrat Secondary School in 1938, when the boys' and girls' school amalgamated. However, no major systemic changes occurred until 1955 when a 'Senior' wing based on the principles of the Marriott Modern school was tacked on to the co-educational establishment which by then was schooling over 180 children aged 11 to 19. Consistent with the Marriott contention that the school should prepare children to earn a living, the Senior School in theory offered a general education 'with a strong infusion of practical subjects' for 120 persons. Pupils were admitted freely, based on the result of a competitive examination. After 1963 when a technical department was added, the syllabus included woodwork and metalwork for boys, home economics, needlework, strawwork and typing (and later shorthand) for girls.

The technical section, which promised a more realistic integration with the island's commercial and occupational life, did not live up to expectations, although it made a valuable contribution in the field of office arts. It shared campus but not status with the academic wing and its local Certificate, unlike the Cambridge Certificate, was no passport to white-collar jobs nor symbol of social advancement. Neither the society nor the students accepted the broader concept of education implicit in the change, and the establishment of a dual institution did not help to change perceptions. Some senior school students merely used the section as a vantage point from which to gain access to the academic wing.

To address this unsatisfactory situation, the school was reorganized on a bilateral basis in 1966. All children were recruited through a common entrance examination and followed a common curriculum for the first two years, after which they were siphoned into one or other of two different but parallel courses according to interests and aptitudes. The pull of the literary curriculum soon led to a blurring of the boundaries and we were back to essentially a classical grammar school in spite of a smattering of a practical subject or two. This particular initiative was a local one with the support of the University of the West Indies.

The impulse for the next change came, as usual from outside, in 1972. This was in the form of junior secondary schools (JSS) to cater to those students who did not qualify for entry to the MSS at eleven-plus. Happily, a decision by the British Government and UNESCO to finance the introduction of junior secondary and comprehensive schools coincided with a popular demand for secondary education. The move also had the sanction of the Moyne Reports, which had recommended junior secondary schools in which practical subjects could be taught. Without any proper evaluation of the first JSS, the second was opened in 1976.

A special feature of the fare for this 'second eleven' was practical subjects, since the students were being prepared for the job market. Negative attitudes to vocational education had changed somewhat, but the three-year practical programme offered was too short to provide students with viable technical skills. In addition, the resources were too limited to provide the rich experiences necessary for effective trade training. The integration of practical and academic training had again failed. In a sense, the great successes of the JSS were the 5 per cent of its students who gained access to MSS Form III at the end of their three-year course. The school, however, whetted the appetites of many students for full secondary education and to fulfil this, they pursued academic courses at the Extra-Mural Centre of the UWI.

In 1976, an Advisory Committee to the Ministry of Education recommended a restructuring of the system to ensure secondary education for all students; and Minister of Education Margaret Dyer-Howe initiated action in 1984 to bring this about. Meanwhile, two private initiatives led to some improvement in the opportunity for secondary education. The first was a small institution, the Academy of Arts and Commerce, founded by J. A. Irish, H. A. Fergus and Bilton Bramble in 1982. It lasted for five years, and offered courses leading to the London College of Preceptors and General Certificate of Education examinations; it was more flexible than the Government school in the acceptable age-range of the students, some of whom were drop-outs from the official system. The second move was made by the Seventh Day Adventists, who created a secondary section out of their primary school in 1983. It was established primarily for its members with an understandably strong religious focus, but opened its doors to children of other persuasions. Although both schools were fee-paying, they suffered from lack of resources and were dependent on Government for aid. They underscored the wide demand for secondary education, but had the capacity to fill only a small fraction of that demand.

Technical-vocational education

Although the need for practical training was recognized in reports and official discussions throughout the first half of the century, no serious, sustained and rational efforts were made to provide technical-vocational training until 1972. Mental and manual training were erroneously regarded as two separate cultures and book learning was given prominence even when it prepared students for nothing.

Not everyone was happy with this philosophy, but money was always the problem. There is a record of a technical school in 1893 for in that year the Legislative Council Minutes speak of a loan of a sum not exceeding £1000 for the establishment of an engineers' workshop as a part of that outfit. This did not last long for, before the end of the century, Montserratian boys were being apprenticed at a technical school in St Kitts.[17] This school, in turn, closed around the beginning of the century for lack of funds, but even before this, the authorities had found it too costly and had stopped financing students. The reason given to the West India Royal Commission (1896–97) was that it was not worthwhile to train boys at public expense when there was no need for skilled labour in Montserrat. The administration supposedly found it more rewarding to vote £1000 for Britain's war fund in 1914 than to establish a trade school. (They bore 'their humble share of the burden now imposed on the empire' with £250 to purchase guava jelly and £750 cash.)[18]

Theoretical recognition of the need for technical education was demonstrated from time to time. One of the objectives of the official education policy for the Leeward Islands (1924–46) was the establishment and maintenance of vocational and professional training regulated by the resources available and the opportunities for employment.[19] Ten years later, Hammond argued for pre-vocational training for pupils 12 years and over in all-age elementary schools. His programme of house-craft, handicraft and husbandry did not seem too creative or job-productive, but his mention of the home, the land and the workshop had a touch of realism. For secondary students, he recommended woodwork, metalwork, technical drawing and general and applied science.

In 1966 Rawle Jordon of the University of the West Indies Institute of Education recommended that a technical school be set up under the aegis of the Public Works Department to teach subjects such as automobile maintenance, electrical engineering, and building trades leading to the City and Guilds Certificates. These ideas had the merit of removing technical training from the shadow of the schools with their basically literary orientation, giving it an importance of its own and relating it to real manpower needs.

Some of these ideas found expression in the 'Senior School', but technical education geared to the production of marketable vocational skills eluded the island until 1972 when the Technical College was established. (In the absence of such formal training, parents took the initiative to apprentice their children with master craftsmen.) The Technical College provided two-year craft-level training for some 80 students in automobile engineering, building trades, electrical engineering, commercial studies and office arts. This college can claim some success. Of the 87 students who completed courses over the period 1975–77, 62 obtained related employment.[20] The college has had to struggle to attain social esteem in an environment in which an academic institution is automatically regarded as superior. Typically, though, the fact that the college takes overseas examinations such as City and Guilds and Royal Society of Arts helped its growth in esteem. Changing attitudes to technical education globally, and comparatively ready access to jobs have reinforced the importance of the college. It further serves the country by retooling adults and upgrading certain skills on a part-time basis. The college still needs to raise some of its courses from craft to technician level and thereby more properly justify the designation of 'college'. There would have to be a consequent improvement in the entrance qualification of the intake.

Reorganization of the system

In 1986, the education system was fundamentally restructured, including the abolition of the common entrance examination (CEE) which gave entrance to the elitist secondary school. This meant automatic universal access to comprehensive-type schooling. One of the significant things about this particular innovation was that the idea originated with a local education advisory body on which there were lay representatives, a delegate of the Montserrat Union of Teachers, and leading educators. The United Kingdom Overseas Development Administration, acting on the idea, commissioned a team headed by a University of London lecturer to produce the project plan; the team included two local educators.

The reference to local participation in this restructuring effort is deliberate, as it may well have registered a shift in the pattern of over-dependence on external sources, ideas and solutions. It is to the credit of the Government that it persisted with the proposal even without the unqualified blessing of a UNESCO mission which attributed peculiar motivating magic to the CEE.

A major objective of restructuring was 'to avoid an element of social stratification in which some bright children gained places in Montserrat Secondary School on completion of their primary school, but others were "doomed" to attend the less prestigious and less academically oriented junior secondary schools'.[21] A Life Skills programme, which combined an academic base with practical activities in commerce, industrial agriculture, craft and hotel work at Form IV was regarded as crucial to restructuring. This was preferred to a watered-down academic curriculum for those students who could not successfully complete the traditional academic programme during their school years.

Through the combined efforts of the Ministry of Education, teachers, and a team of experts from the Wolverhampton Polytechnic in the United Kingdom, the Life Skills idea was transformed and elaborated into a Pre-Vocational Programme (PVP). The PVP has attracted criticism, some of which has been generalized to the entire restructured system. Much of the criticism does not emanate from any rigorous and informed analysis of the system, but comes as part of a recent ripple of anti-British sentiment.[22] The irony is that the British had less to do with the restructured system than with the class-ridden one which it replaced.

There are four basic criticisms: (a) it leads to low achievement at the primary level; (b) instead of automatic promotion from grade to grade, students should be allowed to repeat classes; (c) the PVP creates a cadre of intellectually backward students; and (d) comprehensivization means a general lowering of standards and therefore the CEE should have been retained, to motivate pupils. A Review Body headed by Dr David Pennycuick of the University of Sussex, appointed by Government in 1992 has, however, confirmed support for comprehensivization. It contended that 'performance at the level of the secondary school has not been comprehensivisation per se, but the failure to implement properly some of the recommendations of the Bray Report'.[23] The team went even further than Bray and recommended the abolition of the Grade 6 examination, which has replaced the CEE and is used as the mechanism for streaming pupils for the secondary school.

I have no intention of answering these criticisms, but would point out that, generally speaking, reorganization did not produce these defects. What it did was to reveal weaknesses in learning and teaching, organizing and resourcing which were either endemic in the system or arose from failure to take imperative action ancillary to the innovation. Educational change has to be managed. On the matter of motivation, let me repeat my own comment of 1985:

> One hopes the teachers have not accepted the superficial and simplistic suggestion of some UNESCO consultants that the common entrance examination (and there is nothing 'common' about it) is needed to motivate students. Educators who cannot find other means of stimulating students are in the wrong business. We can at least set examinations and offer sweets or Michael Jackson pins to deserving students, if we are that sold on extrinsic motivation: It is clear that Mrs. Dyer-Howe and her administrators will need stateswomanship, tact and social engineering skills to change the system which really means changing people.[24]

The Pennycuick team recommended a number of amendments, including some adjustment to automatic promotion. If it is heeded, reorganization will not be reversed. On the contrary, the Montserrat system may become a model for the region. An education reform group led by Professor Errol Miller of the UWI which was recently appointed to devise a strategy for education reform in the Organisation of Eastern Caribbean States (OECS), recommended that the entire sub-region should follow the British Virgin Islands, Montserrat and St Kitts and Nevis in providing universal secondary education to all children up to the age of 16.[25]

Adult education

Adult education as an organized activity is of recent vintage in Montserrat. The first mention was made by the Moyne Commission when it advocated that the schools in the British Caribbean should be centres for adult education and for instruction in hygiene and agriculture. The schools were also to be used as library centres. An official 1942–6 Development Plan also emphasized adult education. Noting that literacy is an economic necessity, the author saw the two critical needs of education as primary schooling and opportunities for adult education. It is heartening to note that he did not confine the latter to literacy classes, but recognized vocational and professional training as valid dimensions of adult learning.[26] (Manpower-training for community leadership and nation-building was envisaged as a UWI extra-mural activity from the outset.)[27]

The Government of Montserrat did nothing about these recommendations. In fact adult education was not even mentioned in the 1966–70 Development Plan and, as late as 1980, a UNESCO Report on Montserrat adverted to the lack of a policy on adult education. Meanwhile, apart from the teaching work of church organizations, individuals and community groups conducted non-formal education activities on a voluntary basis. In the early 1950s, the St George's Progressive Society, the Cork Hill Cultural Club, the Kinsale Community Centre and the Salem Progressive Society served their respective communities with arts and humanities programmes, especially in choral music, debates, public speaking and drama.

These voluntary organizations anticipated to an extent the work of the Extra-Mural Department of the University College of the West Indies, which was established in 1948. This department quickly became and continues to be the major purveyor of adult and continuing education in the island. As a single tutor served all the presidencies of the Leeward Islands, the occasional public lecture and choral music were useful programme-fillers at the beginning.

The first tutor for the Leeward Islands, Mr F. W. Case, set up the first Advisory Committee, consisting of 11 persons, in 1949 with Archdeacon P. C. H. Hilbourne as Chairman and the Montserrat Secondary School Principal Mr E. DeV. Archer as Secretary and Correspondent. Eighty-nine persons enrolled for the first courses, in economics, Spanish and commercial studies; and immediate plans were made to add domestic science, elementary mathematics, art and art appreciation to the curriculum.[28] In describing the work of the School of Continuing Studies (the new name), local education officials tend to limit it to purely academic classes. In this first programme, an interest in technical-vocational skills as well as the arts is evident. In addition to its formal certificate courses, the University Centre has offered courses in a range of practical and professional areas including toy-making, food preservation, care of the elderly, management of small business and computer literacy. The appointment of a Resident Tutor in 1964 and the erecting of a University Centre with funds provided by the Ford Foundation in 1970 emphasized the UWI's presence and broadened its role in adult and non-formal education.

A landmark in UWI adult education was reached in 1979 with the introduction of 'Challenge' or external studies, which enabled students to study for UWI Certificates at home and complete the first year of the degree programme in a number of faculties. The advent of the University of the West Indies Distance Teaching Experiment (UWIDITE) facilities in 1992 de-emphasized the divide between intra- and extra-mural and enabled local students to access teaching by the UWI faculty from the three campuses. This development has the effect of ensuring economies at the tertiary level at a time when the cost of university education has escalated everywhere.

Although the Government has not articulated an adult education policy, there are Government units which provide vital adult learning. The agriculture department, through its extension division, instructs farmers in new techniques; and the Technical College, through its evening classes, provides opportunities for adults to learn new skills and to upgrade existing ones, although not enough of this is done. What are needed are an overarching policy and a coordinating mechanism which bring together and give developmental purpose to the work of the various units and organizations which are involved in adult and continuing education. These should include the work of agencies such as the Red Cross, Family Life Services, the Health Department, the Young Women's Christian Organization, the Montserrat Chamber of Commerce and Industry and so forth. These all engage in adult education even if it is not so designated.

With changing economic focus and rapid technological advances, adult and continuing education becomes and indispensable means of constantly retooling the work-force and equipping it with survival skills. This is best achieved through a network of institutions with a central focus. The emphasis may well be on life-skills, including an entrepreneurial orientation. And yet for a people coming from slavery and colonialism, with a penchant for mimicking the metropoles, there will always be the need for 'intellectual inquiry and questioning, the readiness to explore new knowledge frontiers and the encouragement of objective disputation and objective discussion of ideas'.[29] This liberal-education aspect of the adult agenda is perhaps best pursued by the University Centre.

9

Political developments after 1970

A chip off the old block

This chapter focuses on key personalities and issues in the island's politics after the fall of W. H. Bramble. It also examines electoral and political styles as well the question of constitutional advancement.

Percival Austin Bramble, having better formal education than his father, with whom he parted ways, promised a new departure in Montserratian politics. What his critics claimed he inherited was a fair share of that authoritarianism for which his father was criticized. The presence of a former Head Teacher in Executive Council together with his ally in the defeat of his father, the astute John Osborne who later ousted him from power, did not attenuate the tendency towards monocracy. In his first manifesto, John Osborne's People's Liberation Movement (PLM) described the regime of Bramble's Progressive Democratic Party (PDP) as 'one-man-rule'.[1]

After a decade of ministerial government, the concept of a minister and a ministry functioning with a large measure of autonomy was then still alien to the Montserratian political culture. Bramble was the brain power and spokesman for the major policies of the Ministry of Education, Health and Welfare and it was he who determined the parameters for action. Minister of Social Services in his father's government, he retained an abiding interest in that portfolio. He continued to formulate the ideological context of programmes like school meals, nursery education and free secondary education. His very first 'throne speech' spoke of 'the need for government to take its fair share of the increasing wealth its policies will attract, and to redistribute it in a manner that will ensure that the needs of the old, the infirm and the underprivileged are never forgotten'.[2] These policies were dear to his heart and he presided over their implementation from the Ministry of Finance. He thus became minister at large, a process that was easy with apathetic and unimaginative ministers.

Austin Bramble's social services programmes marked him out as left-of-centre, so in a sense he carried forward and sharpened the social policies of his father. It was for this reason that John Osborne, an uncritical worshipper at the shrine of free enterprise, called him a socialist, using the term pejoratively.[3] John Dublin (then Osborne's comrade) dubbed him a communist at the launching of the PLM in 1975. In fact, in Osborne's 13 years at the rudder, he did not change Bramble's programmes, which merely reflected a social conscience and seemed absolutely crucial in a developing society which must cater to the basic needs of its less-privileged, thereby bringing them fully into the line of production. This position was clearly articulated in Bramble's 1970 *Election Manifesto*: 'All of the island's people must be adequately housed, and the sufferings of the aged, the infirm and the underprivileged must be relieved.'

Bramble was no doctrinaire socialist. Indeed he was surprisingly conservative in some of his policies. He opposed a policy of mass secondary education and has consistently defended colonial status for Montserrat. If he was not hostile to trade unions (and Dr J. Irish, his political critic, would argue that he was), he did not suffer them gladly either. Irish continually barbs Bramble on the hostility of the PDP to unions and for generally presiding over an anti-union government.[4]

Bramble was accused of inconsistency when, after campaigning against the alienation of the landed patrimony for expatriate pleasure, he called a snap election in 1973 in search of a mandate to combat racism.[5] This seemed a strange *volteface*, but all that happened was that the realization of the need to attract tourists and investors, who are often inexplicably hypersensitive to nationalistic sentiments, had caught up with the well-meaning idealism of the Bramble 1970 platform. Bramble, however, may have misinterpreted the new thrust for self-awareness, self-definition and self-respect resident in the nationalistic and cultural programmes emanating from the local University Centre under the direction of Irish. Their nuisance value in shoring up the national integrity and self-image against the background of an influx of well-to-do whites, was under-appreciated. The *Montserrat Mirror* affirmed that race relations were good, just three days after the dissolution of the Council, and it is not surprising that precious little was heard of racism after Bramble's return to power.

The only constitutional advance experienced during Bramble's eight-year tenure was the replacement of the Governor as president of the Legislative Council by a local Speaker elected by the Council from outside its members. As a consequence of this move, however, and partly through Bramble's instrumentality, a Montserratian national became the *de facto* Deputy Governor from 1976. Dr Howard Fergus, the local UWI lecturer and Resident Tutor, was the first to occupy that new position. An effort was made in 1971 to establish an element of local government by reintroducing Village Councils 'to form an effective link between villagers and the Government', but it was shortlived. In fact, it drew criticism from the editor of the *Montserrat Mirror* for having civil servants among the Council's membership, for being creatures of the ruling party and for generally ignoring the Rural District Board Ordinances of 1952. This was the last effort at local government in the island.

Bramble's treatment of the racism bogey is conceptually linked with the efforts by post-Labourite politicians to create a welcoming society. North Americans needed only a driver's licence or a similar identification to enter the island. In the avid spread of the red carpet, the Bramble regime, as well as Osborne's after him, have entertained undesirables. In 1978 a false knight, 'Sir Walton Jacob' was welcomed to the island to industrialize it and generally 'to assist in the economic development of the island, to make available funding for local projects, and to do those things which an economic development-type bank can and would do'.[6] Before the imposter could make a second visit, he was arrested for fraud and theft in the United States.

Osborne's duping 'knight' was J. Dominelli who allegedly fled from the United States with $112.8 million in 1985. Promising to invest a handsome chunk of this sum in Montserrat, Dominelli was given VIP treatment. With a warrant out for his arrest, he was bundled on to a US aircraft in Antigua, leaving behind a telephone debt of EC$15 000. The treatment accorded to these big-time crooks is a logical extension of the island's perception of itself as a welcoming society. In addition the incidents revealed the vulnerability of small, poor countries in a hurry to attract investors, but without the administrative capabilities and sophistication to detect gangsters, or the patience to have them properly investigated. The anxiety is that the apparent investor may be lost to another equally poor territory.

Politicians are anxious to demonstrate to an electorate in whom they have excited great expectations, that they can somehow bridge the gap between prodigal campaign promise and actual performance. The 1978 episode occurred in an election year and the 1985 one, in the year after an election. In 1973, Austin Bramble was already concerned about the economy and the role the foreign investor was expected to play. He unfortunately read the tension between that aspect of development and cultural development as racism.

Bramble achieved more in fact, than he is commonly credited with. He was unable to arrest the decline of export agriculture (as were all the other regimes after him) in spite of subsidies, credits and a Development Finance and Marketing Corporation (DFMC). The successful projects which he initiated, however, amounted to the genesis of a transformation of the Montserrat economy. The high-profile projects included Montserrat Air Studios, an electronics assembling company, a philatelic bureau and an off-shore medical school. On the social side, he invested heavily in pre-primary education and day-care centres, instituted a national provident fund which matured later into a social security scheme and, with financial assistance from USAID and the Caribbean Development Bank, established a low-income housing estate on a 3.5 acre site at Parsons. He stuck remarkably close to his election promises, and created a caring regime.

Academic and trade unionist J. A. Irish, who never forgave Bramble for his trade-union policies, attributes the latter's fall from power to the alliance of MAWU with John Osborne's PLM and the support of the 'distressed merchants'. There was nothing distressed about the merchants, and John Osborne was already on the road to victory when Irish openly espoused the PLM cause. We must therefore probe more deeply for Bramble's defeat.

An able and articulate statesman, Austin Bramble lacked some of his father's charisma, but nevertheless filled the role of the over-mighty 'politician-king' in the Montserrat mould.[7] Ironically, his multiple duties in 'running' too many ministries cut him off to an extent from the people, who saw him as aloof, and prevented him from exercising the paternalism which they associated with the leader-in-chief. A merchant himself, John Osborne attracted the support of the merchants with his free enterprise rhetoric as well as some malcontent civil servants spoiling for a salary hike in the face of a worldwide oil crisis. In addition, a somewhat unsophisticated electorate, seeing young Bramble's rule as an extension of his father's, decided that the Brambles had been around long enough. A new generation who were not beneficiaries of the emancipatory work of W. H. Bramble, hopped the anti-Bramble bandwagon and Austin paid the price. The chip off the old block was still the same block, as W. H. Bramble had, with his usual perpiscuity, warned at an election rally.

Bramble never regained power, although he won his Plymouth seat in 1983, but his name surfaces in periods of crisis as a potential saviour; all opposition parties have flirted with the idea of drafting him into their ranks. When, in derisive tones, the *Montserrat Reporter*, organ of the National Development Party (NDP), asserted that 'numerous persons are again challenging Mr Austin Bramble's claim to political astuteness and great leadership capabilities following his big flip-flop yesterday',[8] it was alluding to Bramble's indecisive response to an effort to forge an alliance between the NDP and the PDP for the 1987 election. Most objective observers of Montserratian politics would argue that that leadership capability is in fact a reality in spite of an occasional lapse in judgement.

Bramble has never danced to the music of regional integration, but he gave Montserrat a bright image in the region through his intelligent representation of his country. In urging on CARICOM the need to allocate industries, he was somewhat ahead of political leaders in the smaller islands, who at the time found intra-regional competition difficult, given their small domestic economies. This image has since been sullied and frittered away, and the present regime needs to work hard to restore it.

Opposition parties

In the island's 40 years of adult suffrage politics, it has seen the formation of nine political parties, but so far four of these, the Democratic Party (1958), the United Workers' Movement (1961), the Montserrat Workers' Progressive Party (1966) and the Montserrat Action Group (1973) did not survive their first electoral foray. We may well have seen the last of the United Nation from 1983 also. Although the most recently formed National Progressive Party (NPP) was destined for electoral success in 1991, it came under abortive threats while still in the womb.

Electoral conditions and attitudes did not favour the growth of a genuine multi-party system in the early decades after 1952. Significantly, the first three ministerial governments monopolized all seven electoral ridings and ruled with monolithic party legislatures. Austin Bramble and John Osborne each became Chief Ministers in turn, by breaking away from the parent party. The party was an ephemeral organization, formed for the sole purpose of contesting an election. It had no structure or constitution in any modern sense and, usually, there was room in it for only one dominant figure – the messianic patriarchal figure. There were obviously exceptions to the rule, but the other government members were 'yes-men', backstage players in the cast, helping to win the election and the applause.

Because of their loose and ephemeral nature, party alignments and loyalties were casual affairs, driven by expedience and opportunism. In this unstable electoral milieu, two brothers, E. T. Edgecombe and J. Edgecombe opposed each other in 1952, a son ran against a father in 1970, D. C. Fenton ran against Austin Bramble's Party in 1970 and 1973 and then joined his ticket in 1978, Richard G. Joseph lost in the W. H. Bramble platform in 1970 and won the same constituency under Austin Bramble in 1973. J. B. Chalmers, who was Deputy Chief Minister to John Osborne, is a classic example. After a brief flirtation with the NPP, he joined the opposition NDP for the 1991 elections, and was described in its Manifesto as a national hero for precipitating the collapse of the John Osborne government. In June 1987, David Fenton of the NDP had written that Satan was in complete control of Chalmers, and that he was vulgar, crude and smutty in his views on a particular incident. In fact his constituency opponent of 1987 became his ardent advocate in 1991. He was absolved, anointed and elevated to the status of hero. In the end, opportunism crowned with cynicism was not given a heroic vote.

Let me illustrate the fragile nature of alignments and therefore parties, in another way. Contesting four elections between 1961 and 1978, T. E. Meade ran once as an Independent and then on three different party tickets on the other occasions. Similarly, John Osborne campaigned on three different party platforms and once as an Independent in the four elections between 1961 and 1978. Barrister David Brandt, the current Minister of Communications in the NPP government, has had membership in three different parties and an independent stint in the space of eight years. He occupied the position of Deputy Leader of the NDP when he resigned from the party in 1989. The abler politicians do not fancy a patient and financially unrewarding career in opposition, and the ministerial prizes are few.

One might have expected a party like Irish's United National Front (UNF) to survive, given its trade-union base and its intellectual strength, but it died with defeat in 1983. Perhaps the electoral rejection was too total to suggest resurgence, although timing was Irish's major problem. The UNF received an aggregate of 251, of the 6213 votes cast, and three of the four candidates lost their statutory financial deposits. The Party largely consisted of him, and it was unlikely to survive him. Disillusioned by a decisive defeat aided by a bogus taint of communism applied by the PLM, Irish bowed out and with him the UNF.

Apart from the PDP of Austin Bramble, who functioned effectively as an opposition leader between 1983 and 1987, the NDP formed in 1984 has been the only Montserratian faction to attain any longevity as an opposition force. This was Montserrat's first party with a proper structure and organization which provide for an annual convention, a national committee, constituency branches and district units. In addition to its structure which can facilitate popular participation in decision-making, the party is sustained by the political ambition of its ruling figure, business magnate Bertrand Osborne. A general do-gooder with a record of community service and a leading employer, he commands some popular support as well as the backing of some business colleagues who share his conservative ideology. A leading Roman Catholic layman, he is also buoyed up by strong Church support. The NDP organ, the weekly *Montserrat Reporter*, provides another kind of energy.

After two electoral defects which left it with only one seat in Council, even the mighty NDP has faltered. Fortunately for the NDP, the honeymoon of the problem-plagued ruling NPP was short which gave Osborne some hope of elevation to the cabinet by the coalition route. (It is alleged that he may have moderated his drive to be Chief Minister following persistent comments on the potential for conflict of interest when the leading merchant and principal employer after government is also the chief government executive.) Significantly, after the Chief Minister Reuben Meade was involved in a court case in 1992 which cast aspersions on his integrity, it was Ruby Wade-Bramble and not Osborne who moved the strategic vote of no confidence against the Government. Given the current recession, the NDP will continue to offer opposition (and in many cases Bertrand Osborne has given constructive opposition), but it needs a revival in its ranks if it is to be taken seriously as a viable alternative to the NPP. An acceptable Osborne slate could well offset the conflict of interest problem.

The John Osborne reign

John Osborne's regime deserves special attention if only because it was so eventful in both a positive and a negative sense. There were rifts in his ranks which reflected the unstable nature of Montserratian politics and party system, independence tantrums, significant economic growth, off-shore banking scandals, the most vehement hurricane of the century and finally the arrest of Osborne and his former Minister, Nowell Tuitt, on charges of bribery, corruption and misbehaviour in public office. Not all of these will be examined in this section, but they are cited to illustrate the dynamism of the period.

With 25 years in the Legislative Council, Osborne is the longest-serving politician in Montserrat's history and his 13 years as Chief Minister is also a local record. He reaped handsome revenues from the programmes of his predecessor, but he stimulated further growth with policies that favoured building construction, the island's main employment avenue. His rightist free enterprise rhetoric, uttered as a chorus in every major speech, created a confidence in which the modern sector developed, and unemployment hardly existed in the best years. In 1982, the island graduated from grant-aided status, two years before the time that the British Government had scheduled for it. Osborne was on target in realizing his dream of seeing every Montserratian 'with his own house and car, a good job and money in the bank'.[9] By 1981 the island experienced a growth of 4.6 per cent in the economy, although the agricultural sector remained stagnant.

A ship-building millionaire, Osborne wanted his pride in his personal achievement and self-confidence to be ingrained in the national character. This philosophy is related to two major issues which characterized his regime and impacted significantly on the island's political development – off-shore banking and independence. In pursuit of cash to keep the country solvent and the economy superficially strong, the Osborne government issued hundreds of licences to banks, most of which existed only on paper in a lawyer's office. For the lawyers, it was a lucrative business and their takings might be deemed an indirect contribution to the national income. Government coffers benefited from fees which amounted to only EC$1.2 million in 1987, according to an official report.[10]

Looseness, bordering on irresponsibility in administering the extant laws and rules of security governing off-shore banking, made Montserrat a bastion of banking corruption and a paradise for money launderers. This brought to Montserrat the negative attention of the US Government. In the Legislative Chamber and the Chamber of Commerce, voices were raised against the profligate scattering of licences, as bad publicity mounted in leading international business journals. At least one private firm in the US notched up huge profits by 'manufacturing' and retailing Montserrat off-shore banks. As the Osborne government continued to turn a blind eye, the British acted.

The hawkish Governor, Christopher Turner, spearheaded a task force to investigate off-shore banking. It consisted of a British lawyer in the role of the island's Principal Crown Counsel, a British Financial Adviser with support from New Scotland Yard (NSY) and the Federal Bureau of Investigation (FBI). True to his character and political philosophy, Osborne protested the conspicuous British presence and the prospect of a British bobby as deputy leader of the Royal Montserrat Police Force, but could not halt anything. In fact, much of the blame attached to John Osborne, who as CM and Minister of Finance, took a key interest in the granting of licences.

The British felt that Montserrat could develop as a profitable and respectable financial centre, instead of producing fly-by-night apologies for banks which tarnished the reputation of the island, discouraged genuine investors and brought international embarrassment to the UK. To reinforce its position and provide a rationale for cleansing action, HMG utilized the customary expedient of an Inquiry and Report. Coopers and Lybrand, an accounting firm which advises the Secretary of State at the Foreign and Commonwealth Office (FCO), in polite language indicted the Monteserrat Government for its administration of offshore-banking. Coopers and Lybrand recommended, among other things, that international finances be removed from the control of local Ministers and placed in the Governor's portfolio. In order to do this, constitutional changes were necessary. It is in these circumstances, therefore, that Montserrat received a new constitution in 1990 which reduced the power of the Chief Minister.

Osborne's PLM lost power in the election of 1991 due, it was felt, to rumours and charges of a corrupt regime, ineptitude in handling the aftermath of hurricane Hugo (1989), division among its ranks and a sense that after 13 years it was no longer equal to the task of governance in the face of an incipient recession. The British were convinced that off-shore banking corruption had spread to the body politic, and took the opportunity of Osborne's fall to investigate him and his ministers. As a result, with the assistance of officers from NSY, Osborne and his former Minister of Agriculture, Trade and Housing, Nowell Tuitt, were arrested in 1992 on charges of corruption, bribery, conspiracy and misbehaviour in public office. They went on trial in January 1993 in a historic and dramatic case that brought into action two eminent regional lawyers, with a white north American investor (a man of straw as it turned out) and a former Attorney-General of Montserrat who now resides in the US, following his incarceration for fraud, as star witnesses. In the trial by jury, the two were acquitted, their dignity wounded in the process.

The trial was a sad finale to the career of this self-confident and ambitious politician. He contends that his arrest was a victimizing vendetta by the British for his candour and fearlessness in dealing with them and for his policy on independence. In this he is supported by persons who are not particularly unbiased. Shirley Osborne, for instance, who published an annual magazine, saw her father's arrest as part of England's attempt to recolonize Montserrat. In her view, the British hoped 'that by discrediting and defaming the man, any serious Montserratian drive towards self-reliance will be short-circuited'.[11]

British-bashing becomes popular from time to time in a forward-looking island like Montserrat, but this is too facile an explanation for Osborne's humiliating arrest and trial. He had been forced to defend his honour in a libel case (albeit successfully) against allegations of corruption by the NDP opposition, and the final years of his regime were beset by the suggestion of something rotten in the state. Indeed honesty and integrity were the key issues in the 1991 general election at which Osborne was toppled. If the merit of the historic case is judged solely by the jury acquittal, it would mean that NSY were on a wrong scent, but then the NDP always thought that they too had caught more than a whiff. The *Montserrat Reporter*, in which Osborne's daughter was sometimes a regular columnist, continually harped on the corruption of the PLM with pointed reference to the CM. An editorial captioned 'Honesty and Integrity Essential' questioned: 'How can the Governor and the Queen's Attorney-General sit and watch as corruption consumes the Ministers of the colony... . Should the Chief Minister who has been caught red-handed defrauding the people of Montserrat and his own Government be allowed to seek re-election?'[12] The voice of condemnation came not only from Whitehall, but also from the black Emerald Isle.

The 1989 Constitution Order

In a democracy, a new constitution is normally associated with development and greater self-determination. Regrettably, this cannot be said of the
1989 constitution. One of the positive things it did, however, was to con-
solidate in a single document a number of scattered papers which comprised the constitution up to that point. These included the Montserrat
Letters Patent 1959, the Constitution and Election Ordinances in Laws of
Montserrat Cap 153, the Montserrat Royal Instructions 1959 and the
Montserrat (Governor) Order 1971. This was a sensible improvement. It
also introduced a Bill of Rights which enshrined certain privileges, freedoms and immunities of the islanders. Most of these were provided for by
Common Law, but combining them into a single constitutional document
facilitated ready reference and general awareness of the measure to be
taken to ensure that they are enjoyed by all.

In addition to these, some major changes were introduced. I present
three here: (a) International financial services, 'or any related aspect of
finance', was added to the list of subjects for which the Governor has
special responsibility and discretionary power. The list already included:
defence, external affairs, internal security and the public service; (b) the
Governor was empowered to introduce legislation on matters pertaining
to his reserve powers and under certain conditions to put into effect that
legislation even if it were not passed by the Legislative Council; (c) the
Governor, acting on his discretion, could delegate to a Minister 'or any
other person or authority' responsibility in any area of his reserved
powers.

Many Montserratians found both the absence of consultation and
some measures repugnant. The new constitution was due for promulgation
by Order-in-Council on 18 December 1989, about four days after it was
shown to the Government of Montserrat; and the British Minister
Timothy Sainsbury, who came in person to present the constitution to
local legislators, made it clear that he was seeking reaction and comment
rather than input. Indeed most members were not given the courtesy of a
copy. A livid Osborne rejected it as being retrogressive and sought and
received an audience in England. In this he showed grit and national pride.
While sympathizing with the British Government's basis for acting,
former Chief Minister Austin Bramble also criticized the regressive tampering with the constitution. The British should dismiss the PLM
Government, he suggested. He too led a delegation to England to drive
home this message.

William Bramble Jr, grandson of the illustrious namesake
W. H. Bramble, weighed in, in emotive but compelling tones. 'For if the

dignity of a constitutional roll-back were imposed on an innocent people, without the courtesy of being properly informed and without the opportunity to participate in the process, we would have been treated like an inferior and subhuman species', he told a public meeting. On the issue of a unilateral imposition of the constitution, prominent off-shore banking lawyer David Brandt agreed with Bramble. He and John Kelsick, like himself a lawyer-politician, not surprisingly resented the constitutional reform while admitting the need for reform in the administration of off-shore banking. They felt that it was wrong to penalize a people for the misdemeanour of the politicians. The OECS Heads meeting in St Lucia also recorded their repugnance and their view that this was a setback to the constitution of Montserrat.

Two measures in particular were considered galling – the Governor's power to originate and personally enact laws, and the placing of a critical aspect of finance in the Governor's hands. True, the Governor could delegate powers in finance, but was more likely to delegate these to trusted officials than to local Ministers. While it castigated the Government for 'gross mismanagement', the Montserrat Chamber of Commerce and Industry (MCCI) condemned the move to give legislative power to the Governor since it 'usurps the electorate's right to have representatives of their choice vote on any laws on their behalf'. Responding to the various representations, HMG relented and deleted section 45, which gave inordinate powers to the Governor. Off-shore financial services, HMG's real concern, remained in the Governor's portfolio. With dubious logic the British, supported by Montserrat's Guyanese Attorney-General, Odel Adams, argued that off-shore banking had implications for external affairs and was therefore properly in the Governor's province. Off-shore banking is no more an external-affairs matter than is tourism, but the argument gave the British some kind of rationale.

HMG did get some support for its action. The 15-year old MAWU, whose General-Secretary, Vereen Thomas, was a UNF candidate in 1983, took no particular position. However, she co-signed a letter along with the presidents of the Montserrat Union of Teachers and the Medical Association in which they asserted that for them the 'constitutional crisis' was not a priority, and admitted inadequate knowledge of the old constitution. The sterling support came from Mr Bertrand Osborne and the NDP.

In an early reaction, seemingly without the benefit of indepth study of the constitution, Osborne observed that 'the British Government has good reason to do what it has done'. As the debate heated up, he was less categorical in his endorsement of the British position on every count, but his view was that the CM mismanaged, and the British had good reason to curb him by altering the constitution. The British poet Milton was concerned with justifying the ways of God to men, but B. Osborne justified the ways of HMG to Montserratians: 'My dear friends, you should realize that we are a dependent territory or colony of Britain. If you do not like this, the alternative is independence and then we can have these laws in the hands of people like John Osborne, Dada Tuitt and Auk Jeffers.'[13] The British could have taken comfort from this speech.

B. Osborne obviously wanted to extract political mileage from the affair, but in the process he came over a bit strongly as a defender of the British. John Osborne would fall, but the electorate did not see B. Osborne as the alternative. His response to the constitutional crisis did not help. I see no reason to alter this summative assessment of this episode.

> No one has much to rejoice about in this episode. The British came over as being excessively and unnecessarily authoritarian. Blinkered by personal prejudice and partisan interests, many Montserratians failed to appreciate and respond appropriately to the larger implications of constitutional down-grading. John Osborne may have snatched some face-saving victory, but not enough to totally remove an ugly tarnish from his administration.[14]

The final irony is that John Osborne, Montserrat's Independence Chief Minister, presided over the down-grading of the constitution.

The independence issue

Independence has never been an electoral issue in Montserrat. The question has arisen periodically because her Leeward Islands neighbours, Antigua and St Kitts, have become nations, and the United Nations Decolonization Committee has kept the matter on the agenda. The first CM, W. H. Bramble, rejected Statehood in Association with Britain in 1967 and remained 'wedded to colonialism'[15] seeing England's budgetary dole as indispensable to his country's financial survival. P. A. Bramble was even more firmly committed to colonial status, adding psychological and security reasons to the economic one. He spelt out his rationale in these words:

> Government does not consider Associated Statehood either suitable, necessary or desirable for Montserrat ... . It seems to me that from what we in Montserrat have got, Associated Statehood would be a retrograde step ... Britain has legal responsibilities for us over and above any moral obligation to her forever colonies.

In a tiny territory like Montserrat, an independent Government could very easily abuse its powers and disrespect the rights of its people, and militant minorities could for selfish interests bring about disruption and turmoil. Tiny independent Government may make unreasonable laws and decisions, and impose unreasonable burdens on their people.[16]

Bramble also argued that the powers of intervention and disallowance reserved to HMG were cheap safeguards against tyrannic governments and anarchic factions. In relating size to the quality of governance, he echoed Professor Arthur Lewis, who contended that in small communities of 50 000 to 100 000 persons dominated by a single party, it was very difficult to prevent political abuse.[17] Lewis's solution to democracy and smallness was federation, while Bramble's was colonial dependency. Bramble reflected the conservatism of the populace, who up until about 1980, showed very little interest in independence. However, his argument that Associated Statehood was a backward move is as surprising as is his unqualified acceptance of colonial pupilage. Perhaps Professor Gordon Lewis of Puerto Rico was correct in his perception; he thought he detected a corroding self-doubt in Montserratians.[18] The suggestion that a small territory like Montserrat should become 'independent', under the guardianship of the United Nations, has surfaced. The idea is that this supra-national body guarantees the security and certain rights and freedoms of the ward state. There are conceptual as well as practical problems with such a dependent statehood, and as yet there is really no groundswell of interest in independence on the part of Montserratians.

In 1984, Bramble was just as unswerving in his antipathy to independence. Commenting on reports of a PLM independence thrust, he reiterated his usual tenet.

At a time when widespread political instability in so many parts of the world coincides with economic recession, Montserrat should commit itself unambiguously to maintaining the constitutional status most likely to nurture stability.[19]

An NDP government headed by Bertrand Osborne would hardly be expected to espouse independence. Prior to entering active politics, he told a UN mission on decolonization that independence was neither necessary nor beneficial for a country the size of Montserrat and that 'outsiders would prefer to see Montserrat aligned with the United Kingdom and the free enterprise system'.[20] He took the usual business sector's view that colonialism fosters development since it creates a climate of political stability and confidence which attracts investors. Unfortunately, the empirical evidence does not support this. There are clearly variables other than sovereignty involved, but Antigua and St Kitts have attracted far more investment than Montserrat. The island's commercial sector is predominantly centred on retail merchandizing and a pitifully few off-shore assembling ventures.

Bertrand Osborne's reference to what *outsiders* think is significant as it reflects the depth of our dependency and the distance from independence. A poor developing country must, perforce, induce and placate outsiders, but national maturity and self-determination will always elude a people if critical decisions have to be based on what *outsiders* think. Montserrat's 'outsiders' include a significant expatriate population with views on independence. They make these known often *sotto voce* but often through businessmen and *high* influential persons. Independence is a serpent in their paradise. Too much development and modernization scare them, since they threaten the 'unspoilt' and idyllic haven they dream of. They are unwilling to trust the peace to any indigenous leader, for in their minds a British Governor (whose role many North Americans confuse with a state governor) guarantees that subordination and control of native peoples so necessary for paradise. Prospero, not Caliban alone must be in command.

The periodic visits of UN missions, beginning in 1974, have served to test the independence climate in the island. Beyond that, it has admonished the UK on the economic and educational steps to be taken to prepare islanders to exercise their inalienable rights to self-determination. Britain in turn expresses its willingness to grant independence provided that the majority of the people demonstrate their desire for it either through an electoral platform or some form of plebiscite. The ritual is predictable. What the 1982 Mission revealed, however, was that there had been some change in the views about independence. A few strategic persons including the General-Secretary of MAWU, businessmen and Nominated Member of Council D. R. V. Edwards, saw independence as a legitimate and logical goal towards which the island should strive and for which deliberate preparation should be made. By 1991, Chief Minister Osborne was telling a UN team that 'most of the young people of the territory wanted political independence', although one finds it difficult to substantiate such a claim.

Chief Minister John Osborne is about the only person who has consistently and persistently advocated political independence for Montserrat. I have myself rejected the view of eternal colonial status and suggested that there should be preparation for change, including the building of an effective civil service. Dr J. Irish of the MAWU and the UNF was critical of Austin Bramble's anti-sovereignty stance in 1971 and was prepared to settle for Associated Statehood, a half-way house to independence. His ultimate goal, though, was independence and his cultural programmes consciously or unconsciously were geared to providing the appropriate psychological and spiritual environment.

Motivated by personal and national ambition, Osborne had an early eye on independence. Shortly after coming to power in 1978, he predicted that Montserrat would be independent in five years.[21] Osborne had been supported by the business community in the campaign and therefore had shrewdly omitted independence from his manifesto. It is indeed ironical that this champion of independence has never made it an election issue or formulated any sustained programme to prepare for it. This was due to his pragmatic realization that it would be an election-loser in his conservative country. In fact, he made a tactical change in his rhetoric just days before the 1983 election. He observed that while independence was inevitable, it should be preceded by economic and financial viability. He promised a referendum in 1990 but was, predictably, silent on the idea when the time came. There was evidence that his other PLM colleagues did not share his independence dream. Osborne's most vehement calls for independence came in reaction to some perceived embarrassment or disability sustained in the colonial condition. A typical example occurred in 1983 when the Organization of Eastern Caribbean States (OECS), of which Montserrat is an integral member, decided to intervene militarily in Grenada following a revolt there in which P. M. Maurice Bishop was murdered. Aggressive John Osborne was forbidden by the FCO to send any troops, since to do so would be to involve the British Government when Mrs Thatcher had insisted on a hands-off policy. In any case, only the Governor and not the CM had the authority to order the Royal Montserrat Police Force or the volunteer Defence Force.

Osborne should not have been surprised because the Treaty establishing the OECS denies the right to even deliberate on foreign affairs to a state like Montserrat without the relevant constitutional competence; and Montserrat had made the necessary declaration of non-participation in accordance with Article 23 of the Treaty. He was nevertheless embarrassed by the Whitehall *diktat* which underscored his inferior position *vis-à-vis* his CARICOM colleagues. This issue led to a spate of feverish rhetoric on independence. The manager of the national radio station was instructed to invite citizens to consider the desirability of independence and Osborne's Permanent Secretary was encouraged to collaborate with the University Centre to hold discussions on independence. About the same time, while he was attending St Kitts-Nevis's celebration of nationhood, he told a press conference that his government intended seriously to consider the question of independence over the next six months. No real galvanization of national support followed and Osborne's fervour soon died down.

Osborne's next outburst came in 1988 and sprang from the famous Marquita case in which a five-year-old Montserratian girl was being denied life-saving heart surgery and was threatened with deportation back to Montserrat to die since the Thatcher Government was not prepared to finance the operation. (In any event private persons in England intervened and funded the operation.). The incident spurred Osborne to rant at the British Government, raised the independence banner and compared Montserrat's colonialism to that of Gibraltar and the Falklands. In the exchange between Plymouth and London, the island benefited from a new policy to accommodate a limited number of serious medical cases annually in the UK, but got no closer to independence.

Osborne's latest eruption of anti-British spleen followed his 1993 acquittal. He promptly announced his return to politics to lead a crusade to oust the British and achieve his lifelong dream of a sovereign Montserrat. Claiming martyrdom and heroism in his effort to bring pride and dignity to his people, he is at last expected to make independence the supreme election issue. He may receive the endorsement of the *Montserrat News*, which has dubbed the UK's handling of the case as racist;[22] but even this paper seems to be arguing for enlightened colonialism rather than independence. In his euphoria over acquittal, Osborne must judge whether he can regain power on an independence platform, and in doing so he must be careful not to equate sympathy with solidarity.

In 1993, Montserrat is very little closer to independence than it was 20 years ago. The 1991 Manifesto of the NDP asserted its credo with the usual conservative certainty.[23] The ruling NPP sees independence as inevitable, but this has been said before. Their interest, however is not passive, since they will create 'national songs, national heroes and national place names'.[24] The British recently introduced new mechanisms for the more effective governance of its dependent territories in the region; they take the form of a Ministerial Group chaired by the Minister in the Foreign and Commonwealth Office at Westminster, and a Secretariat in Barbados. They are intended to promote development and good government and appear to be based on the assumption that Montserrat and the rest will remain colonies for the foreseeable future. In this the British are, I believe, right.

Constitutional independence cannot be postponed forever; it is a continuation of the journey from slavery to emancipation, but there has to be conscious preparation. This includes not just the development of physical infrastructure, but an enhancement of the island's administrative capabilities as well. Even then, without a proper work ethic and a change in production attitudes, it will require very brave leaders to take the plunge. This is why an appropriate educational programme on independence is so necessary for all sectors of the society.

The politics of the volcano

The eruption of the Soufrière Hills volcano in 1995 significantly changed the nature and direction of Montserratian politics. Management of the emergency has dominated political dialogue and debate ever since, and fuelled partisan politics, and the fact that the island has had three CMs within the course of a year was a dramatic manifestation of the altered political culture.

The geographical and demographic changes wrought by the volcano changed the political landscape as well. In 1996 when general elections were constitutionally due, four constituencies had been evacuated and 15 to 20 per cent of the population had migrated. In that situation, incumbent CM Reuben Meade suggested that the island ignore party politics in favour of national unity.[25] The *Montserrat Reporter* endorsed the sentiment[26] as did the President of the Montserrat Christian Council who denounced elections on national radio. But to have expected opposition parties to agree to what would have been a prolongation of Meade's regime would be to totally misunderstand Caribbean politics. Crises are vehicles to power whether they are related to fossil fuel as in the 1970s, civil disorder or signal economic failure.

Meade's administration was in trouble on the major matter of housing and there were cracks in his camp on governance generally. His Education and Health Minister, Lazelle Howes, resigned weeks before the dissolution to run as an independent candidate, although curiously she was allowed to serve as a minister up to election time. Another member defected from his government even later and it was only the quick dissolution which averted a 'No Confidence' motion. Aspirants to power saw their opportunity and seized it. Two new parties, the Movement for National Reconstruction (MNR) and the People's Progressive Alliance (PPA) were put together a few short months before the election and there were 11 independent candidates in the record number of 28. The eagles were gathering.

It is no wonder then that a Commission set up by the government to advise whether or not elections should be held when constitutionally due met with hostility, especially from some party leaders and their lieutenants. One such person denounced the Commission as 'a horrendous act of imperialism'.[27] It was seemingly forgotten that hitherto constitutional changes emanated from colonial office *diktats*. A Commission at least had a democratic countenance since the citizens would be consulted on the desirability of holding elections or not. As it turned out, it recommended that elections be held since this was the expressed wish of at least 54 per cent of the population over the age of 18 years.[28]

Not unsurprisingly, given the dissatisfaction induced by the crisis, the incumbent NPP of Reuben Meade lost the election. In addition, the island had its first coalition government. This was considered unusual in a country accustomed to landslide victories or decisive mandates. While no one can categorically attribute this particular outcome to the emergency it is significant that it occurred at that particular time. In addition, the election results could well have reflected the general uncertainty of life at the time. John Osborne's new People's Progressive Alliance (PPA) won two constituencies, Austin Bramble's new Montserrat National Reconstruction Party (MNR) two (excluding himself), the incumbent NPP one only, and there were two successful independent candidates. The fact that there were three political factions of relatively equal strength could also have contributed to the hung results.

Bertrand Osborne emerged as head of a government which excluded the PPA which had attained the largest popular vote, but his regime lasted only eight months. A conservative leader of patrician provenance, he became a victim of dissatisfaction from without and political ambitions from within the ruling coalition. The dissatisfaction was ostensibly over the size of the monetary package offered by HMG to Montserratian evacuees to the region, so this, the island's shortest ever political regime, can be blamed on the volcano and its comparatively volatile political climate. Within his brief rule, Osborne had enough time to dismiss a minister – the former CM, Reuben Meade.

With the fall of Osborne in 1997, politics assumed an aura of instability. He made way for lawyer David Brandt, something of an opposition firebrand who as CM was destined to be a bane of the British. He incurred the ire of Clare Short, the DFID minister with what she insensitively termed his expectation of 'golden elephants'.[29] Brandt himself unceremoniously dismissed a minister, former CM, P. Austin Bramble, and installed in his place a member of the Opposition. This latter act did not endear him to his own Minister of Education and Health, Adelina Tuitt, with whom he had an uneasy relationship throughout the regime. The reign only lasted until February 2001 out of expediency and in the end Tuitt resigned, taking a colleague, Minister Rupert Weekes, with him and precipitating new elections. As a result of the elections, John Osborne became the first come-back CM in Montserrat's history, Reuben Meade's NPP posted its second defeat, and three women, the highest number ever, entered the corridors of power. Not all of these results are attributable to the volcanic crisis but it would seem at least that the housing issue hounded Meade again like a nemesis.

The concept of political instability does have meaning in the context of Montserratian politics with its customary tranquility, but it has to be differentiated from the way it is normally understood, particularly in its effects. With civil servants playing a key role in the administration, the 'musical chairs' of ministers did not seriously affect the general governance of the country. A snap election did slow down the march of vital economic projects and there were the odd times when HMG may have used internal political divisions to its advantage. The old colonial tactic of 'divide and rule' is not exactly dead. On the whole though political instability merely meant uncertainty and lack of cohesiveness at the level of ministers. It was to the British that the people looked for the delivery of development. It is significant that a calypso in the 2001 Christmas 'carnival' competition had as its title 'Vote for DFID'.

The UK–Montserrat relationship is a vital aspect of Montserratian politics. The quality of negotiations with HMG and the resultant benefits to the island was ever an issue. CM Bertrand Osborne was perceived as too conservative and acquiescent. David Brandt, his successor, was in contrast tough and strident but in the end was perceived by aspirants to power to have overplayed his hand and alienated the British. His opponents in the 2001 general election promised a more harmonious relationship with the British benefactors. Opposition parliamentarian Reuben Meade had not been lacking in his attacks on the British but his party brochure promised to 'rebuild good relationships between the Government of Montserrat and the British Government in particular and donor agents in general'.[30]

The volcanic crisis turned the spotlight on British governance of Montserrat. In exposing the plight of Montserrat to the British and global public, the British media assisted the Montserratian cause. Visits of parliamentarians and dignitaries promised more than they delivered but they at least provided valuable public relations for the island. HRH the Duke of York visited twice. Baroness Liz Symons twice, Baroness Scotland once and George Foulkes, Clare Short's deputy, Sir Nicholas Bonsar and Foreign Secretary Robin Cook all also visited.

The plight of Montserrat, including the quality and mode of British governance, initiated a significant constitutional change. It was the Montserrat condition which prompted the publication of the White Paper, *Partnership for Progress*, in 1999 which offered British citizenship on a non-reciprocal basis to the 150 000 persons living in British overseas territories. The British Nationality Act of 1981 deprived Montserratians of British citizenship while it made special provision for Gibraltarians to acquire it; and another Act (of 1983) conferred that special status on Falkland Islanders as well.[31] Montserratians and other Caribbean OTs were ever conscious of the discrimination and they also compared their inferior status to that of neighbouring French territories. The fact that there was an obvious colour difference between Montserratians and the privileged colonies added to the rancour.

New citizenship rights are likely to become a reality in 2001 hopefully including the entitlement to permanently live in Britain and Europe. The

vast majority of Montserratians will welcome the new status although it is
not expected to trigger a mass exodus to the UK. Not everyone, however,
applauds the event. Perennial political activist and maverick member of the
ruling party, Chedmond Browne, has been a tireless campaigner for independence, and soufrière flows have not choked his zeal for self-
government. He told a UN Decolonization seminar in Cuba recently that
'the people of Montserrat are not in favour with the British government's
attempts to manufacture our integration into their empire through making
us British citizens'. In his view, 'this citizenship will not change our
present colonial position and may in fact devolve further what little
administrative authority the elected government has'.[32] From all accounts,
Browne was not speaking for the majority who, even without the perceived benefits of the new status, are compelled to accept imposed laws
such as the decriminalization of homosexuality, for instance, which they
find socially and morally unacceptable. The new status will be a personal
option to Montserratians and other OTs' citizens. Positive or negative, it is
a side effect of the volcanic eruption.

Yet another constitutional change is directly attributable to the volcanic era. A new electoral system was devised in 2000 to address the radi-
cally reduced habitable space and the tiny population of about 5000. A
three-man commission chaired by this author recommended 'voting-at-
large'[33] or territorial voting whereby the island was treated as a single constituency and each elector was entitled to cast as many votes as their seats
were in the Council. The widely consultative commission took the opportunity to abolish the centuries old nominated membership and added two
to the seven elected members which gave each voter nine votes. This move
arguably made for a more democratic parliament as well as a more effective
one since a potentially larger back-bench and opposition could lead to
more effective parliamentary supervision of the executive.

The successful implementation of the new system in April 2001 has
served to establish it on a permanent basis even if with later modification.
The Gibraltar version whereby each elector is given only the number of
votes needed to elect a simple majority (that is, eight of fifteen seats) is
worth consideration. It would make less demand on the voter who in the
April election had to choose nine from 26 candidates. The British Virgin
Islands have a variation which is a mixed system that combines district and
territorial voting. Voting-at-large could well appeal to other micro OTs in
the British *provincia*.

The Montserrat crisis has wrought political changes which may be as
permanent as the geo-physical ones. This may not have been the intention
of HMG in the offer of British citizenship as MP Chedmond Browne
argues, but the changed circumstances would have arrested any drive

towards political independence. This is so for obvious reasons, not least of which is the collapse of the economy and the island's utter dependence on the British purse. Then there is the increased dependency on British civil servants, that well-known mark of classic colonialism. The 2001 election manifesto of the New PLM, Browne's own party, stated that 'the party does not intend to pursue independence at this time'.[34]

The volcano has brought a new level of maturity to island politics. Personal attacks have given way somewhat to principles and issues such as management capability, development programmes and relations with the British even though some of the promises may have been mere wish lists. The 2001 election campaign was conducted to a large extent by paid political broadcasts and debates. In addition, the issues which touched people personally and deeply have bred an increased political consciousness. This was reflected in the avid involvement of the media in political affairs. Both the weekly *Montserrat Reporter* and 'Labour Speaks', an essentially political radio programme broadcast twice weekly by the chief executive of MAWU who eventually contested the 2001 election, attracted popular interest. The eruptions of Mount Soufrière will continue to resonate in the politics of the island for generations to come and feature in the rise and fall of politicians and the fortunes of the island.

10

Disasters and recovery

Was here in '24
Was here in '28
Will be here the day Soufrière
Vomit corruption back in we face
Will be here for the Fire, the Flood
Yeah *I just found joy*[1]

Quite apart from the volcanic eruptions of 1995 (see chapter 11), Montserrat has had its share of natural disasters. It sits in the hurricane belt and has had four full-blown tempests within the last hundred years. Floods and especially earthquakes have been few and far between, but have visited occasionally to remind us that earthly paradise is a myth; flooding invariably accompanies hurricanes. Disasters make a sorry story, but we can identify positive fall-outs in the revival of human and community values. Montserrat's disasters are stories of resilience, the strengthening of familial ties across the sea, the challenge of regional solidarity and a test of the goodwill of the mother country. As we shall demonstrate in this chapter, ill winds do blow good in other ways. Predicting more disasters in the face of hurricane Hugo, peripatetic street preacher Abraham (Hammie) White sang: 'I just found joy' reflecting in a way the irony and ambiguity of some disasters. An inmate of the prison while working without a guard actually said, 'God bless Hugo, it gave me freedom.'

Floods

According to oral tradition, the first flood in colonial Montserrat was in the early seventeenth century, and it came as a divine vindication of the cause of the slave, Harry Powson. The slaves had planned a big country-dance on one of the estates, and this was obviously perceived as a potential for rebellion. Fanny Garvey, an elderly white seamstress, revealed the plan and Harry Powson was singled out as the ringleader. He protested innocence up to the day of his execution, but to no avail. That day the flood came, supposedly in answer to his prayer, and loss of life and property resulted. The incident gave rise to the household simile 'lie lek Fanny Garvey' which persisted into modern times, and the flood came to be called Powson Flood. The superstitious slaves linked yet another seventeenth-century flood with another slave who committed murder and fled to another island.[2]

There is no written evidence on these floods which, if they did occur, were likely to be in the second half of the seventeenth century. Such a drastic reaction to a dance is surprising at a time when the number of blacks was quite small.

Apart from moderate flooding which twinned with an earthquake on Christmas Day 1672, the next significant flood came in 1766 as companion to a hurricane. Fort Ghaut, ever a bane of Plymouth at flood-time, overflowed its banks and carried away several houses. It was so serious that the Assembly had to pass an Act on 10 October 1767 'for cleansing and repairing Fort Ghaut and securing the Town of Plymouth from any future inundations'.

The action taken did not prevent future flood waters from taking the same road. This happened with a massive flood in 1896, three years before a vicious hurricane. Rain deluged the earth from about 7.00 p.m. until midnight, destroying all bridges except Belham Bridge, and the windward section of the island, including Long Ground, was cut off from the rest of the island. Some houses and inhabitants of Cherry Village adjacent to the ill-fated Fort Ghaut were washed out to sea, one or two of whom survived by swimming. Ann Watts, who received £25 to replace her house, and Jane Allen, who received £15,[3] may have lived in this area adjacent to the Ghaut.

F. E. Peters gave the date of the flood as 28 November, but there are primary sources which gave 26 May. What is not debatable is the great damage that was done. An engineer, William Bellamy, brought in to assess the road damage, was paid £40 and the repairs to roads and culverts took several years to complete. The Windward Road, for instance, had to be diverted above Webbs.[4] There were large landslides and several hills and mountains lost vegetative cover. In the rainstorm, a Norwegian boat, the *Grecian* was driven against the difficult windward coast at Furlonge's and was totally wrecked, killing 29 of the 30 persons on board. The sturdy Belham Bridge, constructed by J. Spencer Hollings in the early 1890s, withstood the flood, sustaining only minor damages.

The British tend to act responsibly in times of disaster and with the flood there was no exception. Apart from the Queen's sympathy relayed through the Governor of the Leeward Islands, relief funds of about £1050 came from London. The Lord Mayor made the appeal through the

London newspapers and may have received a more generous response if a parallel appeal was not being made at the same time for the victims of an Indian famine.[5] Since much of the fund-raising activity occurred in January 1897, the November date is most likely the correct one for this flood.

The next flood came in a four-hour rainstorm, illuminated by flashes of lightning, on Tuesday, 18 November 1952, when 11.48 inches of rain were recorded at the Groves Botanic Station. Water, wood and debris all took their toll, washing away bridges, making roads impassable, and launching small houses in the Aymers Ghaut area. The damage was greatest in the southern section of the island. The bridge at Molly John Ghaut was severely damaged, cutting off Aymers Ghaut from Trials and Fairfield, and the ghaut itself changed its course, flooding homes, washing soil and vegetation out to sea. The Kinsale school was gutted with mud and had to be closed for a week.

Apart from the damage to vital infrastructure, crops were badly hit. Several persons were without pipe-water for a long time and lands which were being prepared for the tomato crop were flattened. The official estimate of the cost of repair work and preventative measures was given as £19 255 by Governor Kenneth Blackburne. The bulk of this money was expected as a grant from the British, and in anticipation of the aid, he authorized a start on urgent repairs.[6] No lives were lost, but a Kinsale woman was seriously injured when she fled her flooded house and was slammed into a hedge.

Furious flood waters rampaged over Montserrat again on 3 September 1981, beginning in the early evening. The flood was a by-product of a hurricane in the Windward Islands. Bridges were wasted, roads blocked, including the road between Plymouth and the Trants Airport and villages were cut off; motorists caught on streets-turned-rivers were unable to reach home, and at least six motor vehicles disappeared. Fort Ghaut, turning as usual into an awesome river of sorrow, broke its banks and billowed over lower Plymouth, inundating the market. A house swept into its upstream torrent disappeared with two occupants. The third one, the four-year-old David Williams, was found miraculously stuck in mud, but safe with a torch in his hand. Miraculous escapes are not uncommon in these disasters.

With 12 inches of rain, this flood was rightly described by one journalist as probably the most devastating of the century. The flood bill, which included damage to agriculture, housing, disrupted utilities, and roads, was estimated at $3.5 million,[7] and this did not include the scores of animals carried out to sea. A highlight of the aftermath was the quality of community action which came into play. Private citizens used their own equipment to assist an energetic Public Works Department team in creating a road to the island's only airport and in clearing other roads, for landslides had created havoc all across the island. Very few living Montserratians had witnessed such a deluge.

Earthquakes

Because of their unpredictable nature and their potential for sudden calamity, earthquakes are the most terrible of natural disasters. Even when there are continuing tremors and seismic activity, as happened around the turn of this century at the time of the Mount Pelé (Martinique) eruption, and again in the early 1930s prior to the 1935 earthquake, accurate forecast of a massive quake is not really possible. Fortunately, the island has had only three significant earthquakes in its 360 years of colonial history – 1672, 1843 and 1935. The island did experience an earthquake on 16 March 1985, which measured 6.6 on the Richter scale, and did some damage, but not nearly as much as the two previous ones.

The 1672 earthquake came as a cruel Christmas present on 25 December. Wall buildings were few at that time, but St Anthony's church, which was partly stone, was destroyed.

The earthquake of 8 February 1843, on the other hand, was a terrific disaster which also afflicted the neighbouring islands of Antigua and Guadeloupe. (As these disasters so often transcend national boundaries the case for cooperative preparedness action is clear.) Many homes were destroyed and 'an eye witness stated that the entire face of one of the mountains of Montserrat was laid bare by a landslide, and many years elapsed before it was again clothed with vegetation'.[8] Six people were killed. The Imperial Government came to the island's rescue, but it was in the form of a loan which became a heavy yoke on the island, especially because of the inequitable distribution of the funds. This earthquake apparently forced changes in building styles, and most houses in Plymouth were henceforth built with wooden upper storeys instead of with stone according to F. E. Peters.

The island was visited by a multiplicity of tremors between 1897 and 1902, which only ceased with the eruption of Mount Pelé.

It is not clear whether the earthquake of 1935 was more powerful than the 1843 shock. What we have are more extensive details of the latter. It was certainly far more nerve-wracking and traumatic since it came as the culmination of a long season of tremors and shocks which spread over three years. People sought solace in a fearful religiosity, and church attendance soared as a result of the earthquakes.

The tremors began in 1933 and were fairly frequent although most were not very serious. Activities increased in April and May 1934; the shocks became very severe on the night of 13–14 May and again on 15 May, when buildings sustained minor cracks. A sharp shock rocked the island on 12 December 1934 and damaged several public and private buildings. Most of the devastation was done by three sets of quakes in 1935. The first came on 6 May and the second on 24 August, when the water mains in Plymouth were damaged. The latest, which were felt in Antigua and St Kitts, did further extensive damage. The arrival of a British ship helped to allay the panic.

The damage was severe and widespread. The entire east wall had fallen out of the famous St Anthony's church, with serious cracks in other walls and in some of the arches of the nave. The whole of the apse of St Peter's parish church collapsed overthrowing the altar, and the walls were all badly cracked; the Court House was completely wrecked and the Commissioner's official mansion was damaged enough to make it unsafe for habitation. Like the Canon of St Anthony's, who was using a temporary wooden hut in his garden, the Commissioner was using a wooden hut as sleeping quarters. In fact the official evaluator found most Government buildings too badly wrecked to be repaired. Belham Bridge too, with part of its parapet wall and the face of one arch completely gone, also needed rebuilding. La Barrie, the Inspector of Works, had to build a temporary wooden bridge within three days to reconnect Plymouth and Cork Hill with the northern section of the island.[9]

The visiting Superintendent of Works, J. Purcell Edwards from Antigua, was struck by the fortitude and equanimity of the people in the wake of the disaster. 'One cannot help,' he wrote, 'being struck by the courage with which Montserratians are bearing the almost intolerable strain on their reserves.' He had observed that at St Peter's 'a packed Harvest service was being conducted under tarpaulin stretched from the wall of the school while the church lay in ruins a few yards away.'[10]

I have no figure on the total value of the damage or the amount needed to rehabilitate both the public and private areas, but £4000 were required to rebuild Belham Bridge. The opportunity was taken to elicit technical recommendations on measures for making buildings more earthquake-resistant, apart from making the second storey of a two-storey building of wood rather than stone. Reinforced concrete, for instance, was recommended instead of the volcanic stones which were weak and deemed unsuitable for the stress of earthquakes. The design of the Belham Bridge was faulty; the arches were too flat for the span, and steel girders and re-inforced concrete were proposed. Although the hospital was sturdy, the foundation was not strong enough to withstand earthquakes. In all, it was estimated that buildings would cost an additional 15 to 20 per cent more than usual in order to make them earthquake-proof. There is physical evidence that many of these measures were taken. What is doubtful is whether the cumulative wisdom and experiences are still taken into account in current building styles and practices. Preoccupation with hurricanes as the supreme disaster may have detrimentally minimized earthquake preparedness.

This should not be, for while none has since reached the severity of 1843 and 1935, periodic tremors serve to remind us of our vulnerability to this phenomenon; and some caused damage, though not of disaster dimensions. The 1974 earthquake, for instance, did enough damage to touch the coffers of insurance companies. The island sustained landslides and subsidence and several buildings received cracks, but the earthquake, which registered 7.7 on the Richter scale, damaged Antigua more seriously.

Hurricanes

Montserrat grabbed world headlines in 1989 when what was perhaps the worst hurricane of the century harassed the island for over eight hours on 16 and 17 October. Advances in telecommunications and global sympathies for victims of disaster placed the island in the limelight, but it had in fact experienced several severe hurricanes before. Of these the best-documented struck in 1899, 1924, and 1928, but some nine or 10 others are on record. The disasters wrought by hurricanes come not only from winds, but also from the flooding which usually accompanies them.

Montserrat's first hurricane in historic time occurred in 1667, although it very likely sustained damage from one which hit the Leeward Islands the previous year. They were particularly busy during the eighteenth century. The first one came in 1737, accompanied by heavy flooding, when, as often happens, waters broke through Fort Ghaut and rampaged over the town. The security of the island was imperilled as several forts, so vital to the island's protection from French attack, were destroyed. Two came in fairly quick succession in 1740 and 1744 and did damage mainly to crops.

The 1766 hurricane was powerful, working dual destruction through wind and water. According to one source, half the town was destroyed, with many dead and hundreds homeless. Roads and bridges needed extensive repairs; much of the rehabilitation was done on a communal basis, the sugar lords using their human chattels to do the work. A heavy hurricane attacked the Leeward Islands in 1772, destroying almost every house in St Kitts. Montserrat did not fare as badly, but crops, housing and shipping suffered. Another hurricane in 1792 did light damage to crops on Montserrat while it pounded Antigua and St Kitts.

Hurricanes were less busy in Montserrat in the nineteenth century, but there was one in 1816 and two came in successive years, 1866 and 1867. The 1816 storm struck on 16 September, destroying food crops, leaving the poor and the slaves destitute. The loss was all the keener since the other important source of food supply was North America, and shipping between Montserrat and that continent was very infrequent. In some respects the island was at the mercies of the infamous Dudley Semper and his smuggling escapades. The 1866 hurricane, described as 'unusually severe', must have severely punished the entire British Leeward Islands, but no details on Montserrat were available to me.

One of the most terrific storms to hit the island prior to the mighty Hugo came on Monday, 7 August 1899. It thrashed the island for about six hours from 11 a.m. to late afternoon; and Anguilla was also hard hit. Writing from personal contact with adults who experienced the visitation, F. E. Peters painted this picture of what happened:

> The whole island was devastated, all churches and school-rooms except the Plymouth Wesleyan and Kinsale were thrown down, the crops destroyed; there was great damage to roads. Following the disaster, there was great distress among the poorer classes; the finances of the island were low; sugar, the staple product was selling for little or nothing; the estates could not afford to employ much labour and relationship between the Government and people was strained owing to the disturbance of the previous year. The Mansion House Fund was opened in aid of sufferers, and the Imperial Government came to the assistance of the planters.[11]

The 'disturbance' to which Peters alludes is the Fox Riot which was referred to in Chapter 5.

The next big hurricane crept upon the island around midnight on 28 August 1924 when most persons were asleep. It spared Plymouth and the south, but took only two hours (1.00 a.m. to 3.00 a.m.) to devastate the north and east of the island. There were 36 deaths, scores of serious injuries and 938 homes were destroyed, rendering an estimated 5000 persons homeless. Crops and estate houses were damaged everywhere, especially at Bethel, Farms, Farrells and Roaches. Many churches in the danger zone were destroyed, including the Anglican churches of St Peter's and St James, the Methodist church at Salem and the Christian Mission buildings at Cudjoe Head and Harris. The damage was estimated at £100 000.

Damage statistics apart, it was a horrifying night, sad with human suffering; branches, galvanized iron, and debris flew about; babies were separated from mothers, some surviving miraculously; and families were scattered. A Harris woman, her collar-bone broken in the storm, gave birth two days later to a daughter who was nicknamed 'Baby Gale'. Mary Elizabeth Brown, alias 'Sister Jane Ann' was by her own account a year old at the time of the hurricane. She was blown from her parents' arms but was found when someone accidentally stepped on her. The suddenness of the storm, the waste and the wounds demoralized the people. Relief came quickly from other Caribbean territories, with Guadeloupe and Dominica in the lead.

The housing problem was particularly acute and, although some folks tried to knock up hovels from wreckage, the results were described as 'decent pig sty'. As often happens, the disaster triggered observation and new recommendations on the structure of houses. In 1899, the Senior Medical Officer, in his role as a member of Executive Council, had recommended a Government housing scheme which would have allowed people to repay in instalments. In 1924, Methodist parson Rev. J. F. Studley not only recommended government-aided housing for the poor, but also stipulated that the houses be built of concrete with shingled roofs, and should measure 15 by 10 feet. The owner would pay 75 per cent of the cost over a period of 10 years while Government would bear the other 25 per cent. There is no evidence that these proposals were adopted.

The island recovered remarkably rapidly from the ravages of the 1924 hurricane, and the 1928 tempest met an island comparatively prosperous, about to take off materially and intellectually. Cotton pests were under control and a good harvest was expected. Immediate plans were on hand to generate electricity, manufacture ice and publish a local newspaper (two previous newspapers, the *Jack Spaniard* and The *Montserrat Herald*, which had courageously championed the cause of the poor, were put out of circulation due to official antagonism and lack of moral and financial support from the very people they purported to help). In the very year of the hurricane, a grammar school was established for boys. The hurricane set back all of this development.

Heralded by an intolerable heat, the hurricane came about 5.00 p.m. on 12 September, spilling over into the next day. Unlike 1924, there was warning and preparation. Word that a hurricane of considerable intensity was approaching came from Washington. Signals were sounded from St George's Hill and the Commissioner, Major H. Peebles, journeyed to several districts, urging people to bar up and prepare for the storm.

The hurricane bombarded the island for ten hours. Plymouth fared the worst, but the entire island was severely hit. The storm came like a pestilence on the poor, destroying their homes and crops; telephone wires were all down and nine inches of rain caused flooding; the lime industry was wrecked, over 350 persons were treated for casualties and the death toll was put at around 42,[12] with at least one from nearly every village. (The little village of Molyneaux lost four.) In the words of Commissioner Peebles, 'the village of Salem presents a sad and sorry plight, most houses being flat.' But this was true of many other villages, including St George's Hill, where almost all the houses were demolished and the contents blown away. The fury of the storm can be gauged by the fact that a large crane capable of lifting five tons was moved some 500 yards from its moorings on the pier.[13]

The damage and desolation were stupendous. All the public and corporate buildings in Plymouth were either totally or partially wrecked. These included the warehouse, the court house, the Coconut Hill Hotel, the grammar school, the hospital, and the Montserrat Company's depot. Government House, the Treasury and Post Office, the prison and the dwelling house at the Grove were damaged, but deemed habitable. Some high-class mansions, such as 'The Bend', belonging to a Miss Barry, and the Montserrat Company's house at Richmond were razed. Churches were, as usual, high on the casualty list with the St Patrick's church, the Wesleyan church and school, the Roman Catholic church, presbytery and school and the St Anthony's church wrecked. Then there was the usual story of broken bridges, blocked roads and popular destitution. People passed the night under nooks within, or boulders without, most of them in water. More than 600 houses were totally destroyed and the damage conservatively estimated as £150 000. The estimated cost of repairs to government buildings, property and roads was £11 713.[14] The British Government provided a grant of £10 000 and a further £5000 as a non-interest-bearing loan. (This was unfavourably compared with the £800 000 which the French voted for Guadeloupe as a grant.)

The relief measures which were executed after the storm were very impressive. In fact, the preparations that were made and the efficiency with which they were carried out, were not bettered in 1989. Relief supplies were well managed. Government took over all provisions in the warehouse and listed all provisions in private warehouses; a large depot was built to receive all relief stores. Those who could buy did so, and the infirm and old were given free food. Accountability was in evidence as a careful check was kept on the issues; and the over 2600 adults and 2000 children had to sign for the clothing they received. When the records showed a shortage of 5335 feet of lumber and 83 bundles of shingles, it was explained that this was 'due to the people on two occasions rushing the depot and breaking down the barbed wire fence'.[15] The depot referred to here was the central depot for storage and distribution of lumber which was built at the sea-front adjacent to the jetty.

The efficiency of the relief administration may have been due to the quality of the district committees. Planters figured predominantly among the district chairmen, but there is no evidence that they acted in a partisan manner. They included names like Jeffers, Mercer, Shand, Horner, Otway and Griffin – all prominent planters or business persons. The Commissioner lavished praises on the Chairmen and also singled out Rev. W. Sunter for his indefatigable work in reconstruction. The police and the civil service were also commended for 'not sparing themselves day or night'. Voluntary work was significant, especially that given by Roman Catholic nuns who, on their own initiative, went on foot to South, Windy Hill and Molyneaux with food and medical supplies. Once again assistance came from the immediate sub-region. What was new, however, was the input of Montserratians abroad as a body. The Montserrat Progressive Society of New York, for instance, sent large quantities of clothing.

The recovery process started speedily. Within a week, water was restored in Plymouth; a refuge barrack to house 200 people was erected alongside the sea north-west of the town; and in the north, three acres of land were put under the cultivation of vegetables and ground provisions. This provided employment and guaranteed a future food supply. A prompt visit by the Governor of the Leeward Islands, Sir Eustace Fiennes, accompanied by doctors Heath and Griffin on 16 September helped to reassure the people and trigger the reconstruction process, since Fiennes was able to authorize certain expenditures. Restoration of normalcy would take a long time. One of the effects of the storm was the dislocation of the grammar school, and many boys had to go abroad for schooling. The Cambridge Syndicate provided some relief by waiving the examination fees in 1929 because of the losses the island sustained in the previous year. The boys' well-to-do parents would have been pleased.

Fortunately the island had a long respite from hurricanes after 1928, although it felt the effects of hurricanes David and Allan in 1979 and 1980 respectively which whipped the Windward Islands. In fact the Plymouth wharf was severely damaged. Hugo, the first named hurricane to devastate Montserrat, belonged to the same league as the big wind of 1928. It was, however, the worst of the century, judged by its velocity and the havoc from which no corner of the island escaped. With winds gusting well over 165 miles per hour, Hugo rampaged furiously over the entire island and colossally damaged vegetation and nearly every building. The lush-green island became a desert-brown, and decapitated houses and scarred roofs spoilt the landscape. The hills looked as if a fire had raged through them and scorched them. That only 11 persons died was miraculous and may be due partly to the fact that most people were already indoors when the storm began.

> It was no Mona Lisa the picture that we saw
> More like the field of Flanders at the ending of the war

was the way Peter Lake, a resident, described the desolation.

Most church buildings bowed to Hugo without divine deference to any denomination. Rome, Wittenberg, Geneva, Coptic Africa, USA – all felt the lash. Many of them were razed like the temple in Jerusalem whose ruin Jesus had predicted with uncanny accuracy. Notable exceptions were the Bethel Centenary Methodist church, whose conical spires escaped with peeling only (it is famous for resisting hurricanes), the below-road Pentecostal church at Dyers and the Church of Christ building at Trials. The Plymouth pier, sitting in a shelter-less roadstead, vanished. One of the significant losses was an ancient landmark – a large tamarind tree, just inside the southern entrance to the St Anthony's Church yard. Hugo floored the aged tree which had weathered many a hurricane, and British soldiers completed the wreck with sticks of dynamite. According to oral sources, slaves who accompanied their masters to church sheltered under this tree during divine worship. Not allowed to enter the place of the 'holy', they listened at a distance. There is nothing so new about apartheid. Hugo's scourging added to the troubled history of the church building itself.

The damage done by Hugo was unprecedented. It affected 98 per cent of the houses, 50 per cent severely and 20 per cent totally, leaving nearly a quarter of the population of 12 000 homeless. The damage, excluding the airport, was assessed at EC$645 750 000, and of this EC$350 million was the estimated value of the damage to middle- and upper-income property.[16] Hugo's damage was more conspicuous than that caused by his predecessors partly because of the level of development attained by the island. Montserrat is a developing country, but it balances its recurrent budget and the citizens enjoy a creditable standard of living in spite of the insubstantial base of its externally oriented economy. The standard of housing was particularly high.

A house for the Montserratian is not just a shelter; it is a solid symbol of possession of a stake in his or her island; it is a concretizing of his roots and has spiritual value. Many put virtually all their lives' earnings – past and future – in their homes. For the under- and non-insured, therefore, the loss was catastrophic (not counting the irreplaceable curios, keep-sakes, books, business papers, data on diskettes and more). Some persons were left with heaps of rubble and ruin to mark the spots where their houses once stood. They camped and cooked their meals during the day, still identifying with the property in which their lives were rooted.

Predictably, attention was focused on the structural styles of houses. In 1928 when all lordly plantation houses, except those designed and built by S. W. Howes at Trants and Woodlands, sustained major damage, resident chronicler T. S. English attributed the widespread destruction to the work of amateur architects. Noticeably, some small houses with galvanized covering and hip roofs survived Hugo, while loftier modern structures crumbled. It is evident that the post-1928 generation built with hurricanes in mind. By 1989 the country had become careless and architectural attractiveness was not combined with hurricane worthiness. Hugo's winds, accompanied, it was felt, by tornadoes, would be ruinous in any context, but in addition to hip roofs, it was clear that houses with shorter eaves fared better.

A technical study on the structural damage commissioned by the United Nations Development Programme (UNDP) immediately after Hugo, recommended that new roofs be hipped with pitches of 20 to 35 degrees.[17] Another investigation commissioned by the British Overseas Development Administration (ODA) noted that 'Montserrat has a reputation for the quality of its buildings which in general are of better design and construction than those in some other parts of the Caribbean'. It nevertheless made some recommendations, some of which had obtained and generally went out of practice: the super-structure of buildings needed to be tied to the sub-structure by holding-down bolts or steel reinforcing rods; verandahs, which are so vulnerable to hurricane damage, should be constructed as a separate element to the main roof structure.[18] Both studies produced several illustrations to show that buildings constructed in the traditional idiom suffered much less damage. They also showed that special attention has to be given to building near hill tops because of increased wind-speeds on steeply rising ground, as well as in valleys where the funnel effect also increases wind velocity. The lessons of Hugo and the studies it generated should assist not just Montserrat, but the rest of the Caribbean in constructing hurricane-resistant buildings.

In 1928 it was suggested that it would take 20 years to restore the island to the pre-hurricane state. An identical figure was cited for Hugo. In fact it took far less. This is because materials were quickly secured (some as a gift from Jamaica), and tradesmen rushed in from other parts of the region, some as volunteers and others as job-seekers. A commendable aspect of Caribbean cooperation and integration was in evidence. The problem came later as jobs became scarce and the local population started to revolt against the 'foreigners'. Government felt obliged to step in with the regulatory expedient of the work permit. Interestingly, a local newspaper reminded the government and people of their debt to their Caribbean neighbours, and the editor was obviously opposed to what he described as Government's 'stringent labour policy proposals'.[19]

An interesting area of 'assistance' took the form of outward migration and in a sense demonstrated the interdependence of Caribbean people. Montserratians have always emigrated in significant numbers since the turn of the twentieth century, but Hugo gave momentum to the process. Children went to Antigua, Barbados, the USA and elsewhere to attend school. The Government of Antigua offered to school Montserrat's sixth formers, although the offer was not generally taken up by parents. The post-Hugo trek was not confined to children. The vulnerable group, the aged, sick and infirm went on 'holidays' to US cities where they could be cared for by relatives. It was difficult for them to endure the inconveniences along with the personal traumas of their illnesses when the single hospital was torn apart. Most of them returned when the situation became tolerable.

One of the good things that Hugo did was to revitalize and hone the links between overseas Montserratians and their homeland. Montserratian organizations in Boston, New York, Canada and the United Kingdom were reactivated and went into action garnering relief. A new organization, the Aston Montserrat Association (Birmingham) came into being for the occasion. Aided by cheap fares provided by US air-carriers, many came from North America to see the damage firsthand and to bring supplies. Scores also came from the UK although there was no corresponding fare relief from BOAC. This was a kind of self-help, and it was heart-warming that Montserratians in 'exile' were not prepared to leave overseas aid for their stricken homeland entirely up to outsiders without kinship connections. There are very likely more Montserratians in the UK and the US than the eleven thousand plus at home and that rekindling of their patriotism was a positive and most welcome development.

Hugo aid came from a multiplicity of sources – regional governments, the British, French, the USA, the European Economic Community, international organizations, denominational affiliations and more. One of the many lessons that the hurricane taught was the need for a sophisticated organization and mechanism to collect, coordinate and distribute relief. The 1928 story of Mary Elizabeth Brown (already referred to) cannot be tolerated. In her second hurricane in 1928 when she was five, her family lost most of their clothes and she had to live in her father's shirt for a long time. She reported that: 'My mother stood in a line and never got a thread of cloth to put on us although she was actually there before they started sharing.'[20] This may not have happened in Hugo, but many scandals and stories of selfishness, greed and corruption abounded. What was also lacking in the Hugo preparedness were the plans for housing the homeless for long weeks and months while permanent shelter was being prepared.

An *ill* wind, Hugo blew a large shot of capital into the economy and many made mini-fortunes. It came largely in the form of insurance pay-outs. Contractors proliferated as tradesmen upgraded themselves to grab bigger shares of the loot. With people anxious to rebuild and a scarcity of workmen, building costs escalated to unconscionable levels and poor folks without insurance groaned. John Osborne's PLM government, which worshipped fanatically at the shrine of free enterprise, failed to protect the weak. This is another area of post-hurricane management that merits attention. In the instant-riches post-Hugo season, builders reportedly exploited foreign workers.

Hugo blew some good. Some persons took the opportunity to improve their homes. Some of the good, however, turned out to be deceptive in its effects. Much of the sudden monies were spent on consumer items. This remains to be ascertained, but in some cases it may well have been at the expense of restoring buildings to a durable state. In any case, the monies were not used productively or wisely and two-and-a-half years after the hurricane, dozens of unlikely persons faced financial collapse. The Hugo boom had hidden the onset of recession and obscured the island's basic unproductiveness.

There is no evidence that Government itself anticipated the bust and the cessation of the good times. No voices were raised against the sterile spending spree. This is further evidence of the complex and many-sided nature of post-hurricane governance – a governance which must include mechanisms to ensure the timely draw-down on aid for capital works. The British responded generously as far as the announced figures were concerned, but three years after the hurricane, major infrastructure, such as the island's only hospital, has not been rehabilitated. It is hoped that the new British Secretariat in Barbados, with its emphasis on partnership for good government, will eliminate some of the bottlenecks in the future. Hugo seems to belong to a new genre of hurricanes in the velocity of its winds and their behaviour. It should have generated new thinking on disaster preparedness and management. The Hugo experience remains a fertile field for research with practical and vital implications for the entire Caribbean region.

The contrast between Montserrat on the morrow of Hugo and Montserrat two years later was mind-boggling. Nature healed quickly, restoring the lush-green and lively vegetation; and a resilient people moved equally promptly to rebuild their homes. We owe it though to another generation to replant the trees. Many were permanently lost.

11

The volcanic awakening

Precursor studies

Although *'The Catalogue of Active Volcanoes of the World'* lists Montserrat's Soufrière Hills among the volcanic centres,[1] government publications on disaster preparedness were absolutely silent on volcanic eruption. This included a 260-page 'Disaster Preparedness' document published in 1995. The 18 July seismic events of that same year and their sequel changed that posture for several generations to come and have also fundamentally transformed the course of the island's history.

There is no totally satisfactory and logical explanation for the neglect of the volcano and its potential hazards except the imprecision of volcanology as a science, the ambivalence of the predictions as a result of that imprecision, and the long time-lapse between the last eruption and 1995. Montserrat is one in a volcanic arc of islands in the Lesser Antillean chain. With the exception of Barbados, Antigua and Barbuda and Guadeloupe in part, all the others from Saba in the north to Grenada in the south are almost totally volcanic in origin and house dormant volcanoes. As we observed in Chapter 1, the island is comprised of three mountain ranges which are all volcanic centres, the youngest being the Soufrière Hills where the latest drama has occurred and is still occurring.

The use of the word 'dormant' to describe all the volcanic masses that made the island, entrenched a conceptual confusion that prevented prompt administrative response even when fairly clear warning was given. The Soufrière Hills volcano did not really awaken in 1995, although it provided an awakening for the unsuspecting populace and a succession of sleeping administrations. Constant fumarolic activity, gas emissions on the flanks of the volcano and hot streams and springs, some surfacing near frequented areas, spoke constantly of a living volcano. Tar River in the east, which gave its name to an estate south of the village of Long Ground, was known to generations in that area as Hot River. It was fed by the hell of Soufrière.

Extant scientific accounts of the volcano date back to 1811 to a visit by N. Nugent, a medical doctor and an honorary member of the British

Geological Society. He observed Galways Soufrière which he 'conceived might be the crater of an inconsiderable volcano'.[2] He found no crater, but his description of fissures, sulphurous exhalations and a boiling rivulet were evidence of an active volcano. J. Davy, another medical doctor, was, as we observed in Chapter 1, captivated by the romantic environment of Galway Soufrière but learnt of two craters, one of which was the Upper Gages Soufrière 'now a lake of clear water at the summit of one of the highest mountains'.[3]

Even more attention was paid to volcanic activity in Montserrat by serious scientists in the twentieth century. With the knowledge of Perret's 1934 experience (noted in Chapter 1), no one should have been surprised that volcanic gases and ashes posed a potential hazard to the health of Montserratians. Perret's account was pointedly titled *The Volcanic-Seismic Crisis at Montserrat*. This 1934 crisis which manifested itself mainly in earthquakes was obviously volcano related although this was not popular knowledge outside the scientific community. It soon attracted other volcanologists, notably MacGregor,[4] Martin-Kaye[5] and Rea,[6] a doctoral student; and this interest continued for up to seven years before the great eruption, with the famous predictive publications of Wadge and Isaacs who focused on hazards.[7] The establishment of the Seismic Research Unit (SRU) at the St Augustine campus of the University of the West Indies in 1959 (whose original name was the Volcanological Research Department and which channelled research on Montserrat), also focused attention on the eruptive possibilities of the island's volcano. Its own scientists, Shepherd and Tomblin, published works on Montserrat especially after the crisis in 1966–7.[8] It should not have been a secret, therefore, that the Soufrière Hills volcano was spoiling for a crisis throughout the twentieth century.

But government managers seldom read scientific journals if at all and management was always a burning issue in this crisis. Besides, the interests of the scientists tended to peak with crises which generate research and publication and fade away thereafter. The 1980s, however, and in particular the decade between 1985 and the 1995 climactic crisis, was a particularly productive and vitally relevant period of research on the Soufrière Hills volcano. It was in 1985 that Baker published, concentrating on radiocarbon dating to determine ages and eruptive sequence, and pointing out that the delimitation of hazard zones around the Soufrière Hills was fraught with a great measure of uncertainty. He nevertheless went on in the same article to predict, with somewhat doubtful logic, that the lava flow hazard to the island was small.[9] This demonstrated something of the ambivalence that attached to volcanic forecasting and therefore the dilemma that civil authorities faced even if they were studious readers and able interpreters of the available scientific data.

Wadge and Isaacs, also working in the 1980s, have been justifiably esteemed as the most reliable prophets on Montserrat's volcanic hazards. Improving on Baker's digital model for mapping volcanic hazards, they contended that the volcano posed a considerable potential threat to the southern section of the island. They regarded central Montserrat as also being in danger if the eruption were an energetic one. In addition, they offered a three-stage process that would comprise the next eruption including a second stage of major activity. In their view, mudflows would be associated with the next eruption.[10] The work of Wadge, from the University of Reading, and Isaacs, from the SRU of the UWI, provided the government of Montserrat with a basis for practical planning, if the appropriate enlightenment existed. The value of their data is underlined by the fact that the posse of post-eruption scientists took quite a while after the eruption started to improve on the predictive value of Wadge and Isaacs.

If the Wadge-Isaacs findings were cloistered in a learned journal, Montserratian planners might have had an excuse for their inaction, and there might have been some rationale for the deafening silence of disaster planning on volcanoes. In fact the publication of the article was closely linked with a regional seminar which the UWI hosted on 25–26 April 1988 to assess the volcanoes of the Lesser Antilles. Montserrat was represented at the seminar at a senior official level but there is no evidence that the official reported back to the government. This says something about the official but it does not exonerate the government which was actually sent a report captioned *Volcanic Hazards from Soufrière Hills Volcano, Montserrat West Indies: A Report to the Government of Montserrat and the Caribbean Disaster Preparedness Prevention Project*. Wadge and Isaacs went unheeded both locally and regionally.

In this report, these two scientists were not as equivocal as their colleagues usually are even now, in their effort to avoid dogma and action based thereon which might prove erroneous. They made it clear that the Soufrière Hills volcano 'will erupt again' and that the three seismic crises which the island experienced in over a period of roughly 100 years – 1897–8, 1933–7 and 1966–7 – were strenuous efforts being made by the volcano to erupt. They showed too that radiocarbon dating of the volcano proved that a series of eruptions had occurred between 24 000 and 17 000 years ago. There is an unusual positiveness about the tone and language of Wadge and Isaacs. They were even more positive in advocating that emergency plans should precede future eruptions and in identifying areas that would be affected by the eruption. Given the nature of their science and its relative youth, their level of verity was remarkably high. They bear some quoting at length:

We suggest that eruption emergency planning should allow for three different types of eruption:

1. A small eruption within English's Crater. The only community that should be directly threatened by pyroclastic flows would be Long Ground which should be evacuated as soon as the eruption starts. There would also be a hazard from mudflows, specifically in Fort Ghaut in Plymouth.
2. A moderate to large eruption. Most of southern Montserrat should be evacuated. The only two communities that would be relatively safe are Richmond and Cork Hill. The sequential hazard zone map gives a guide to the priority of evacuation in the event of such an eruption.
3. A collapsing dome/lateral blast eruption. This is a very remote but dangerous possibility. The conditions leading up to it may be detectable in advance and once diagnosed immediate evacuation of the relevant 180 degree sector of the volcano would be required.[11]

The Report alas was destined for dusty alcoves like so many others.

Two other persons made volcanic predictions of a kind but mysticism and vision were even less likely to provoke action where science failed. The first was peripatetic street preacher Abraham White of Harris village in the vulnerable east who prophesied a trinity of disasters just prior to hurricane Hugo.[12] The other, also of Harris origin, was Montserrat's most accomplished creative writer, Archie Markham, who wrote after Hugo of the day 'the volcano vomit corruption back in we face'.[13] The day was six short years away but none of these Cassandras was heeded and the eruption caught the island napping.

Eruptions and evacuations

Seismometres installed around the volcano by the SRU of the UWI recorded large swarms of earthquakes between 1992 and 1994.[14] These are generally signals of imminent volcanic activity. But when on 18 July 1995 villagers living to the west of the Soufrière Hills heard a sound like the roar of a jet engine overhead, they did not know it was the volcano. No one had prepared them for this. For the next three years, people's lives were governed by eruptions and evacuations at the whim of Soufrière and the will of government figures – a will that was informed more or less by the advice of scientists who developed their discipline in the laboratory of growing devastation.

This wake-up call placed the island on a three-year alert during which islanders experienced almost every kind of physical manifestation of a volcano and learned of its destructive and deadly consequences the painful way. The first major phreatic (ash and steam) eruption occurred on 20 August blackening the sky over Plymouth for 15 minutes and bathing it in thick ash. This prompted the first evacuation of southern Montserrat. By September the yoyo of evacuation and returns started when with the passage of hurricanes Luis and Marilyn residents were allowed back in their homes. It was luck rather than management that no one was incinerated, for hurricanes were still regarded as the dominant disaster. There was no evidence that the situation at Soufrière had changed. The overriding thought was to get people out of tent-like accommodation, but then they could have landed in the fire.[15]

With continuous dome growth between August 1995 and 25 June 1997 when the first fatalities occurred, there were about five major eruptive events and three evacuations. One of these events was a powerful pyroclastic flow on Mother's Day 12 May 1996 preceded by incandescent lava which was first observed for sure on 30 November the year before. This flow reached the sea for the first time channelled by the Tar River bed. Another first came on 17 September 1996 when a 45-minute magmatic explosion destroyed the Tar River Estate house and catapulted incendiary rocks which gouged houses at Long Ground, the village closest to the eastern flanks of the volcano. It also showered pumice fragments on the southern section of the island. The dome had reached its highest volume to date of 28 million cubic metres and the ash cloud produced skied to about 14 km (46 000 ft).

A climax of the dome build-up and intensive seismic activity – some of it cyclic with eruption and flows every eight hours – came in the big bang of 25 June 1997 which swept through almost all the eastern villages with a surge reaching into Belham near Cork Hill in the centre of the island. With the resultant fatalities, the issue of management came into sharp focus. The editor of the *Montserrat Reporter* has consistently sought to place the blame squarely on the head of the Governor and 'management',[16] which presumably included the CM and other government ministers. But that is too facile a conclusion. By June 1995 the science of soufrière and the response to the mountain had advanced from July 1995 when residents of Long Ground were entertaining hundreds of tourists on the margin of the volcano and there were no strict exclusion policies in place.[17] There was still a level of unpredictability and this was aggravated by the fact that the Soufrière Hills volcano behaved in an atypical and idiosyncratic manner even for volcanoes. Strong comparisons were made to Martinique's Mount Pelée with the growth of an andesite lava dome, pyroclastic flows and destructive surges, but unusually, the destructive activity came towards the end of the extrusion of the dome rather than at the beginning. This made management complicated and was partly responsible for progressive evacuation northwards.[18]

In June 1995 though, the warnings were loud and voluminous. The first scientists from UWI had arrived within a day of the onset of obvious activities and within six months some 40 international ones would have sojourned. There was general agreement on the precursor activities even if there was uncertainty about preparation time. The presaging activities of the June eruption were accompanied by warnings to avoid the very areas which were devastated. Some contend (in personal conversations) that the authorities sent the wrong signal to the people of Farms (an area of fatality) by keeping the adjoining William H. Bramble airport open. Any element of truth in this accusation has to be qualified by the fact that the airport and its environs were under a heightened state of alert. A hot telephone line was in effect between the observatory, the airport where a scientist was stationed on duty and the Vere Bird airport in Antigua; airport workers had conducted evacuation drills and simulations; and children were not allowed at the airport unless they had to travel.

The harsh sad fact is that people took chances even with the advancing knowledge of the scientists whose forecasts had proved wrong sometimes, but right at others, as journalist Polly Pattullo observes in her eminently readable and valuable *Fire from the Mountain*. She did not however attempt to refute allegations that 'because no one cared enough, because the official priorities were of expendiency rather than principle, nineteen people had died'.[19] It is not so simple and indeed not true. In explaining the fate of a Spanish Point family who narrowly escaped with foot-burns to their four-year-old daughter Mary, she suggests that 'a stubbornness combined with religious fatalism proved a rationale to remain at Spanish Point'[20] which is south of the airport. To stubbornness and fatalism, I would add belief in divine benevolence, although this is not a sufficient explanation for the fatalities.

Evidently an eruption of the nature and magnitude of the 25 June event might have killed people including scientists on any given day. According to the weekly *Montserrat Reporter* (the island's only newspaper), three weeks before the eruption CM Bertrand Osborne and Acting Governor Howard Fergus ordered farmers who cultivated lands under the crater rim of the volcano to stop visiting those areas immediately. This order was based on scientific advice. Influential persons criticized the order to leave immediately and counselled that the farmers should be given proper time to harvest their crops along with individual advice on workable arrangements.[21] It is cozy and 'comforting' to lay the blame for death at the door of the administration, but that would be simplistic at the very least. Grim necessity, deprivation, dislocation and uncertainly over the behaviour of a capricious volcano all figured in the fatal decisions of the victims.

A formal inquest into the June deaths could not deny that the 19 ignored danger warnings even though the tone of the report was decidedly anti-authority. The inquest had to concur with the Foreign Office in London which stated that 'On May 23, the farmers were told to stop farming in the area nearest the volcano. It is inconceivable that they were not aware of the dangers'.[22] It was suggested, however, that the administration was negligent and guilty of what was termed 'contributory causes' especially in the case of farm workers and those who died adjacent to the William H. Bramble airport. Significantly, although lawyers represented families of victims at the inquest, government culpability was seemingly insufficiently grave to warrant litigation for damages.

Legal niceties and the pleasure of demonization aside, some of the unfortunate dead were victims of economic deprivation, dislocation and the psychic pressure of restricted movement as well as of their own negligence. To the extent that the governmental authorities failed to provide alternative farming sites and livelihood for farmers and comfortable alternate dwellings for evacuees, and to the extent that they rejected a policy of forceably ejecting persons from the danger zone and policing every access thereto, to that extent, they are guilty of causing these deaths. But this is an open-ended debate with the jury still out on a definitive conclusion on how much blame to attach to whom in this sadly complex matter.

One can hardly fault the volcanologists on the June tragedy. Questioned by a juror at the inquest, this author rejected the suggestion that persons lacked information either in total or in an assimilable form. In the early months of the crisis, Dr William Ambey and his UWI colleagues educated the public in their various communities and on radio employing multiple message delivery modes. The Montserratian populace generally, including children, learned much of the lexicon and grammar of volcanoes and it was true to say that the rank and file of Montserratians trusted the judgement of SRU's William Ambey and to a large extent that of his colleagues, Richard Robertson and Lloyd Lynch. Even when the SRU was reportedly sidelined in favour of the scientists of the British Geological Society during the regime of Governor Frank Savage, the quality of the work was not in doubt within the accepted limitations. (Monitoring the Montserrat volcano had become a profitable and prestigious profession and scientists served as adjunct administrators when it suited them and purely as information providers at other times.) The reasons for the marginalization of the SRU were never made clear to the public except that

Ambey reportedly preferred to report to CM Reuben Meade rather than to the Governor.[23]

Although it was the fatal one, the June 1997 eruption was not the most powerful. In fact an even more powerful dome collapse of 21 September overwhelmed Whites and Trants including the air terminal. Half of the 45 million cubic metres of the dome became fiery rivers of debris which created new beaches at Trants and Tar River and deposited heavy ash in the north. No place was sacred though some were safe. Surge deposits at Trants were 400 degrees celsius.[24] The worse was yet to come when the southern flank of the volcano collapsed on Boxing Day and delivered a knock blow to the entire St Patrick's district with a lateral blast that spread northward to Kinsale where some houses were burnt. Through this major collapse, the volcano expressed its devastating mission in several ways. A pyroclastic flow down the south east reached within 300 metres of the sea producing a delta; the volume of material which entered the sea generated a small tsunami which washed up boats and debris at Old Road Bay on the mid-western coast; and the ash cloud which reached as high as 47 000 metres went south as far as St Vincent, spraying it with fine ash.[25]

From March 1998, the volcano made no landmark waves until 28 July 2001 when a major dome collapse deluged the south, covered the middle of the island with ashes and exported it liberally as far north as the US Virgin Islands and Puerto Rico. But between those dates it continued to be active, more or less. Apart from being discomfited by drizzles or deluges of ash throughout the eruption saga, almost invariably people were required to move as the island map was periodically being re-written to delineate habitable and exclusion zones. In accordance with Wadge's gospel, Belham River, which skirts the river of Cork Hill, was the main divider between north and south making nomads of persons in the central zone of the island. A massive 4 August explosion which shed gravel in the north prompted a move of the dividing line to Nantes river putting most of the village of Salem, a large community which housed significant commercial businesses, in the vulnerable zone. By 21 September a new central zone was created between the Nantes and Lawyers rivers and this placed Salem squarely into the exclusion zones.

By March 1998 the island had lost lives, population and habitable space and certain semi-permanent designations of safe zone, flexible or central zone and exclusion zones were created. In October1998 the re-occupation of Salem was authorized and a daytime entry zone between Belham and the Plymouth environs was promulgated. This enabled residents to supervise and repair properties in a controlled regime which vitally involved the scientists. Everyone welcomed the reclamation of Salem but since, along with other central areas it was never physically affected except for heavy ashfall,

some questioned the wisdom of the evacuation in the first place and consequently the credibility of the scientists. This was natural considering the
economic loss, and the only plausible answer was the one offered by the
authorities – that they preferred to err on the side of caution and that 'the
people's safety has always been paramount'.[26] The ambiguous noises which
emanated from scientists themselves did not flatter their cause. The magazine *Nature*, referring to a survey, reported that the scientists on the island
had lost credibility in the eyes of the inhabitants because of wrong predic-
tion including false alarms resulting in unnecessary moves. Professor
Stephen Sparkes of Bristol University, who served as chief scientist at the
Montserrat Volcano Observatory, admitted to mistakes, blaming them on
the inexactness of volcanology and pointing to the need for a partnership
with sociologists and disaster managers. It is not clear, however, whether
the Professor put forward any such proposal locally. Some scientists were
reported as saying privately that politicians made unrealistic demands on
their expertise.[27] Perhaps; but maybe this was one of the prices the scientists
had to pay for their high profile as saviours in the society. This business of
private dialogue was a problem because in some minds there was always
suspicion that scientists gave differing messages to the local government
and the British government. The London *Sunday Times* (7 December)
quoted former chief scientist Simon Young as saying in London that there
was no evidence that the volcano would stop.[28] That message was never
conveyed to Montserratians. Young did deny the statement but these
murky rumours heightened the stress level induced by the volcano. Perhaps
the real truth is that the volcano made playthings of us all, confusing and
confounding our skills.

The social impact

The 'sugar revolution' used to be a stock topic in West Indian history.
Montserrat has added a 'volcanic revolution' with AD 1995 as the bench-
mark beginning of the new era. Huge social, economic and political
changes have taken place. (The politics of the volcano is dealt with in
Chapter 9.)

The main social problem connected with the crisis was shelter and
shelter culture. Driven from their homes by fear of fire and by administrative edicts, large numbers found themselves in shelters such as schools,
churches, tents, tent-like structures, and, after a while, hastily constructed
wooden buildings. Space and toilet facilities were inadequate resulting in
overcrowding, lack of privacy and inadequate sanitation. Some sheltered
with relatives and friends in the north but neither this situation nor the

governmental shelters possessed the quality of permanence. Citing D. Alexander, UWI sociologist Christine Barrow observed that shelter was a last resort and was universally condemned, associated as it was with homelessness and low social status.[29] In the Montserrat case shelters came to stay for a long time and took on a culture of their own and a politics withal.

In May 1997, 22 months into the eruption, there were 37 shelters, 15 of which were churches, with a population of 775 persons.[30] The number peaked to 1498 by August of the same year.[31] Much of the social evils of the volcano, some real and a few imagined, were blamed on shelters. Jury chairman and coroner Rhys Burris, a British magistrate, blamed some of the June deaths on shelters. To the commonly stated woes, his panel added rowdy conduct, exposure of children to distasteful conduct and possibilities for child abuse as reasons why persons chose to remain in forbidden territory.[32] If Burris is correct it is perhaps fortunate that only a small number of affected citizens arrived at that conclusion. The jury seemed to have exhausted all of the possible evil consequences of shelter dwelling. Dorris Murrain, who left her native Corkhill, pinpointed one of the negative impacts – the frustration of able-bodied persons confined to a small space doing nothing.[33] This frustration was inherent in shelter culture.

Shelters were absolutely wretched, in one case with 114 persons sharing four toilets, but one nevertheless has to apply some test of objectivity to some of the condemnatory statements. The most frequently cited comment is the one made by lawyer David Brandt to the effect that shelters were worse than cattle sheds in the UK and more like the barracoons in which our people were kept prior to transportation from Africa.[34] It was this kind of vigorous and graphic rhetoric that brought Brandt to power and helped him to win concessions for his country even if it did not endear him to DFID Minister Clare Short. So whatever the level of veracity that the statement contained it was functional especially when the international press quoted it and silently endorsed it. Erick Kelsick, a Plymouth merchant, was no friend of the Reuben Meade government, so one is not surprised that he nearly paralleled Brandt when he accused Meade of purchasing prefabricated barns to house the evacuated.[35]

The delay in providing housing or upgrading shelters was perhaps worse than the state of the shelters themselves. They should have been temporary holding bays. On the surface Eric Kelsick was justified in castigating the Reuben Meade government for lack of planning and the British government for a wait-and-see, spend as-as-little-as-you-can attitude.[36] And the policy of delay found resonance in Governor Frank Savage's recommendation that the British build 1000 homes in the north of the island in contrast to Meade's lack of urgency at best, depending as he was on uncertain and unrealistic assistance from CARICOM.

Without excusing British parsimony or downright meanness, criticism of Meade has to be attenuated by what we know of the status of the science of volcanoes and the fact that the scientists did not always sing from the same song sheet. In his scathing attack on the local government as 'vacillating, incompetent and overoptimistic particularly in respect of the redevelopment of the safe zone and making provision for the homeless',[37] former Governor David Taylor was lacking in objective analysis. Even though the British International Development Committee cited the decision of the Reuben Meade government not to apply for aid to construct housing as a significant cause of the appalling housing conditions after two and a half years, it did not offer that as a sufficient cause for the delay. They too correctly associated the atypical and unpredictable behaviour of the volcano as an associate cause.[38]

Housing aggravated or triggered other social problems. By utilizing churches and schools as shelters for such an extensive period, the occupants delayed the rehabilitation of education and consistent pastoral care. Loss of proper accommodation restricted the legitimate efforts that church and school might have made to ease the psychic burden. The disaster and its attendant dislocation and sense of helplessness produced stress in young and old. The local Director of Health thought that stress and related problems like loss of sleep and hypertension hastened death among the aged and aggravated ill-health at all ages. Recognizing the stress of both teachers and students working in cramped conditions, Bonnerjea *et al.* drew attention to the need for appropriate professional support from a psychologist or some such service.[39]

Education, which is generally regarded as pivotal for any recovery and rebuilding (sometimes over-emphasized as a panacea), was also affected. As elitist systems go, the island's comprehension education system performed well producing GCE and CXC results averaging well over 60 per cent, to use one measurement index. Between 1995 and 1998, enrolment (from nursery to secondary) dropped from 2672 to 620 or over 80 per cent and the teaching population fell from 200 to 27.[40] Some of the latter migrated and others were made compulsorily redundant. Housing and education were integrated as push factors. Not only was the technical college closed, but plans to establish a community college had to be shelved.

Prodigious efforts had to be made to maintain or resuscitate education because there were periods of disruption and hiatuses. Schooling at first had to take refuge in hot cramped tent-like structures or even a bar while the St John's school sited in the privileged north was commandeered as a temporary hospital – understandably so. Teachers had to cope with unprecedented disciplinary problems attributed to the newly induced social conditions. A teacher offered this insightful comment to researchers:

> These children are crushed in shelters or cramped houses where they are not wanted. When they come here (to school) they desperately need their own space. I've had these fights in class – over a chair, over a book – when they are really fighting over personal space.[41]

In addition it was generally felt by teachers that migration of the brighter children impacted negatively on the learning culture and classroom atmosphere.

Apart from some sluggishness in the rebuilding process (which further fuelled migration) education as a sector was fairly privileged. Teachers had vested interest in their jobs and academic results, parents recognized its value as an instrument of social advancement and the government and even DFID seemed to have accepted that it was the foundation of development. This is why it was disappointing that a 1998 DFID study charged with 'assessing the full range of educational needs'[42] saw no immediate role for technical education. This was at a time when the physical rebuilding was getting into gear in the north. This was reflective of the stereotypical thinking and business-as-usual manner which has bedevilled the management of the crisis.

The recovery in education has been significant. There are two well organized and comfortably housed primary schools with a third on the way. Secondary school is available for all in newly rehabilitated quarters with a current enrolment of 292; and there are plans to restore the lost Sixth Form immediately and to build a community college in the short run. Except for the two nursery schools which are crowded, classroom space is adequate and teacher:student ratio which was good before the crisis is even better now at 1:20 in the primary school (2000), even though this is in part a function of emigration.

One of the lessons worthy of emphasis is that migration and evacuation issues were central to the fate of the island and much of the migration was driven by the imperative for parents to find overseas centres of education. In such crises therefore, next to very basic needs such as food and shelter, education must be regarded as a prime agenda item. This realization was a belated one in the Montserrat case and not necessarily fully grasped even now. It is important for the government of Montserrat to take the opportunity of reconceptualizing the entire system in a creative way to meet the peculiar needs of the tiniest of micro states struggling to be reborn after the mightiest of natural crises. To merely copy existing patterns is to pour an unwelcome libation on the sacrifice of disaster. The main financiers, HMG, need to be guided by a corresponding enlightened thinking lest they find themselves feeding a dependency which begets dependency.

Massive migration was another response to the crisis with educational needs, housing, unemployment and, to a lesser extent, fear as push factors. Some reasonably comfortably housed residents of the safe zone migrated in order to access education for their children and jobs or doles for themselves elsewhere; some left for health reasons especially those with or predisposed to respiratory diseases, and yet others like Eric Kelsick feared the ultimate eruption.[43] The most reliable estimates of population suggest that by 1998 the island had lost some two-thirds of its population of over 10 000. By 1999 a sprinkling of returnees had increased it to about 4500 and it has since probably stabilized at around 5000.

The traditional mother country, where every Montserratian had relatives due to the mass migration of the 1950s and 1960s and where life's prospects were bruited as better, was the main draw. The Caribbean where there were friends and relatives was the second choice, especially Antigua next door from which they could keep an eye on the homeland. The figure popularly associated with the UK was over 3000 and 2000 for Antigua. Migration was more than a demographic phenomenon. The island was losing its sinews of wealth in its skilled and able-bodied and the future of its human resource in its youth. An already embattled commercial sector lost out on its consumer market and families were fragmented by both internal and out-migration. Bonnerjea *et al.* summed up some of this well along these lines: The expenditure reflows circulating in the economy decreased to the level where shops shut and business leave. 'Continued migration, far from being a solution to the country's problems, exacerbates them.'[44]

Lodging with relatives and friends had its own social problems. Strained relationships developed as the immigrants out-stayed their welcome and assumed the status of refugee as educator-calypsonian Randy Greenaway has popularized in his near classical 'Refugee in Meh Own Country'. And even within the island the crunch for space led to the separation of family members on a larger scale than in external migration. The negative social effects of this situation are yet to fully manifest themselves.

A comment seems necessary on the fate of the Montserratians diaspora created by the emergency as they occupy what may be termed Montserratian 'social space' overseas. The voluntary outrush to the Caribbean and the UK preceded planned packages and welfare benefits. The scattering of Montserratians throughout the region gave positive meaning to regional co-operation particularly in Antigua where a large number had established themselves by mid-1997. More generous than most, Antigua benefited more than most. She received an aid loan repayment waiver amounting to £1.25 million from the UK government and a development grant of £3 million in addition to rents paid by Montserratians. The grants to Antigua were a recognition of the principle that HMG had to bear responsibility for Montserratians who had sought refuge in the Caribbean.

In August 1997 DFID agreed to make a grant of EC$10 000 to all adults and $2500 for each child under 18 years of age to Montserratians who had relocated to CARICOM countries provided they were resident on the island on 16 August 1997. This was intended to assist new residents to resettle over a period of six months and was based on average Montserratian salaries together with an amount necessary to establish a new home. They were means tested to ensure that they did not possess assets totalling EC$42 000 outside Montserrat. After some agitation the scheme was extended to all Montserratians resident in the island at the onset of volcanic activities. Transportation costs only were provided to those relocating to third countries. The GOM was allegedly opposed to the relocation grant[45] apparently judging that large-scale assisted evacuation would deplete the population and render the island unviable as a political entity. Their priority was the development of the north instead. It would have been difficult to defend this stance after the serious events of June and August 1997 so they used the relocation package to bolster their argument for a better deal for remaining residents who had no access to social welfare (as obtained by those who chose the UK option).

A Voluntary Evacuation Scheme instituted in April 1996 established Montserratian entitlement to income support, general welfare and employment in England but they had to get there at their own expense. This changed by the magic date of August 1997 to a totally financed scheme. Over the next year, pockets of Montserratians were settling in Birmingham, Hackney, Stoke Newington, Leeds, Leicester, Manchester and Preston where they connected with Montserratians of a former migration wave. It did not all happen smoothly and the lack of planning for reception, for initial housing measures to counteract the protracting bureaucratic niceties in the UK, came in for harsh criticisms especially by Bernie Grant and Diane Abbott, British politicians of Montserratian provenance or connection. Grant pulled no punches. Montserratians were being treated as refugees and asylum seekers rather than as British he thought. 'They have suddenly been thrust, if they are lucky, into cold damp mildew-ridden council flats in Tottenham, Hackney or Deptford.' In one case, a man of 35 years, his 17-year-old son and a 16-year-old daughter were placed in one room. Montserratians who were accustomed to a high standard of housing were not hesitant to protest. Many of them had stood at rigid attention for the national anthem of the mother country for years and had sung 'patriotic' songs like 'Children of the Empire ye are brothers all' and the ironical 'Rule Britannia'.[46]

The slack (there is a pun on the word) left by the British government was taken up by philanthropic organizations, churches and individuals including Montserratians and Montserratian organizations. Strategies for dealing with evacuees to the UK closely mirrored the British attitude to the situation in Montserrat in a sense. They were not informed by the spirit and character of an emergency. The International Committee of the House of Commons chaired by Bowen Wells, with Abbot and Grant as major players, made a positive contribution. Their uncompromising description and analysis (albeit exaggerated at times) and their generous recommendations helped to alleviate the situation for Montserratians both in the UK and at home. They helped to remove bottlenecks, reduce bureaucratic humbug and establish benevolent infrastructure. An example of the last was the Montserrat Project, later the Montserrat Support Trust which was eventually headed by a high profile Montserratian evacuee. This supporting facility funded by British money took over the voluntary work carried out by Montserratian voluntary organizations and the Red Cross. Montserratians are now reasonably comfortable in the UK and are unlikely to return in any significant numbers unless the forces that drove them away – unemployment, housing, education and volcanic uncertainty undergo dramatic change.

The psychological effects apart, the volcano has not significantly impacted directly on the health of the population except for exacerbating the health of those with respiratory diseases. There was also a reported increase in respiratory tract infections and eye and skin irritation during the early days of the crisis. Fear over the toxicity of ingested ashes directly or through foraging animals led to a series of investigations. Dr J. Baxter of Oxford University found that in addition to physical risks from volcanic activity, there existed the danger of a lung disease called silicosis from christoballite, a chemical found in the ash.[47] Baxter's work intensified the wearing of ash masks. Although he regarded the risk of silicosis as slight in the safer zones he cautioned against giving Montserratians the possibility of attributing future illnesses to ash exposure and risking claims of compensation on the British government. The issue then arose in whose interest was he reporting. This led to an accusation of conspiracy with HMG. A. B. L. Anderson (MD) did not fully trust Baxter who, in his view, subordinated the interest of Montserratians to those of his paymasters. 'So Peter do not expect your *ex cathedra* pronouncements to be greeted with ringing hosannas',[48] he wrote.

In addition to ash and psychic distress the general standard of health care deteriorated. After a period of indecision, the Plymouth Glendon hospital was replaced by makeshift premises in the north in 1997. This quotation from Sir Kenneth Calman, the British Chief Medical Officer, adequately sums up the new conditions. 'The hospital premises are grossly substandard; there is no adequate sanitation system to dispose of waste at the hospital; the wards and operating theatre are separated by a mile.'[49] And while the volcano did not create the 250 elderly persons who he met in institutional care and the 120 in need of regular medication, the emergency situation and its management considerably reduced the national capability for attending to them. While Calman did not totally exculpate GOM for the belated response to the health situation, he categorically blamed HMG. Indeed he was 'appalled' that vulnerable persons were allowed to exist in such degrading conditions after over two years. A diagnosis and recommendation of British provenance is more likely to yield results than a locally generated one, and action followed Calman's report. However, in the style of protracted response characteristic of the crisis, 18 months elapsed between the identification of the need for the St John's hospital to the initiation of the building. The hospital was finally commissioned in 1999. Fortunately nurses from the region made up for the loss of local nurses through migration.

A positive note on health care is worth sounding in this story of overwhelming gloom. The conditions in shelters and disruptions in health maintenance were fertile grounds for communicable diseases and epidemics. Education and health surveillance by health authorities coupled with the general social discipline of the people prevented a secondary disaster.

The economic impact

It is difficult to clinically isolate social from economic factors since education, health and migration, which all affect human resources, took their toll on the economy. That said, the pounding which the economy took resulting almost in total collapse, continues to be obvious. No precise dollar figure has been assigned, but the island plummeted from relative prosperity even after its most disastrous hurricane in 1989 to abject dependence on HMG for budgetary aid and consequently financial control from Westminster. Between 1991 and 1994, for example, the island enjoyed an average annual growth rate of about 2.0 per cent. By 1997 the volcano had destroyed Plymouth, the commercial capital, and much of the infrastructure, the economy experienced negative growth of –7.61 per cent in 1995 and –20.15 in 1996 and the preliminary figure for 1997 also indicated negative economic growth. Damage to buildings was estimated at some EC$172 million or £40m and a probable figure of EC$1.0 billion has been assigned to total losses. For obvious reasons tourism which produced an estimated 30 per cent of popular income earnings, steadily declined. Visitor arrivals for the first five months of May 1997 totalled 8305 compared to 41 731 for the same period in 1995.

Two flagship industrial ventures, Montserrat Rice Mills and W & W Electronics which accounted for over 90 per cent of manufacturing exports, ceased operating after June 1997. The former, an industry worth about US$11.8 million in foreign exchange earnings annually and employing a total of 78 people in addition to trucking, involved completing the processing of rice grown in Guyana. The latter was an assembly-type business dealing in computer and electronic components. Labour costs in Montserrat are not cheap but the commercial success of both industries was largely a function of the tariff differentials which DTs enjoy within the European Union.[50] The flight of the American University of the Caribbean (AUC) an offshore medical school which in some ways was analogous to an assembly plant (students, cadavers and lecturers were all imported and the final product exported), left a yawning gap in the economy. To these big three, should be added the dozens of small businesses which folded up, or in a few cases, migrated as AUC and W & W did.

Agriculture contributed a minor annual average of 3.2 per cent of the GDP prior to 1996 but it provided a substantal livelihood for about 300 farmers. As most of the farming zones were in Long Ground, Lees, Riley's, Amersham and St Patrick's which were at once the most fertile and the most hazardous areas, evacuation plunged the sector into the doldrums.

To these problems, one has to add the loss suffered through the woes of the Montserrat Building Society – a well-run savings and mortgage granting financial institution. As property insurers withdrew, its assets became nearly worthless and the savings of many, including the poorest, were threatened with annihilation while savers were still liable for mortgages on burnt-out properties. It is a credit to their integrity and good management that they have recovered somewhat although abandoned by the British government. Clients received 35 cents in the dollar on their savings in 1997, another 35 cents in 1999 with a hope of the full amount in 2001–02. All entreaties by Montserratian victims of the volcano and the MBS collapse, to save the institution or compensate them for their loss fell on obdurate ears. HMG took a legalistic posture and resorted to evasive and obscure arguments about precedent and lack of precedent.[51] This was another instance of British refusal to treat this tiny outpost struck by an unprecedented disaster as a unique case requiring unconventional management strategies and magnanimity.

The decision by insurance companies to unilaterally reduce their liabilities on properties by 40 per cent in the unsafe zone, an act of dubious legality – and to totally terminate coverage even for hurricane damage in August 1997 – was the *coup de grace* on the economy. Between 1994 and 1997 it had chalked up an estimated 44 per cent decline.[52]

Redevelopment from this litany of losses would have required urgency, ingenuity, cohesive action and generosity and none of these was in rich supply. Delay for one reason or another runs like an unresting thread of evil throughout the story of the volcano. The concept of 'managed delay' emerged locally to describe DFID's attitude to the disbursement of funds earmarked for development. A sum of £24 million has been approved for the year 2001 but up to mid-July no project had started. GOM and DFID trade blame for the delay but the reality is that the money is not likely to be spent, with the consequence that the sum for the following year will be reduced. A government collapse followed by election only explains part of the delay and on current management style, no account is likely to be taken of that eventuality. The requisite generosity needs to go deeper than naming and figures. The following statement, attributed to a government official, may well be an exaggeration but it illustrates the concept of the alleged 'managed' or 'strategic delay':

> Using the money in the time specified is the greatest Montserrat's problem. Not because the government does not want to use it and get back on their feet, but because the British themselves tie it up. When we make proposals and send them to DFID, we have to wait an eternity before we get a response. When we do, it is because London has sent down consultants to do feasibility studies. Then others come to review what the first team did. By the time the project is approved, the time will have passed. It all a game that the British play.[53]

From the seemingly generous £75 million projected for the period 1998–2001, DFID's local staff have to be housed and remunerated, the volcano monitoring has to be funded, as well as the heavily subsidized external transport service. The transport service illustrates both lack of ingenuity and lack of local consultation. A consultant appointed by DFID in July 2001 discovered that the ferry and the helicopter together which transported passengers between Antigua, the international gateway, and Montserrat operated at an annual deficit of EC$8.9 million. With a capacity for 302, the ferry load is seldom more than 20.[54] The subsidy meant less real development funding for the island. GOM's suggestions of less expensive ferry options, purchasing and operating the ferry, for instance, were reportedly not entertained by DFID. Decisions on a fixed-wing aircraft to replace the expensive helicopter have stalemated because of conflicting views between GOM and HMG on the site of an airport.

A temporary government headquarters (GHQ) may well become a permanent memorial to DFID's folly of ignoring informed local advice. Budgeted to cost £758 000, it was eventually constructed, albeit with some unavoidable cost overrun, for over £2 250 000 and to the satisfaction of no one. This sum could have produced a more accommodating structure and a permanent one to boot. This was another example of the man-made disasters which have retarded recovery from the natural disaster and which continue to affect redevelopment. As was noted earlier, in an ill-considered remark the British Minister for DFID, Clare Short, said that the Montserratian people would soon request golden elephants; (she herself would call her remark 'off-the-cuff').[55] In the GHQ they nearly ended up with a white one. In the next section, we isolate and summarize some of the management issues that have surfaced in the analysis of official response to the emergency.

Management of the emergency

'Mismanagement' or an equivalent phrase is the most frequently used evaluative term employed in studies of the volcanic crisis. An IDC press notice on the Montserratian dilemma highlighted 'mismanagement' and 'confusion'; journalist Pattullo wrote of 'a tortuous management hierar-chy'; sociologist Christine Barrow identified 'crisis management' and a senior Montserratian official reportedly bewailed that 'we had no leaders, we were tossed on the sea'.[56] There were instances of poor management as we have recognized in this chapter, but enough allowance is not made for the fact that the volcano kept administrators guessing, although this very fact should have been factored into the planning earlier. In the condemna-tory ethos, inadequate account is taken of the success stories and there were successes.

Confusion in leadership and aid provision is the most frequently cited cause for mismanagement. While the FCO held administrative responsibil-ity for Montserrat, aid administration rested with DFID. In the early months of the emergency, ODA's arm, the British Development Division in the Caribbean (BDDC) as well as the Emergency Aid Department (EMAD) in London were also involved. Pattullo wrote of a triangular arrangement of power meaning Westminster, the Governor and GOM. This does not capture the full complexity though, for the Governor was at once a representative of HMG and part of GOM and one or other role was dominant depending on the circumstances. Savage was able to claim with some veracity that he had different priorities to those of the GOM.[57] He was able therefore to lay the blame for housing at the door of CM Reuben Meade. It is generally agreed though, GOM apart, that the greatest management sin of the crisis was the absence of a single decision-making authority backed by money.

The generally preferred solution was a British assumption of the total administration without any specific proposal on how this was to be done. The IDC's preference, for example, was for direct rule. In their view high-handed imperialism would have better served Montserratian interest than democratic involvement. I do not think however the latter was an avoidable choice. In any case an Electoral Commission established by the Governor in 1996 found that the majority of the electorate regarded direct rule through the Governor or by whatever mechanism as retrogressive and an anathema.[58] Even under direct rule, effective co-ordination would still have been necessary. After mid-1997 when under the grant-aided status, HMG and its various agents have assumed more and more effective authority but some aspects of the management problem have not been solved. The Clay Report identified three critical management problems facing the investment programmes as 'lack of delegated authority, high staff turn over and poor consultation with GOM'.[59] One has to add to these the multiple departments and pockets of administration involved and general indecision. GOM had its deficiencies, among which were lack of experience in dealing with emergencies, but there is nothing to suggest even in 2001 after several ministerial visits that HMG's direct hand contains the panacea for the Montserrat malaise. Perhaps it does, but it has not been demonstrated.

It is not that nothing has been achieved under British supervision. An almost new hospital has been built in the north, there is a new, albeit infamous, government headquarters, two housing estates have been built though one is far less functional than the other, many residents have benefited from a modest grant for assisted housing, infrastructure like water and roads have received the attention necessary for development; and GOM knew that it had a three-year budget of £75 million 1998–2001.

Unfortunately there is no strong evidence that the lessons of the last five years have been fully grasped. Without a specially staffed development unit, the institutional capacity of both DFID and GOM is still deficient; DFID and GOM still blame each other for tortuous delays in project implementation; potential for strains still exist between Plymouth (or is it Little Bay) and Whitehall and large sums from the aid package are being unwisely and peripherally spent. The case of the leased ferry which plies between Montserrat and Antigua, the island's international gateway, and the large sums which allegedly go to the agents is but one example. And sadly, before the management problems can be solved, DFID has given notice of steady aid reduction over the next three years. This apparently means reduction of the amount available each year if the GOM has not fully spent what was budgeted for, in the preceding year. The principle of self-reliance is laudable and there is nothing about the history of the island to show that it relishes the inherent embarrassment of budgetary aid. But unless appropriate management structures are instituted for the new milieu, what is being offered is a recipe for failure, grovelling dependency and 'miserization'.

12

Arts and culture

Culture is a complex concept, but we use it here to mean mainly certain creative manifestations of the people of Montserrat which are associated with entertainment, identity, expression and survival. These express themselves in activities like music, theatre, literature and certain customs. In short, we are dealing mainly with the cultural arts. Montserrat's culture reflects both African and European traditions and reinterpretations, as well as trans-Caribbean influences, and as culture is dynamic, new influences continually bear on the core culture. For instance, American television and the relative ease of communications generally between North America and the island have already made new imprints on the culture. Basketball draws greater crowds than cricket and cheer-leaders are replacing folk-mummers in Christmas festival parades.

Ritual and folk music

We noted in Chapter 4 that a 1736 law banned the playing of certain musical instruments by slaves for the entertainment of their colleagues, in the interest of plantation security. This suggests that there were recognized musicians 'retained' to provide recreation and give temporary respite to the crudeness and drudgery of plantation life. They obviously created songs with the drum as the dominant instrument. Celebration in the form of song and dance took place on all plantations at year-end and this was really the origin of our surviving Christmas jollities. By law, Christmas holidays lasted for three days. This creativity emerging from African drum music and folk religion survived the ban and cane-slavery to find rich expression in ritual music which has lingered until the present day.

The *jumbie dance*, which is the purest manifestation of folk religion in Montserrat, is the matrix of a distinctive ritual music. It is a religious-therapeutic dance practised to induce temporary spirit possession and divination. The sound and tempo of the music produced by the instruments help to produce in the worshippers a trance-like state which brings special devotees into communion with the world of the dead. The purpose of the dance is to obtain cures for chronic ills, to lift an *obeah* spell or otherwise prognosticate; the benign spirit of a dead ancestor speaks through a medium, an entranced or 'turned' dancer.

The musicians, themselves mostly *obeah* men, used four instruments – the tambourine, or *babla* drum, identical to the African *babala*, the French *réel*, a fife and a goat-skin drum. (The player beats this drum and rubs it with his hand to produce a characteristic sound which gives the name 'woo-woo' to the band. The sound was supposed to be effective in attracting spirits.) An iron triangle completes the ensemble. In some bands a concertina replaces the fife.

There is some uncertainty over the relative extent of European and African influence on jumbie music. Following Messenger,[1] Jay Dobbin identifies both the woo-woo and *babla* drums with the Irish *bodran*,[2] but he ignores the fact of the African *babala* drum. European influence is undoubtedly present in the French *réel*, and the waltz, polkas and quadrilles, but the *babla*, the rhythms, the body movements and the religious base are African. The folk religion reflects the syncretic nature of the ritual. For as Dobbin, a Roman Catholic priest, confirmed, certain Roman Catholics 'blend together the *jombees* with the poor souls in Purgatory'; and religious aids such as 'altar candles, rosaries and saints' medals, become as potent obeah charms as the magical compelling powder'.[3] As Hodge Kirnon too, reminds us in his very valuable historical essay on Montserrat,[4] magic, supernaturalism and mysticism are fundamental features of both religion and obeah.

Ironically, however, Judaeo-Western Christianity is one of the causes of the near extinction of the *jumbie* dance and related magical-religious practices of African derivation. (The tension between Europe and Africa is endemic to the island's culture.) Most Montserratians under 20 have never seen an authentic *jumbie* dance and some even older saw it only when it was staged at the University Centre as folk art in the early 1970s. In 1990, when a dance was held at Sturge Park, ostensibly to lift a losing spell off Montserrat's cricket in the Leeward Islands tournament, it provoked a storm of protest and denunciation from staunch Christian adherents. The elements of folk art, ancestral religion and humour were completely missed in decrying the devilry and backwardness of the practice. The cricket match was reportedly merely a screen to mount the dance for public education and entertainment. In any event, it was poor art, and too feeble a reflection of reality to have invoked any self-respecting spirit. The dance is still occasionally practised at a christening or at a wedding feast, but even then it is just a ghost of its former self.

Masquerades have a celebratory element, but they too are essentially folk rituals. Masquerades are masked, dancing mummers in colourful costume – a tall head-gear, ribbons, small mirrors, bells and a masque. Like minstrels, they danced from house to house, accepting gifts of drink and money. Masquerades were danced at Christmas-time (in Montserrat, eight days long) to celebrate a period of plenty and respite from toil. The prominent masque and ritual dancers which are symbols of war, guardianship and fertility make the dance strongly African. The dancers crack cart whips to make way for themselves, dis-cipline each other and ward off evil spirits.[5] The original dancers also used the 'hunters' or cart whips to symbolically beat their estate masters in retaliation for their long oppression.

Masquerade bears some dress resemblance to the Belizian and Jamaican *jonkonnu*, but the ritual dances and the musical ensemble are unique. A troupe contains from six to nine dancers and the captain is distinguished by a gold ring in the nose of his mask. Music is supplied by a fife, a kettle drum played with two sticks to give an infectious syncopating rhythm, a boom drum, a boom pipe which emits a 'boom' sound and a *shak-shak* or maracas. Again, this dance blends Europe and Africa with Caribbean colours. The folk religion and the drum beat are African, but there are Westernized steps in the quadrilles and polkas. Masqueraders also dance to folk songs which are rooted in and created from Caribbean experience. The incorporation of European elements in this ritual dance, especially the instruments, was a means of making it acceptable to European planters. The slaves were con-scious of the loss in the compromise but accepted it in the interest of the sur-vival of the art-ritual. It was for the same reason that masquerading was perhaps emptied of its religious content.[6] Once an adult art traditionally asso-ciated with Christmas, it is now practised by children and danced at odd times for tourist entertainment. Masquerades are the richest expression of African folk art in Montserrat.

Folk songs are essentially secular, but they are used extensively in the *jumbie* dance and masquerade ritual music. There is no contradiction here, since the sacred and the secular are one in the Montserrat spiritual universe and creole world-view. Born out of pre- and post-emancipation slavery, many of the songs survived European intervention and oppression and are therefore critical in defining and dynamizing the culture. Written largely in creole, they pulse with the raw realism of people's lives and subliminal yearnings. The themes are varied – *obeah*, farming, etiquette, young lust in old men, infidelity, disappointment and historical events. Some are satirical and others are sung to engender the communal spirit.[7] They are invaluable to Montserratians's self-definition as a people.

Songs with historical themes are of particular interest. It is not sur-prising that a significant event like emancipation inspired songs. But so did a crowd hero ('Run Run Ben Dyer Run') running to elude arrest; and so did the arrest of family members for illegal distillation of rum and the skill of the lawyer who secured their freedom.

> If nuh me fo' lawyer Moore
> Dey woulda rot in Antigua gaol

The fate of Telecuma for estate larceny is treated in one of the oldest folk songs.

> Me mi tell Telecuma nuh fo trouble de buckra sheep
> Now de skin pon ee back ago feel um feel um

The African influence is unmistakable in the name Telecuma and the Ibibio word *buckra* (he who conquers). A song like this gave slaves a chance to laugh at their own misfortunes – the therapeutic and life-sustaining laugh in place of weeping.

The quality of the creative talent is not in doubt in these songs. Note, for instance, the lovely liquid movement of 'Me mi tell Telecuma', set against the harshness of 'trouble'. What is surprising or perhaps not so surprising in our Britannic colonial atmosphere, is that generations of post-emancipation children were never taught these songs in schools. They were songs of rural illiterates. Children sang, instead, of British life and countryside – London Bridge, Loch Lomond and the braes of Bonnie Doone interspersed with negro spirituals written by white men.

It was not until the early 1970s when something of a creative renaissance was generated by the UWI Extra-Mural Centre that these songs were revisited, researched and given national prominence. They are now sung in schools and by choral groups. Credit for this work belongs to Dr James Irish who, as UWI Resident Tutor, founded the Emerald Community Singers who popularized these songs at home and on international stages. The new spirit coinciding with the spirit of Caribbean independence in the 1960s and 1970s generated a few indigenous composers; they turned to another genre of songs which glorified the island home and were sung along-side the folk songs. Together they nursed a nascent national consciousness.

Tea meetings and concerts

The Montserrat tea meetings were associated with the upper classes and were show cases for some of the best natural talent in the country. The *Montserrat Herald* of 26 March 1898 listed tea meetings, soirées and concerts as entertainments which attacted townfolk to the country. The emphasis on 'much taste and refinement'[8] for tea meetings must have excluded the humble folks. The latter, however, had their day in the Sunday afternoon 'penny' concerts held in the village centre. Missionary fund raising was often the cause, but the event was a secular one.

In these concerts, people developed their talent and personality in songs and speeches before a participative and appreciative audience, who banged their coins on the table. Conscious of kinship bonds, the relatives of a performer led the plaudits. The programme was unrehearsed and items were offered on the spot. His tongue loosened by liquor, the chairman kept the concert lively, soliciting 'collection' between lines of oratory like:

> Hail to the Lord's anointed
> Great David greater son
> He came in the time appointed
> His reign on earth began

Typically, the sacred and the secular merged in this rich manifestation of community life. Speech-making was a prized item even if parts of the speech contained unknown Latin phrases (*tempus fugit*) and nonsense words. There was a formality about the rhythmic preamble to a speech. Invariably it began:

> As I was in yonder corner I heard the most noble chairman call my name. As I looked around and see so many lovely ladies, it charms my heart to say a word or two out of my *rignum, signum, dignum.*

Interspersing the monologue with 'Master Chairman, can I proceed', the orator invites participation from an approving audience in a chorus of: 'Proceed until morning'. Tea meetings have ceased since the 1930s, and penny concerts died in the mid-1950s with the mass exodus of rural folks to England.

Literary organizations

In 1925, Hodge Kirnon wrote of a defunct literary organization which acted as a powerful intellectual stimulant in the society. The programmes consisted of debates, discussions, impromptu addresses and other literary activities. The members were of the middle-class intelligentsia whom Kirnon referred to as 'wide-awake men'. The leading figures included

T. N. Kirnon, Austin Taylor, Fred Peters, W. Graham, Fred Nanton, P. Arthurton, and James T. Allen (father of W. H. Bramble, of political fame). An old students' association of the Montserratian Secondary School was also formed around 1941 which included fifth-formers as non-paying members. Established by the headmaster, Mr G. G. Lamacraft, it debated topical issues, encouraged its members to pursue further studies, and sponsored a scholarship to the school. The Endeavour Club, established in Plymouth in 1948, though less literature-oriented than the Kirnon group, took up the torch of informed discussion, but it was an elite, even snobbish group, with a very restricted membership.

The masses had a chance to share in the tradition of debate through the village community clubs and societies which also sprang up in the late 1940s, adding choral music and drama to their agenda. With the establishment of the Leeward Islands Unit of the UWI Extra-Mural Department in 1949, these clubs received a fillip. In July 1946, Ellen Peters, later to become a noted trade unionist, debated the issue: 'Does Tradition Hinder Progress?' at Kinsale;[9] and on 6 August 1949 a singing and elocution competition was held in Plymouth.[10] The functions of these 'literary' organizations have largely been assumed by the local UWI Centre.

Journalism was, to some extent, an offshoot of Kirnon's literary group. In 1898, the famous James T. Allen, together with James R. Peters edited and published The *Montserrat Herald*, which appeared fortnightly. Kirnon, who was sympathetic to the newspaper, recognized its deficiencies in layout and arrangement of news material (see Figure 21), but in his view it was:

> virile, fearless and outspoken. Without the slightest fear or attempt to palliate any vital issue, it exposed official negligence, incompetence and bungling; also judicial stupidity, oppressive measures and other political and economic injustices. It was hated and despised in high places.

It is no wonder that the paper was banned or that draconian regulations were introduced to curb journalism; and the imprisonment of J. T. Allen for one year may have been associated with the legal battles stemming from his publication.

The *Montserrat Herald* breathed the same spirit of its predecessor, the *Jack Spaniard*, a stinging newspaper published by Richard Piper. It was even more radical than Allen's newspaper in ventilating the burdens of the poor and the tyranny of their oppressors. It too had run foul of officialdom and went out of circulation for lack of financial support. These examples of literary men championing the cause of the poor is a valuable cultural legacy.

String and steelbands

The organ and the piano are the most obvious abiding European contribution to the music of Montserrat. It is still a mark of respectability and prestige to have the organ played at one's funeral, especially in the so-called established churches. In the first half of the twentieth century, the upper crust of society and a few struggling middle-class persons purchased pianos to enable their children to practise Brahms and Beethoven. The purpose was not just to develop and give rein to an innate desire for harmony, sound and music textured in art. It was not just a desire to embrace and appreciate what the great masters had created and passed on as part of man's universal heritage. They desired for their children to be refined and *cultured* in the Arnoldian elitist sense.[11] This skill and adornment would open social doors to their offspring, it was hoped.

Although the string band was somewhat overlooked by the 'respectable' classes, its creole energy ensured its survival. Essentially a folk band, it is a natural accompaniment to traditional songs, providing music for dances and other occasions of merriment, especially at Christmas time. It consists of six instruments and the music predictably reflects the combined European and African heritage. There is a guitar, the Hawaiian ukelele which rings out the basic melody, a triangle with its ringing, tingling sound, the boom pipe, giving depth and body to the harmony, and the fife and *shak-shak*. The cultural revival of the 1970s helped to rescue this rich ensemble from the invasion of sophisticated brass bands and stereo sets and won it general acceptance. The bands play at hotels and night clubs, but so far nothing has been done to alter its essential character.

Along with the string band, dance music was supplied by bands in which saxophones and guitars were dominant. One such band was constantly advertised in the newspapers of the 1940s and 1950s as 'Music by Sam and Pam', conveying the household names of the two leading musicians Samuel White and Thomas Nathaniel Irish. These bands, which were the precursors of the brass bands of the 1970s, enjoyed more respectability than the string band and were hired for Town Hall dances – town hall being the Council Chamber. Joe Taylor's band played at the more exclusive Cloverdale Hall for the upper classes. Against such bands, the steelband had to struggle for a place in the musical firmament.

Ryner's Village occupies an important niche in the creative history of Montserrat. Its William Brade featured prominently in the genesis of both the trade union movement, and the steelband. An impresario bringing in bands from Antigua, Brade encouraged the birth of the music in Montserrat. The steelband prototype, dubbed a 'street band', appeared in 1949 when young men using old bits of iron made 'very good harmony';[12] they paraded the streets nightly in Ryner's Village and Kinsale. In that same year the Hell's Gate Band of Ryner's Village was formed, borrowing a name from Antigua.

The steelband developed rapidly, for in 1950, it won official recognition when it was programmed in Empire Day celebrations at the Cenotaph. Recognition, however, did not come easily or evenly. An erudite snob who was born too soon to be able to realize that the steelband is 'arguably the only acoustic instrument to be invented in the 20th century (and by West Indians)',[13] denounced the steelband as hooliganism. Incensed that a demonstration of steelband music was held on the exalted grounds of the Montserrat Secondary School, he charged that such music was degrading to the moral minds of children. He was generous enough to give credit to the 'Steel Band Gang' (his words) for synchronizing harmony on crude bin-top covers, but mean and myopic enough to contend that 'such music tends to lower the moral tone and principle of classical music in the mind of the ambitious scholar'.[14] Such hifalutin' nonsense; and yet he undoubtedly spoke for a number of like-minded citizens. Writing on Empire Day (24 May), and employing a quote from the English poet Alfred, Lord Tennyson to denounce the steelband, the writer gave his letter a sad but familiar irony. It is the folk (in a creole sense of the word) who are the authentic creators and carriers of culture. With his closed anglophile mind, Mr 'Montserratian Citizen' could not envision that classical music would be played on pan or even that steelbands would be adopted by English schools three decades after he wrote.

By 1952 the steelband had developed rapidly and had spread to other villages, notably Harris in the east of the island. The Rising Sun of Harris won the first national steelband competition held in Plymouth on 28 September 1952.[15] Promoter and impresario William Brade supported the development of pan music by inviting steelbands from Antigua where pan had reached a high pitch following its transport from its native Trinidad. The steelband quickly became integrated into the life of the people and was used on varied occasions. The Blue Sky Band welcomed the Montserrat cricket team in August 1952, fresh from its first-ever away victory in the Leeward Island tournament; and, around the same time, members of the Excelsior steelband were prosecuted for their role in trade-union picketing and strikes.

Pan music declined by the end of the decade. Interest was focused on calypso at the beginning of the 1960s and it was combo bands and brass instruments that were used to accompany them, not steel or string bands. One adult band has survived mainly, it seems, for its tourist value. Any real revival rests with the emergent school bands, if these are taken beyond the mediocre stage to classical heights, as befits the association with education. It would also need to be again integrated with the life of people and not just treated as an exotic exhibit.

Calypso and carnival

Like steelband, calypso is Trinidadian in origin, but it has pervaded the Caribbean region, adopting new homes everywhere. In Montserrat, the calypso competition for the monarch of the year (which invariably ends up in controversy) is the single most popular show in the longest Christmas celebration in the world. After about 30 years of practising the art, Montserrat has earned an honourable niche in the world of calypso, due in large measure to the internationally acclaimed Alphonsus Cassell (Arrow).

So profound and so extensive has been Arrow's influence in the music world that for many persons abroad, the name Montserrat is synonymous with Arrow. There are, however, several other stars in the Montserratian calypso firmament who contributed to the development of the art form. In 1962, when Justin Cassell (Hero), the brother of Arrow, won the first national competition, only five calypsonians were in the lists. By 1979, the number had grown to 40 with 23 in the quarter-finals.[16] Hero, who sang calypso of the classical type, with trenchant criticism and searching social comment, won the crown 13 times. After becoming calypso king of the Organization of Eastern Caribbean States (OECS) in 1986, he retired from the local competition. Other key names are: Alfred Christopher (Christo), one of the earliest kings, Everton Weekes (Reality), a leading composer and one-time king (1980), Winston Christopher (Young Warrior), Cyril Fergus (Lasso) and Franklyn Dyer (Falcon). Most of these sang in Trinidad, the mecca of calypso and in North America and produced albums of appreciable quality. North, however, has approached the rarefied heights of Arrow, the doyen of Montserratian calypsonians with small single-digit rating in the calypso universe.

Born in 1951 of an upper middle-class background, Alphonsus Cassell received sixth-form education and could easily have gone on to obtain an academic degree and a white-collar position as did most of his brothers and sisters. He chose instead business and entertainment, and calypso was his vehicle to success in both. His real livelihood interest was business, for in his words, entertainment was at first merely an expensive hobby.[17] He chose business for the sense of independence it gave him, an independence which, as it turned out, enabled him to transform his hobby into a profession. Arrow first competed in 1968 and retired from the local competition in 1974 to make way for emergent artists; inevitably, he went to Trinidad in 1972, where he came under the influence of Sparrow, the Gamaliel of calypso.

Cassell rapidly became a professional calypsonian, constantly improving the quality of his art and earning a steady income as an artist. He began with a single in 1970 and a first album, *Arrow on Target*, the following year; he had recorded seven albums by 1980, and his famous soca/calypso album *Hot Hot Hot* reportedly sold over 75 000 copies in 1982. By 1985 he had captured the heart of Trinidad (having attended carnival every year since 1972); and when Arrow sang 'Raise you han' if you want to jam', people raised their hands all over the Caribbean and beyond.

With his keen commercial eye, Arrow looked to North America for exposure and support in a manner somewhat reminiscent of West Indian writers who looked to England for sponsorship and clientele in an earlier era. Spreading his feathers abroad, he did much to further internationalize the calypso in entertainment odysseys that have taken him to every continent except Australasia, infecting crowds as they dance and wail in diverse tongues. It is 'Hot Hot Hot' in Morocco as it is in Montreal, Japan, Germany or Guatemala. We no longer look outside for legitimization of our accomplishments in the Caribbean, but the appearance of Arrow on *Soul Train* and *Top of the Pops* is a useful barometer of his global appeal and the ubiquitous acceptance of this Caribbean art, of which he is so great an apostle.

Arrow is an outstanding creative artist in a dual sense. In his early days he was an exponent of the classical calypso – the national conscience warning against profligate squandering of the landed patrimony in 'Hold on to Your Property', the upholder of creole language in 'Dis is Awe Culture', the celebrator of national resilience in the face of vicious adversity in 'Man Mus' Live'. However, he searched for his own form, his own musical idiom.

From about 1979–80, the music rather than the message became dominant in his work. In the words of local journalist David Edgecombe, 'everything from soca, meringue and cadance to salsa, rap and scratch is incorporated in his music and the 'fusion' results in an international flavour which appeals to many tastes'.[18] It was music for party and jump-up with a brief but catchy storyline. In developing this new form, he consciously drew on French and Spanish Caribbean material, recreating the whole in his own image. This new calypso genre (that is what it was), made good commercial sense and brought big dollars. Arrow drew criticism for departing from the rubrics of classical calypso. Gordon Rohlehr, Professor of West Indian Literature at the University of the West Indies, Trinidad, and an authority on calypso, adverted to this change in the work of Cassell (in conversation with me). He reasoned that the change was deliberate, the artist catering to people's taste with an eye on album sales.

Arrow accepts Rohlehr's analysis, but insists that he experiences satis-faction in making people happy. As producer, the entrepreneur and enter-tainer unite in him to good advantage. By producing his own albums, he is able to ensure the integrity of his styles and trends and hit the target of the authentic Arrow every time. The artist and the businessman (he is manager and proprietor of Arrow's Man Shop) found harmony in Arrow without any great loss to art and with great gain in entertainment. Short in physical stature, Alphonsus Cassell is a tall artist and his small island has grown with him.

I shall now turn to carnival. Montserrat was Irish Catholic, and not French Catholic, and its Roman Catholic population after emancipation was a fully anglicized one. It is therefore not surprising that carnival was foreign to the island until 1962, when one was first organized by the Montserrat Junior Chamber, a young men's organization with emphasis on leadership training and community development. From Trinidad and the Windward Islands, carnival had come to neighbouring Antigua as a non-Lenten August festival. Montserrat could not long resist the event, so the question was posed in the *Observer* in April 1958: 'Will Montserrat benefit from an organised yearly carnival?'

Carnival found resistance as the steelband had done. A headmaster, R. R. Mason, gave 'a definite and unhesitating No'. He saw potential for violence and no moral, financial, educational or spiritual benefit. Indeed, he cited T. A. Marryshow as describing Trinidad, the mother of carnival, as 'a land of calypso and cutlass, or in other words a land of music and murder'.[19] In his view, the majority of our beautiful girls had gone to England, so a beauty contest was not viable; we had nothing to advertise, but Depot sweet oil, black soap and plastic (a local white rum); a change was needed from the monotonous masquerade show, but carnival was not the answer. The country said 'Yes, teacher' to the faulty analysis and so carnival was postponed for another four years.

Carnival could not long resist the forces of modernization which pushed for it. The festival emerged in 1962 to buttress tourism. If Antigua had carni-val in August, Montserrat could have it at Christmas and graft it on to the traditional Christmas festival. In the early years some folks lamented the absence of the natural energy and spontaneity of the indigenous celebration with its 'monotonous masquerade'. (Mason was nearly unique in finding the masquerade monotonous; it is happily incorporated in carnival.) However, carnival has become an integral part of Montserrat's life and has provided opportunities and outlets for a variety of arts and talents. By blending native and imported elements the organizers have achieved a pleasing cultural *pot-pourri* with a unique Montserratian flavour. There has been some loss: folks no longer 'sing out' from door to door to remind us of the coming season, but the proliferation of transistor radios, cassettes and television would have rendered this custom obsolete anyhow. Perhaps the real loss is in mummers like Miss Goosie, a high-rise puppet masking a person, John Bull in sack cloth and terrifying horns with a satanic forked stick, and the Moko Jumbie who walked on stilts and entertained the crowd with ugly antics.

Theatre and literature

Montserrat has never developed and sustained a reputable theatre company, but there have been valuable ephemeral efforts at dramatic productions and playwriting. Popular theatre emerged in the mid-1950s, mainly through village-based community organizations. While the University College of the West Indies (now UWI) did not start these groups, it saw them as valuable vehicles for developing drama and musical arts and has since been active in drama promotion in the island in one form or other. Montserrat participated in the first Leeward Islands Festival of Music and Drama organized by the UWI Extra-Mural Department and hosted in St Kitts in 1956.

The year 1957, when the island hosted the festival, was a landmark in drama development. Montserrat presented a judicious mix of four plays: an English comedy, a West Indian farce by Wilfred Redhead, a play written by F. W. Blackman, principal of the Secondary School and one by local playwright Vincent B. Browne. The island staged the winning play, with outstanding performances by George Edwards, William Graves and Iris Brown of the Salem Extra-Mural Drama Group.

Apart from isolated efforts such as the establishment of the Plymouth Renown Club in 1958 with educator and musician Edwin R. White as its first president, the next burst of activity surfaced in the 1970s. The first local UWI Resident Tutor, Dr James Irish, formed the Montserrat Theatre Group (MTG) in 1971, which featured in the national arts festival the following year. Management of MTG fell to David Edgecombe, Howard Fergus and others, but after about 15 years it faded away, unlike its companion organization, the Emerald Community Singers, which was University Centre-based. A Montserratian Amateur Dramatic Society (MADS), set up by Vincent Browne in the late 1980s, was very shortlived.

The UWI Centre has invariably been involved in theatre on the island at several levels – workshops, productions, scholarships and infrastructure. But although the MTG served the island well for many years, it too collapsed. The failure to develop a stable and permanent company is due to lack of the dedication needed in amateur theatre. It was to counterbalance this that the MTG started to pay performers, but this brought problems of its own. Training in stagecraft ought to be extended to theatre management in any new thrust in theatre development.

Montserrat has fared rather better in playwriting than in theatre. The plays of Edgar White, who is London-based, have been internationally published and performed at, among other places, the Edinburgh Festival, on Broadway and in Africa. His play on Marcus Garvey was staged in Barbados in 1987. White lives in England but his Montserrat and Caribbean background informs much of his work. *Big Business and Other Plays* by Vincent Browne was a 1991 publication, but this local drama laureate has been writing for the stage since the early 1950s, and has produced 16 plays, some of which have been staged overseas, including the Caribbean Festival of Arts (CARIFESTA) in Guyana in 1972. David Edgecombe, currently Director of the Reichhold Centre in St Thomas, completes the quartet of Montserratian playwrights of international stature if we include Archie Markham the poet, who was originally a playwright.

It can be inferred from this survey that a body of plays, albeit of uneven quality, occupies the Montserratian house of literature. Other forms exist. In the late 1960s teacher and journalist (now lawyer) Dorcas White made Montserrat's first creative writing publication in *Songs of the Soul*, a small personal volume of philosophical reflections in verse; and in 1972, Dr James Irish published *Alliouagana Voices*, which gave this first outlet to local writers, apart from the newspapers which carried the occasional poem, usually of a political nature.

On becoming Resident Tutor in 1973, I established an ongoing Creative Writing Workshop (now the Montserrat Writers Maroon) with the avowed aim of stimulating creative writing and developing a Montserratian literature. A supporting mechanism was an annual St Patrick's Day creative writing competition. This has produced creditable pieces in the genres of short story and poetry which have been published in regional and international literary magazines and anthologized at home and abroad. This writer apart, significant names that have emerged include Violet J. Grell, Elcia Daniel, Jamaal Jeffers, Ann Marie Dewar, Yvonne Weekes and Jacqueline Browne. The emphasis for the future has to be on strict attention to quality in an effort to distil a lasting literature from extant and emerging pieces.

We are yet to produce a home-grown novelist, although there are two names on which the island has at least marginal claim. The first is Ruel White, who was born in Montserrat in 1950, emigrated to London at the age of four and has since lived there. A writer of songs and lyrics, his first published piece of literature was a short story which appeared in *New Beacon Review* in July 1985. Since then, he has published at least one novel.

The other novelist is Mathew Phipps Shiell who was born in Montserrat on 20 July 1865 to Mathew Dowdy and Priscilla Ann Shiell, who were Irish. Schooled at Harrison College in Barbados where, among other things, he learnt chemistry and Greek, the gifted young man wrote (not published) his first novel at age 12 and went on to produce 24 in all. It is not known if he was related to the great estate magnate and slave-owner Queely Shiell (266 slaves in 1810) or to William Shiell, who managed the estates and was President of the Council in 1842. None of his novels are set in Montserrat, but his poetic, 'picturesque' and 'overcharged' style may have been influenced by the awesome beauty of the island which he described as a 'mountain-mass, loveliest of the lovely, but touchy, uncertain, dashing into tantrums, hurricanes, earthquakes, brooks, bubbling-hot soufrières (sulphur-swamps), floods, fit nurse for a poetic child'.[20] This extravagance seemed to have been characteristic of his style.

Meanwhile Archie Markham, who had migrated to

> ... a far land where half my life
> was scheduled to be lived

became one of the leading West Indian creative writers in England. At first he wrote and directed plays, but it is as story-writer and poet (especially poet) that he excels. With the aid of a number of writing fellowships and positions as writer in residence, he has published several collections of his work and edited several books and magazines. Among his latest work was *Hinterland* (1989) containing the works of 14 West Indian poets writing from both sides of the Atlantic. Markham currently teaches in a Master's course in creative writing at the Hallam University of Sheffield.

In his words, 'someone in academic power in Barbados', reportedly denied Markham's right to be a West Indian writer.[21] Whatever else he is not, he is a Montserratian writer. Yes, he draws inspiration and experience from the immediacy of his environment, whether it is Papua New Guinea or Ulster, but he is nourished by abiding influences of home – his grandmother, his schooldays, the ruined house of his childhood and the physical and social space which these encompass; he periodically returns physically to the source to drink, breathe and write. With his unique style characterized by a trenchant but subtle humour, a wry, unobtrusive irony and astute political comment, Markham is Montserrat's broadest entry point to international literature.

Customs

Marronage, denoting communities of runaway slaves, was unknown to tiny even if mountainous Montserrat, but Montserrat had maroons, an

African communistic practice. This is the voluntary cooperative activity of a number of persons who combined to assist one or more persons in a particular task. Typical tasks were the building or moving of a house, the preparing of land for planting, and the harvesting of a big crop. In the 1970s, when the Government tried unsuccessfully to establish cooperatives with the help of the American Peace Corps, it might have been prudent to look into the history of maroons for guidance and inspiration.

Another communal activity associated with economic survival is what was termed 'minding'. A more successful person gave a reliable neighbour one or more head of stock to rear for one-third or one-half of the offspring.[22] Sometimes the contract was expressed as: 'half improvement and half increase'. It was all done by mutual agreement on a friendly basis, mostly without any legal document.

The 'box hand' was another valuable example of cooperative activity for economic advancement. A number of persons contributed equal sums regularly to a common pool and each in turn obtained the entire sum, which could then be invested in a big project. This was a useful mechanism for compulsory saving, especially in pre-bank days and in the days when such institutions were not fully trusted. In any case, it was certainly safer than burying money in the earth or wadding it on to the person.

Cricket, more than a game

Montserrat has had its moments of shame in cricket, the game at which West Indians have outstripped the British from whom they learnt it; but the island has also had its run of glory. Indeed, many justifiably contend that the little island has produced world-class cricketers in persons like Nathaniel Fox, Sylvester Davis and Jim Allen. In his model Leeward Islands team, chosen from players ranging from 1946 to 1963, Kittian cricketer and cricket journalist Austin Eddy included Davis and D. R. V. (Frank) Edwards. In his view, this team at its peak could have held its own in a test match anywhere.[23] It is surprising though that Eddy placed Davis at eleven in the batting order below Antiguan Hubert Anthonyson.

The island began playing in the Leeward Island tournament from its inception in 1913. Antigua and St Kitts were regarded as the front-line teams, while Montserrat and Nevis, which did not enter until 1949, were regarded as weaker teams. Individual cricketers have nevertheless registered outstanding performances. R. A. Piper, for instance, held a Leeward Islands record with seven wickets for 20 runs in a match against Antigua in 1925. It took the island 21 years to win its first tournament, which it did at home in 1934, repeating the feat in 1938. The heroic names included Nat West, James Pyke, Willie Harris, Dick Weeks, Charles E. Greenaway, Joe Fergus and Cyril Taylor. Taylor had also featured in the 1930 tournament in Dominica when the team was captained by his father M. A. Taylor, an estate manager, and included two of his brothers. In the 1938 match Eddie Roberts, an off-break bowler, distinguished himself by taking a hat-trick (that is, wickets in three successive balls) against Antigua.

Years of hope and frustration followed the 1938 triumph. In 1946, for instance, led by a Kittian, Edgar Berridge, Montserrat defeated Antigua in St Kitts. Antigua had considered its victory over Montserrat as a foregone conclusion and had reportedly omitted its pace-bowler Challenger, so that he could rest for the epic St Kitts–Antigua duel. Montserrat, however, lost to St Kitts, with George McMahon setting a new record of 167 runs. Montserrat flattered with a response of 81 for no loss, but soon collapsed, a pattern which became familiar in succeeding years.

It should not be surprising that in this period Montserratian cricket reflected the class-based nature of West Indian cricket of the era and indeed of the society itself. Hardly any ordinary citizen made the team, especially if he were from the rural area; and captains were either white, white-inclined or upper-middle class. If he possessed this colour or class qualification it was relatively easy for a non-Montserratian cricketer to gain the captaincy, as Edgar Berridge did when he became Commissioner's Clerk and Commander of the Defence Force in Montserrat. A white Antiguan, Clement Gomez, who was Curator at the Department of Agriculture, captained the team for many years including the victorious years, 1934 and 1938. From all accounts, both Gomez and Berridge had more than colour and position to commend them, since they were actually able cricketers.

The financial demands of the game reinforced the class element. With an indigent Sports Association, most cricketers had to finance themselves, including their passages to Leeward Island tournaments. It was therefore possible for persons with marginal ability, but with money and middle-class 'manners', to make the team and even the captaincy. It was reportedly on this basis that Stuart Mercer skippered the team in 1939. He could pay his way and sponsor someone else. Cricket reinforced the class divisions.

Even among the Plymouth clubs, the social divide was evident. The Pickwicks, headed by Clement Gomez, attracted the upper crust such as planter Wilfred Griffin. A couple of cuts below, the Wanderers, headed by M. A. Taylor, included the cricketer and indefatigable cricket administrator William 'King' Graham. The Wanderers themselves catered to a certain level of clients but M. A. Taylor reportedly rose above the snootiness to encourage and foster local talent from whatever class. Other clubs catered for lesser mortals. Interestingly enough, there was also a Pickwick Cricket Club in Barbados which catered to white men. Montserratian whites and white equivalents very likely copied the name and behaviour from Little England. A Pickwick Club still exists in Barbados.

The exclusiveness of the sport had attenuated somewhat by 1951 when gold finally came. Montserrat notched up its first away victory with Sydney Meade, a senior civil servant as captain. The 'man of the match' was Sylvester Davis with 97 runs not out, and 11 wickets. The local newspaper described him as 'the best all-rounder in the Leewards today and the best cricketer Montserrat has seen'. It was a superb performance, but he was supported with outstanding performances by Sydney Meade and H. Mason.[24] Played in Nevis, the match gave inspiration to the Nevisians, who had not yet won the tournament. The victorious players returned to a jubilant Montserrat that greeted them with a motorcade and steelband music.

Montserrat seemed to be developing a winning habit when two years later it won the tournament at home, defeating St Kitts for the first time with what Eddy described as 'the best Montserrat team'. Full of expectations, an unprecedented crowd streamed into Sturge Park for the occasion, and 'the colour of the grounds was bathed with a galaxy of beautiful ladies'.[25] Ably assisted by Sydney Meade and Theodore Bramble, George Edwards (then teacher George, now Rev. George Edwards), routed the Antiguan and Kittian teams in turn. This was Montserrat's last taste of victory. Montserrat continued to produce outstanding individual cricketers such as George Allen, Jim Allen, Fitzroy Buffonge, Alford Coriette, D. R. V. Edwards and Kingsley Rock and has at times come close to winning, but the prize has since eluded them.

Quite apart from victory on the field, one of the things which the game has lost is the national following and the occasion of fun off the field. A cricket match was a community event whether it was played between two country teams on a crude pitch, at Hyde Park in Harris, a village which has produced many persons (including women) who are knowledgeable of cricket, or whether it is a formal tournament at Sturge Park. A match was a social occasion which assumed the flavour and atmosphere of a party, where liquor flowed like runs. The reality is that cricket no longer occupies the pre-eminent place it did as a national sport, especially with so many other recreational avenues open to the populace. And yet because of the international status of cricket, it still possesses the potential to evoke national pride and bolster collective self-respect. A victory in the Leeward Islands tournament can still work wonders for the game in Montserrat, and there is much in the past to still inspire such a victory.

Radio

Even with the pervasive influence of television, radio continues to be a powerful purveyor and shaper of culture. It does this both through its 'educational' function and by its decisions on what people hear. The home of three radio stations, including Radio Antilles with its regional outreach, Plymouth is an important Caribbean media capital. It all began in a basement in Olveston in 1952 when, on his own initiative, Frank Delisle (the founder of Leeward Islands Air Transport (LIAT) also in Montserrat at Olveston), established Radio Montserrat. It was the first national radio in the Leeward Islands and was rooted in voluntarism. Delisle set up his private transmitter in his own home, but monies provided by Colonial Development and Welfare purchased some of the equipment. An unpaid broadcasting committee kept Radio Montserrat on the air twice weekly until 1957, when it moved to its new studio at the Grove. It has been particularly useful in promoting cultural and community events and in assembling discussants around development issues. Its cultural programmes helped to set trends, develop tastes and give public exposure to artists.

The next landmark was in 1966 when the powerful Antilles Radio Corporation, a subsidiary of Deutsche Welle of West Germany, started its operations here. Transmitting with 200 000 watts covering the Caribbean and beyond, it was said to be the most powerful radio station in the Western hemisphere. Its leadership was German, but its programme and focus were Caribbean, and its Caribbeanness in news and culture did much to break down some of the stifling anglophile conservatism of the Emerald Isle.

Concluding note/cultural identity

In arts and culture Montserrat has a rich and goodly heritage, but much of it is inchoate and uncoordinated, without developmental focus. This is so in spite of the salutary work of a National Trust formed in 1970 to preserve the cultural patrimony, among other things. What is still needed is an explicit cultural policy which gives focus and purpose to the arts as an aspect of national development – a policy that recognizes the economic implications of the cultural arts. Such a policy will demonstrate some political will and sophistication, and justify the provision of promotional resources.

Unrepentantly colonial, up to 1970 Montserrat experienced no real sense of nationhood or cultural cohesion. Britannia's rule was absolute. A cultural awakening sparked by activities of the UWI Centre in the early

1970s generated change. Folk stories, songs and dances were researched and staged and some respectability was given to 'nation language' as a valid medium of communication and as a vehicle of art. This, as we have seen, met with resistance and criticism. Montserratians are still not fully certain of what they are, but some semblance of a cultural identity is struggling to be born, and the 'rhythm of Africa' is at last finding a respected place in the cultural amalgam. The Montserrat National Trust contributed significantly in the area of historical research and work on flora and fauna but, founded and dominated by expatriates from a different culture, it has had its limitations.

The decision in 1985 to make St Patrick's Day a national holiday and to celebrate Montserratian heroes past and present with activities rooted in creole culture is contributing to the development of a national and cultural identity. A recent decision by the Government to create a national song (1993) is a healthly signal. It needs to go further, and follow most of the former British colonial territories in the region and give the name of a local hero to the national airport. At present, it carries the name of a former Governor of the Leeward Islands, who also became Governor of Jamaica. Developments like these will have a cumulative impact on the emergence of a distinctive Montserratian identity – one which is strong enough to recognize the composite nature of the culture without losing its soul. Montserrat can be colonial in constitution, if it thinks it has to be, without being crassly colonial in identity and mentality. In more senses than one, complete emancipation is yet to be won.

Notes

Introduction

1. E. Goveia, *Slave Society in the British Leeward Islands at the End of the Seventeenth Century.*
2. D. Hall, *Five of the Leewards.*
3. A. G. MacGregor, 'The Royal Society Expedition to Montserrat B. W. I. The Volcanic History and Petrology of Montserrat with Observations on Mt. Pelè in Martinique' *Philosophical Transactions of The Royal Society of London*, p.13.
4. CO 152/415/15 J. P. Purcell Edwards, Superintendent of Works Antigua to T. E. P. Baynes, Commissioner of Montserrat.
5. N. Nugent, 'An Account of the "Sulphur" or "Soufriere" of the island of Montserrat', *Transactions of the Geological Soceity*, pp.185–90.
6. F. A. Perret, *The Volcanic – Seismic Crisis at Montserrat*, p.22.
7. CO 152/415/15, *op. cit.*
8. For a detailed study of Montserrat's soil, see D. M. Lang, *Soil and Land Use Surveys No.22 Montserrat.*
9. *Ibid.,* p.6.
10. J. Davy, *The West Indies Before and Since Slave Emancipation*, p.409.
11. N. Nugent, *op. cit.,* p.186.
12. H. Coleridge, *Six Months in the West Indies*, pp.180–1.
13. D. W. Steadmon, *et al.* 'Vertebrates from Archeological Sites on Montserrat, West Indies', p.1.
14. J. R. Blankenship, *The Wildlife of Montserrat*, p.66.

Chapter One   Settlement

1. I. Van Sertima, *The African Presence in Ancient America: They Came Before Columbus.*
2. S. E. Morrison, *Admiral of the Ocean Sea*, Vol.2, p.399.
3. R. Bullen, (private Correspondence with Mr and Mrs E. Herman of Old Town, Montserrat).

4. J. Rouse, *Prehistory of the West Indies* (a pamphlet).
5. D. R. Watters, *Transect Survey and Prehistoric Site Location on Barbuda and Montserrat* (Dissertation), Department of Anthropology, University of Pittsburgh, 1980. (Typescript).
6. D. R. Watters, 'Montserrat's Amerindian Heritage' in *Montserrat: Holiday 1995–1996,* Government of Montserrat, 1995.
7. J. B. Petersen, 'Archaeology of Trants, Montserrat, Part 3:Chronological and Settlement Data' *Annals of the Carnegie Museum,* Vol.65 No.4 pp.223–61.
8. T. S. English, *Records of Montserrat*, p.47.
9. A. Gwynn, 'Documents Relating to the Irish in the West Indies', *Analecta Hibernia*, p.209.
10. C. S. S. Higham, *The Development of the Leeward Islands under the Restoration 1660–1688*, p.36.
11. Higham, *op. cit.*, p.123.
12. D. Akenson, *If the Irish Ran the World Montserrat 1630–1730*, Liverpool, Liverpool University Press, 1997.
13. Higham, *op. cit.,* p.139.
14. G. Mendes, *The Leeward Islands Review*, 1937, p.9.
15. D. Akenson *op. cit.*
16. V. T. Harlow, *Colonizing Expedition to the West Indies and Guiana 1623–1677*, p.83.
17. Cited in A. Gwynn, 'Documents relating to the Irish in the West Indies', p.184.
18. Gwynn, 'Early Irish Emigration to the West Indies', p.391.
19. M. D. Higgins, *Montserrat and Its Irish Connection* (Unpublished Lecture) Montserrat, March 2000.
20. *Calendar of State Papers, American and West Indies*, Vol.LXI, No.70.
21. E. Curtis, *A History of Ireland*, 1961, p.233.
22. This information was supplied by Niall Brunicardi of Ireland, a researcher on the Irish in the West Indies.
23. M. D. Higgins, *op. cit.*
24. D. Akenson, *op. cit.*
25. J. Oldmixon, *The British Empire in America*, Vol.2, New York, Augustus Kelley Publishers, 1969 (1741).
26. S. English, p.82.
27. CSP LXI, No.70.
28. A. Gwynn, *op. cit.*, p.209.
29. D. Akenson, *op. cit.*
30. *The Laws of Montserrat*, No.6 of 1668.
31. R. S. Dunn, *Sugar and Slaves*, p.35.
32. CO 1/41, 193–243.
33. J. du Tertre, *Histoire Générale des Antilles*, p.199–205.

34. Gwynn, 'Documents', *op. cit.*, p.279.

35. CSP 550, No.52.

36. CSP 1689–92, No.43, p.204.

37. CSP 550, No.52.

38. CSP 1697–98, No.828.

39. *The Diary of John Baker*, p.11.

40. Gwynn, *op. cit.*, p.222.

41. CSP 1669–74, No.76/77.

42. A. Burns, *A History of the British West Indies*, p.339.

43. CO 153/1, quoted in R. Berleant Schiller, 'Free Labour and the Economy in Seventeenth Century Montserrat'.

44. J. Black, *The Blathwayte Atlas*, Vol.1, Providence, 1970.

45. CSP 1689–92, No.2060.

Chapter Two   Sugar

1. CO (CSP) 390/6, p.117.

2. CSP 1681–85, Col. paper, Vol.LXV, No.9.

3. Gwynn 'Documents' pp.214–19.

4. L. M. Pulsipher, 'Seventeenth Century Montserrat: An Environmental Impact Statement', p.9.

5. D. Akenson, *If the Irish Ran the World: Montserrat 1630–1730* 6, Higham, p.184.

7. C. and R. Bridenbaugh, *No Peace Beyond the Lines*, p.82.

8. CSP 1574–1660, Vol.XI.

9. Gwynn, *op. cit.*, p.205.

10. *Ibid.*, p.216.

11. *Ibid.*, p.223.

12. *Ibid.*

13. Higham, *op. cit.*, p.149.

14. CSP (Entry Book), Volume XXIX, p.290.

15. D. Watts, *The West Indies: Patterns of Development Culture and Environmental Change Since 1492*, p.336.

16. *Ibid.*

17. English, p.224. He suggests that the faulty arithmetic is due to some confusion between sterling and currency.

18. *Acts of Montserrat*, No.36 of 1693.

19. Goveia, p.103.

20. B. Edwards, *The History Civil and Commercial of the British Colonies in the West Indies*, 1793, quoted in T. S. English, p.37.

21. Goveia, *op. cit.*, p.122.

22. M. G. Lewis, *Journal of a West Indian Proprietor*.
23. Dunn, p.141.
24. CSP, Vol.XLIII, No.173.
25. R. Pares, *War and Trade in the West Indies*, p.246.
26. Du Tertre, 1667–71.
27. Higham, *op. cit.*, 1921, p.48.
28. CSP 550, No.41.
29. Burns, p.379.
30. Pares, *op. cit.*, 1963, p.181.
31. CO 155/1 (Council Minutes).
32. CO 152/9.
33. *Ibid.*
34. D. R. Crandall and B. S. Dyde, p.17.
35. Burns, p.584.
36. Dunn, p.129.
37. Stapleton Papers.
38. *Acts of Montserrat* No.112 of 1736.
39. Dunn, *op. cit.*, p.125.
40. H. Beckles, *A History of Barbados*, p.41.
41. R. Berleant-Schiller, 'Free Labour and the Economy in Seventeenth-Century Montserrat', p.558.
42. R. Sheridan, *The Development of Plantations to 1780: An Era of West Indian Property*, p.94.
43. F. Watkins, *Handbook of the Leeward Islands*, p.198.
44. L. Pulsipher and C. M. Goodwin, *Galways Plantation, Montserrat, West Indies*, 1981, Field Report (Department of Geography, University of Tennessee, Knoxville, 1982).
45. Pulsipher, 'Galways Plantation, Montserrat' *Seeds of Change* p.143.
46. Pulsipher, *ibid.*
47. C. M. Goodwin, *Sugar Time and Englishmen: A Study of Management Strategies on Caribbean Plantations*, p.60.
48. J. R. V. Johnston, *The Stapleton Sugar Plantation in the Leeward Islands*, pp.175–9.

Chapter Three   Slavery

1. D. Akenson, *If the Irish Ran the World: Montserrat 1630–1730*.
2. D. Somerville, *The Early Years of Montserrat*, p.15.
3. From the author's notes made from records at the County Hall in Bristol.
4. *Acts of the Assembly of Montserrat 1668–1740*.
5. Goveia, p.243.

6. Dunn, p.128.
7. K. Kiple and V. Kiple, 'Deficiency Diseases in the Caribbean', p.174.
8. R. Mann, L. Meadows, W. M. Bass, D. R. Watters, 'Description of Skeletal remains from a Black Cemetery from Montserrat, West Indies', *Annals of Carnegie Museum*, Vol.56, 1987, pp.319–36.
9. R. Edwards (ed.), *Equiano's Travels*, 1967, p.78.
10. CO 155/1, Council Minutes, 1693.
11. CO 155/6, Council Minutes, 1721–2.
12. CO 151/1, Council Minutes, 1692.
13. Dunn, *op. cit.*, p.239; E. Goveia, pp.20–1.
14. CO 155/6, Council Minutes, 1723–4.
15. *Ibid.*, 1698.
16. Watkins, p.32.
17. CO 153/22. Correspondence, Commander-in-Chief to the Governor.
18. H. A. Fergus, 'St. Patrick's Day in Focus', *Montserrat Reporter*, 27 March 1992.

Chapter Four   Irish and African emancipation

1. H. Coleridge, *Six Months in the West Indies in 1825*, p.282.
2. English, p.282.
3. L. T. Ragatz, 'Absence Landlordism in the British Caribbean', p.16.
4. CO 393/1, Bathurst's approval of Semper's appointment, 23 October 1826.
5. J. Gyorgy, 'The Other Emerald Isle', the *Gazette, Montserrat Reporter*, 11 March 1992.
6. J. Messenger, *Montserrat: The Most Distinctively Irish Settlement in the New World*, p.301.
7. D. Akenson, p.180.
8. M. D. Higgins, p.6.
9. J. C. Wells, 'The Brogue that Isn't' *Journal of the International Phonetics Association*, Vol.10, 74–9.
10. A Demets (Bishop), *The Catholic Church in the Emerald Isle of the West*, p.26.
11. English, p.264.
12. CO 318/64.
13. G. E. Lawrence, *Montserrat and its Methodism*, Vol.1, p.141, and R. Berleant-Schiller, 'Montserrat during the Emancipation Process 1810–1826', p.7.
14. CO 318/64.
15. F. E. Peters, *The Abolition of Slavery*, p.8.
16. *Ibid.*, p.6. See also CO 318/64 (Official Report on the Colony).
17. Goveia, pp.97–8.

18. R. Berleant-Schiller (1994), p.6.
19. F. E. Peters, *op. cit.*, p.8.
20. Lawrence, p.20.
21. Hall, p.24.
22. T. S. English, *op. cit.*, p.290.
23. J. Sturge and T. Harvey, *The West Indies in 1837*, p.88.
24. *Ibid.*, p.82.
25. See SO 7/64 *Sixth Report of the Stipendiary Justice of the Island of Montserrat*, and R. Berleant-Schiller, *Land and Livelihood in Montserrat after the End of Slavery*, pp.5 and 6.
26. *Ibid.* John C. Collins to T. S. Warner. Letter accompanying Sixth Report.
27. CO 7/54 Address of the Assembly sent to the General Council of the Leeward Islands, 20 February 1838.

Chapter Five   Establishing a free society

1.   CO 7/54 President Hamilton to Governor W. G. Colebrooke.
2.   Davy, p.427.
3.   Government House Archives, 82–106, Legislative Council Minutes, 1861–1913; D. Hall, pp.161–3.
4.   CO 7/99.
5.   Hall, *op. cit.*, p.172.
6.   Government House, *op. cit.*
7.   Berleant-Schiller, 'Land and Livelihood in Montserrat after the end of Slavery', Preliminary Conference Draft, 1992.
8.   Hall, *op. cit.*, pp.174–5.
9.   CO 7/143, Address to the Legislative Council, Antigua, 13 August 1870.
10. CO 7/143, The Leeward Islands Federation.
11. Government House 82–106, *op. cit.*, 7 October 1886.
12. Hall, *op. cit.*, p.180.
13. CO 7/64, Letter to Governor W. G. Colebrooke, 1 November 1839.
14. W. K. Marshall, 'Notes on Peasant Development in the West Indies since 1835', *Social and Economic Studies*, Vol. 17, pp.252–3.
15. R. Berleant-Schiller, 'Free Labour and the Economy in Seventeenth Century Montserrat', pp.540–61.
16. Berleant-Schiller (1992), p.8.
17. CO 7/91, A. Brinn, to Colonial Office.
18. Hall, *op. cit.*, p.147.
19. CO 7/64 Henry Hamilton's Comment on the Stipendiary Magistrate's Report for 30 August 1839.
20. CO 7/64 Ninth Report of the Special Stipendiary Justice, 1 March 1840.

21. Berleant-Schiller, *op. cit.*, p.9.
22. Government House, 82–106, *op. cit.*
23. CO 7/64 Report on the Leeward Islands to M. Stephen, February 1840.
24. Government House Archives 82–18, *Montserrat Book of Acts 1827–1869.*
25. Berleant-Schiller, *op. cit.*, p.12.
26. Lawrence, Vol. 1, p.68.
27. CO 7/72, The Governor Charles A. Fitzroy to Lord Stanley regarding Montserrat.
28. *Ibid.,* Stipendiary Magistrate's Report for April and May 1842.
29. CO 7/91, A. Brinn to Colonial Office.
30. CO 7/64, Correspondence of Thomas S. Warner, 1 December 1839.
31. Government House Archives 82–18, *op. cit.*
32. *Ibid.*
33. Government House Archives 82–106, 1868.
34. Watkins, p.177.
35. CO 7/102.
36. H. Kirnon, *Montserrat and Montserratians*, p.24.
37. CO 177/30 Legislative Council Minutes 1881–1901.

Chapter Six   Alternatives to sugar: Cotton becomes King

1. R. Beachey, *British West Indies Sugar Industry*, p.63.
2. CO 7/64, Thomas S. Warner's Report to the Governor, 1 December 1839.
3. Hall, p.112.
4. *Ibid.,* p.132.
5. West Indian Royal Commission Report, 1897, p.129.
6. CO 7/64, Francis Burke to Stanley, Secretary of State, 1841.
7. Hall, *op. cit.*, p.130.
8. West Indian Royal Commission Report 1897, p.128.
9. A. Aspinal, *The British West Indies*, 1912, p.194.
10. Sturge Family Papers seen by the author at Waterworks in Montserrat when they were in possession of Joseph Sturge, a grand-nephew of the first Joseph Sturge.
11. The Beasley Report, 1953, p.20.
12. *Montserrat Observer*, 31 January 1942, p.3.
13. *Report on the Presidencies of the Leeward Islands Colony for the Year 1936*, p.37. (Advocate Co., Ltd, Barbados.)
14. CO 950/156. Commissioner T. E. P. Baynes's memorandum to the West India Royal Commission 1938 (Moyne Commission).
15. CO 950/537 Letter of T. E. P. Baynes to the Moyne Commission, October 1938.
16. CO 1042/339, The Montserrat Development Association; Note by the Governor, K. W. Blackburne, 30 June 1953.

17. *Colonial Report: Leeward Islands 1953 and 1954,* London, HMSO, 1956, p.63.
18. A. Tyrrell, *Joseph Sturge,* 1987, p.232.
19. Montserrat Company, *Minutes of Directors, 7* July 1934. Sturge Family Papers.
20. Colonial Reports, *op. cit.,* p.61.
21. CO Memorandum of G. J. Retheus to the West India Commission, p.3.
22. CO 950/545, Letter to Lloyd from T. A. Twyman, 13 April 1939.
23. CO 537/6118, *Leeward Islands Reports 1950.*
24. CO 950/550, G. J. Retheus, *op. cit.*

Chapter Seven   Trade unions and politics

1. *Leeward Islands Federal Department of Labour Annual Report 1947,* p.33 (Labour Report).
2. Memorandum by Federal Labour Officer to the Acting Commissioner, 25 November 1945. File M38/29 Government House Archives.
3. CO 950/545, The West India Royal Commission Record of the First Session in Montserrat, 3 January 1939, p.7.
4. Beasley, p.13.
5. *Rules of the Montserrat Trades and Labour Union,* 1946, p.1.
6. Labour Report, *op. cit.,* p.7.
7. *Leeward Islands Report,* 1951, p.8.
8. *Montserrat Observer,* 8 June 1946, p.1.
9. Labour Report, *op. cit.,* p.47.
10. *Ibid.,* 25 March 1950, pp.5–6.
11. *Ibid.*
12. CO 537/7366, *Leeward Islands Report 1950,* p.4.
13. *Montserrat Observer,* 5 March 1949, p.4.
14. CO 537/7366 *Leeward Islands Report, June 1951.*
15. H. Fergus, *History of Alliouagana: A Short History of Montserrat,* p.39.
16. *Montserrat Observer,* 5 March 1949, pp.3–4.
17. CO 537/7366, *Leeward Islands Report, April 1951,* p.14.
18. *Montserrat Observer,* 24 January 1953, p.1.
19. CO 1031/513, Blackburne to Wallace from Government House, Antigua, 3 July 1953.
20. CO 1031/135, *Leeward Island Reports, June 1953.*
21. CO 1031/513, *op. cit.*
22. *Montserrat Observer,* 11 July 1953 (supplement page).
23. *Montserrat Observer,* 21 December 1957, p.5.
24. CO 1031/2283, Governor A. T. Williams on the Constitution, 1958, Government House, Antigua.
25. CO 1031/513, *op. cit.*

26. *Montserrat Observer*, 14 February 1953, p.6.

27. *Ibid.*, 17 August 1957.

28. S. B. Philpott, *West Indian Migration. The Montserrat Case*, p.29.

29. HMSO, *Montserrat 1965 and 1966, 1968*, p.3.

30. HMSO, *Montserrat: Reports for the Years 1963 and 1964*, 1966, p.4.

31. *Montserrat Mirror*, 22 April 1967, p.3.

32. A, Solomon, 'Montserrat, a wee bit o' Ireland in the Caribbean' *Travel-Holiday*, October 1984, p.46.

33. *Montserrat Observer*, 24 August 1957, p.5.

34. *Idem*, 31 August 1957, p.4.

35. J. A. Irish, *Life in a Colonial Crucible*, p.85.

36. *The Workers' Defense: A MAWU Newsletter*, Vol. 2, No. 1. p.4. 1984.

37. H. A. Fergus, 'Problems of Micro Parliaments in Caribbean Micro States', p.31.

Chapter Eight   Education in the twentieth century

1. Government House Archives 82–106, File 30/1933, *Visit of Mr. Marriot, one of the Education Commissioners* (Montserrat Commissioner's Office).

2. CO 950/547, Memorandum from Montserrat Association of Teachers to the Royal Commission to the West Indies.

3. CO 950/545, Commissioner's Memorandum to the Moyne Commission (Education), p.2.

4. Lawrence, p.75.

5. *Ibid.*, p.74.

6. CO 1031/490, Education Policy of the Leeward Islands, 1942–1946.

7. HMSO, *Colonial Reports Leeward Islands 1953 and 1954*, p.91.

8. CO 7/64 Stipendiary Magistrate's Report 194.

9. Government House File 30/1933, *op. cit.*

10. HMSO, *Colonial Reports Leeward Islands 1953 and 1954*, p.93.

11. *The Hammond Report, Part IV*, p.41.

12. D. F. Browne, *A Survey of the Development and Growth of Secondary Education in the Island of Montserrat, West Indies*, p.15.

13. Government House Archives 82–441, File 30/1993, *op. cit.*

14. *Ibid.*

15. *Ibid.*, Commissioner T. E. P. Baynes to the Acting Colonial Secretary, Antigua.

16. *Ibid.*, Minutes of a Committee of Management Meeting of the Montserrat Grammar School.

17. H. DeR. Walker, *The West Indies and the Empire*, p.24.

18. Government House Archives 82–106, Minutes of Legislative Council, 23 September 1914.

19. CO 1042/355 *Leeward Islands – Education Objectives*.

20. D. Jeffcock, *An Evaluation of Technical College Training in The Eastern Caribbean*, p.6.
21. M. Bray, *et al.*, *Secondary Education in Montserrat; a Report on the Potential for Expansion and Restoration*, 1985, p.9.
22. S. Osborne. 'Let's Talk', *The Montserrat Reporter*, Vol. VI, no. 27, p.7.
23. *Review of Educational Performance: Montserrat* (Pennycuick Report), p.13.
24. H. A. Fergus, *Rule Britannia: Politics in British Montserrat*, p.80.
25. E. Miller *et al.*, *Foundation for the Future: OECS Education Reform Strategy*, p.80.
26. CO 1042/355.
27. P. Sherlock, 'The Extra-Mural Work of the College', *Pelican Annual*, 1956.
28. *Montserrat Observer*, 26 August 1950, p.5.
29. A. Pearse, quoted by H. A. Fergus in *Bulletin of Eastern Caribbean Affairs*, Vol.16, no.2., 1990, p.17.

Chapter Nine   Political developments after 1970

1. *Manifesto of the People's Liberation Movement*, 1978, p.3.
2. *Minutes* for Opening Session of the Legislative Council 1971, Council Chamber.
3. 'Montserrat, A Right about Turn' (Interview) *The Caribbean and West Indies Chronicle*, June/July 1979, p.14.
4. Irish, 1991, p.33.
5. Irish, p.8.
6. *Montserrat Mirror*, 10 March 1978, p.1.
7. For an elaboration of the idea of the 'politician-king' see my 'Electoral Behaviour in Montserrat', *Caribbean Quarterly*, Vol.27, no.1, 1984, pp.32–41.
8. *Montserrat Reporter*, 14 August 1987, p.1.
9. *Manifesto of the People's Liberation Movement*, p.2.
10. Rodney Gallagher, *Report on the Survey of Offshore Finance Sectors in the Caribbean Dependent Territories*, London, HMSO, 1990, p.104.
11. *Montserrat Magazine*, 17 August 1992, p.8.
12. *Montserrat Reporter*, 23 September 1991, p.4.
13. *Montserrat Times*, 24 November 1989, p.12.
14. H. A. Fergus, 'Constitutional Downgrading for Montserrat: Tampering with the Constitution', *Caribbean Affairs*, Vol.3, no.2, 1990, p.66.
15. O. C. Mathurin, 'Electoral Change in Montserrat and Antigua', T. Monroe and R. Lewis (eds), *Readings in Government and Politics of the West Indies*, 1971, p.147.
16. P. A. Bramble, *Montserrat Mirror*, 8 October 1971, p.5.
17. A. Lewis, *Agony of the Eight*, 1965, p.16.

18. G. K. Lewis, *The Growth of the Modern West Indies*, p.137.

19. P. A. Bramble, *Montserrat Times*, Vol.3, no.43, 25 November 1983, p.1.

20. B. Osborne, in *Report on the United Nations Visiting Mission to Montserrat*, 1982, p.20.

21. J. A. Osborne (Interview), 'Montserrat: A Swing to the Right and Independence?', *Caribbean and West Indies Chronicle*, June/July 1979, p.14.

22. *Montserrat News*, Vol.III, issue 5, p.2.

23. 1991 *Manifesto, National Development Party*, p.25.

24. *National Progressive Party Manifesto* 1991 p.12.

25. Quoted in the *Montserrat Reporter* Vol.XII No.16 Friday 26 April 1996, p.1.

26. 'Now Is the Time', *Montserrat Reporter* Vol.XII No.20 Friday 24 May 1996, p.1.

27. H. A. Fergus *et al.*, *Montserrat: The Report of the Elections Commission*, Montserrat, Government of Montserrat, 1996 p.15.

28. *Ibid.*

29. *Observer* 24 August 1997, p.1.

30. The National Progressive Party: The Candidates (NPP Brochure, back page).

31. FCO, *Partnership for Progress and Prosperity: Britain and the Overseas Territories* London, HMSO, Cm4264, 1999.

32. H. Durand & B. Roach 'Montserratians and British Citizenship' *Montserrat Reporter* Vol.XVI No.26 p.12.

33. H. A. Fergus *et al.*, *The Report of the Election Commissioners 1999* Montserrat, Government of Montserrat, 1999.

34. *New People's Liberation Movement*: The New PLM Manifesto 2001, p.13.

Chapter Ten   Disasters and recovery

1. E. A. Markham, 'Here We Go Again', *Hugo Versus Montserrat*, p.87.

2. F. E. Peters, *Montserrat, Her Disasters: A Souvenir of the Great Hurricane of September 12th, 13th 1928*, p.7.

3. Government House Archives 82–106, *Council Minutes* 1816–1913 (1896 entry).

4. *Ibid.*

5. CO 507/7.

6. *Montserrat Observer,* 6 December 1952, p.4.

7. *Montserrat Times,* 25 September 1981, pp.1 and 7.

8. Peters, *op. cit.,* p.9.

9. CO 152/455/15, J. Purcell Edwards, Superintendent of Works, Antigua to Commissioner T. E. P. Baynes.

10. *Ibid.*

11. Peters, *op. cit.*, p.11.

12. CO 152/408/11, p.1. H. Peebles to the Colonial Secretary in Antigua.

13. Peters, *op. cit.,* p.17.
14. CO 152/408/11, *op. cit.,* Appendix C.
15. CO 152/413/9, Hurricane Report by Commissioner H. Peebles.
16. *Hugo News I* (Official Newsletter of the Montserrat Hurricane Relief Effort).
17. Consultant Engineers Partnership, Ltd, *Hurricane Hugo in Montserrat,* para. 1.6 (1).
18. E. H. Riley, *Montserrat: Assistance in Reconstruction Post Hurricane Hugo,* 1989.
19. *Montserrat Reporter,* 25 September 1992, p.4.
20. M. E. Brown's letter to the author.

Chapter Eleven   The volcano awakening

1. J. B. Sherpherd *et al., Summary Proceedings of Lesser Antilles Volcanic Assessment Seminar.*
2. N. Nugent, 'An Account of "The Sulphur" or "Soufriere" of the Island of Montserrat' *Transactions of the Geological Society,* London, 1, 185–1, 790, 1811, p.187.
3. J. Davy, *The West Indies Before and Since Emancipation,* London, Frank Cass & Co. (1854) 1971, p.428.
4. A. G. MacGregor, 'The Volcanic History and Petrology of Montserrat with Observations on Mt. Pelé in Martinique' *Philosophic Transactions of the Royal Society B.557,* Vol.229, 1938.
5. P. H. A. Martin-Kaye, *Reports on the Geology of the Leeward and British Virgin Islands* (By Authority of the Governor of the Leeward Islands) 1939.
6. W. J. Rea, *The Volcanic Geology and Petrology of Montserrat, British West Indies,* PhD Thesis, University of Oxford, 1970.
7. G. Wadge & M. C. Isaacs, 'Mapping the Volcanic Hazards from Soufriere Hills Volcano, Montserrat West Indies using an image processor' *Journal of the Geological Society,* London Vol.142, pp.279–95.
8. J. B. Shepherd, J. F. Tomblin & E. Wood, 'Volcanic seismic Crisis in Montserrat, West Indies 1966–67', *Bulletin Volcanologique,* 35, pp.143–63.
9. P. E. Baker, 'Volcanic Hazards in St. Kitts and Montserrat, West Indies' *Journal of the Geological Society,* London Vol.142, 1985 pp.279–95.
10. G. Wadge & M. C. Isaacs, *op. cit.*
11. G. Wadge & M. C. Isaacs, *Volcanic Hazards from Soufriere Hills, Montserrat West Indies: A Report to the Government of Montserrat and the Caribbean Disaster Preparedness and Prevention Project,* 1986.
12. E. A. Markham & H. A. Fergus (eds), *Hugo Versus Montserrat,* 1989.
13. E. A. Markham, 'Here we go Again' *ibid.,* p.87.
14. G. E. Norton, *The geological features of the Soufriere Hills volcano: past history, re-awakening, explosions and the monitoring programme of the Montserrat Volcano Observatory.*

15. *Ibid.*

16. B. Roach, 'A Failing Management' *Montserrat Reporter*, Vol.XIII No.24 p.7.

17. H. A. Fergus, *Eruption: Montserrat Versus Volcano*, Plymouth, Montserrat UWI School of Continuing Studies, Montserrat 1996.

18. G. E. Norton, *Ibid.*

19. P. Pattullo, *Fire from the Mountain: The Tragedy of Montserrat and the betrayal of its people*, 2000 p.5.

20. *Ibid* p.11.

21. B. Roach, 'Increased Fears of the Volcano' *Montserrat Reporter* Vol.XIII No.19 6 June 1997.

22. Staff Correspondent, 'Inquest Finds 19 Who Died Ignored Dangers'.

23. For a discussion of this issue, see Polly Pattullo, *Fire from the Mountain*.

24. C. Buffonge, *Volcano Book 3, Events in Montserrat during 1997*.

25. G. E. Norton, *op. cit.*

26. C. Buffonge, *Volcano Book 4 1998 and 1999* p.34.

27. *Nature*, Vol.392, 23 April 1998.

28. 'Staffer, Leave we Must?' *Montserrat Reporter* Vol.XIII No.38, 12 December 1997.

29. C. Barrow, 'The Persistence of Shelters and the Politics of Crisis Management during the Montserrat Volcanic Emergency' (Draft Book Chapter), Cave Hill Campus UWI 1999.

30. B. Roach, 'What a Dilemma' *Montserrat Reporter* Vol.XIII No.18, 30 May 1997.

31. Provided by the Emergency Operations Centre, Government of Montserrat.

32. 'Jury's Riders and Coroner's Statement' *Montserrat Reporter* Vol.XV No.1, 15 January 1999.

33. 'Fed Up of Shelter Life' *Montserrat Reporter* Vol.XIV No.3, 23 Jan 1998.

34. P. Pattullo, *op. cit.*; C. Barrow *op. cit.*

35. E. Kelsick 'Thoughts on the Staging of Elections in Montserrat during the Volcanic Crisis' *Montserrat Reporter* Vol.XII No.32, 30 August 1996.

36. E. Kelsick, 'On the Montserrat Dilemma' *Montserrat Reporter* Vol.XIII No.39, 23 December 1997.

37. 'Ex Governor Exposes British' *Montserrat Reporter* Vol.XIII No.4, 31 Jan 1997, p.12.

38. International Development Committee, *Montserrat (First Report)* London, The Stationery Office, 1997.

39. L. Bonnerjea, C. Cameron, I. Laughlin and A. Mathurin-Jurgensen, *Montserrat: Social Situation & Social Policy Review* London, London School of Economics, 1997.

40. E. Clay *et al.*, *An Evaluation of HMG's Response to the Montserrat Volcanic Emergency* Vol.1, London DFID, 1999.

41. J. Bonnerjea, *op. cit.*, p.37.
42. S. Passingham & J. McCredre, *Montserrat Education Sector Review* Montserrat, Department for International Development, 1998.
43. E. Kelsick, *op. cit.*
44. J. Bonnerjea *et al.*, *op. cit.*, p.16.
45. International Development Committee, *op. cit.*
46. 'Our Disaster is a Non-Ending Debate' *Montserrat Reporter* Vol.XIV No.8 27 Feb 1998, p.6.
47. P. J. Baxter *et al.*, 'Christobalite in Volcanic Ash of the Soufriere Hills Volcano, Montserrat, British West Indies, Science', *Science* 283: 1999, 1142–5.
48. B. L. Anderson, 'Beware Professional Advice of Doctors Paid in Advance' *Montserrat Reporter* Vol.XV, 9 April 1999, p.4.
49. K. Calman, *Report by Sir Kenneth Calman, Chief Medical Officer, Into the Health and Health Service Implications of the Montserrat Crisis*, London, 1997, paras 6.2.2– 7.9.
50. The statistical data in paragraphs one and two, were taken from: *Government of Montserrat, Sustainable Development Plan, Montserrat Social and Economic Recovery Programme – A Path to Sustainable Development 1998 to 2002*, 1998; E. Clay *et al.*, An Evaluation of HMG's Response to the Montserrat Volcanic Emergency London, DFID, 1999.
51. E. Clay *et al.*, *op. cit.*
52. *Ibid.*
53. 'GOM Breaks Bottlenecks at CPP Talks?' *Montserrat Reporter* Vol.XVI No.19, Friday 1 June 2001, p.10.
54. H. Durand, 'Consultants Suggest Obtain New Ferry, Hike Copter Fares' *Montserrat Reporter* Vol.XVI No.24, Friday 6 July 2001.
55. International Development Committee *op. cit.* para 44.
56. P. Pattullo, *Fire from the Mountain*, p.113.
57. International Development Committee Report, para 48.
58. Government of Montserrat, *Report on Electoral Commission*, Plymouth, 1996.
59. E. Clay *et al.*, *op. cit.*, p.44.

Chapter Twelve   Arts and culture

1. J. C. Messenger, *Ethnicity*, 2, p.297.
2. J. Dobbin, *The Jombie Dance of Montserrat, p.52.*
3. *Ibid.*, p.17.
4. Kirnon, p.20.
5. J. A. Irish, *Alliouagana in Focus,* p.20.
6. E. K. Brathwaite, *Folk Culture of the Slaves in Jamaica,* p.14.

7. See A. Dewar, *Music in the Alliouagana Cultural Tradition* for a comprehensive survey and valuable analysis of Montserrat's folk songs.

8. H. Kirnon, *Montserrat and Montserratians* 1925, p.22.

9. *Montserrat Observer*, 20 July 1946, p.1.

10. *Ibid.*, 6 August 1949, p.4.

11. Matthew Arnold, 'Culture and Anarchy', *The Portable Matthew Arnold*, ed. L. Trilling, 1949.

12. *Montserrat Observer*, 16 July 1949, p.1.

13. *Time for Action: The Report of the West Indian Commission*, p.279.

14. *Montserrat Observer*, 27 May 1950, p.3.

15. *Ibid.*, 4 October 1952, p.1.

16. D. Edgecombe, *Montserrat Reporter*, 26 January 1985, p.6.

17. Interview with Alphonsus Cassell (Arrow) 20 January 1993.

18. Edgecombe, *Montserrat Reporter*, 28 February 1988, p.8.

19. The *Observer*, Saturday, 19 April 1958, p.8.

20. A. R. Morse, *The Quest for Redonda*, 1979 (Preface).

21. E. A. Markham (ed.), *Hinterland*, 1989, p.196.

22. Kirnon, p.48.

23. A. Eddy, *In Defence of None*, 1983, p.151.

24. The *Observer*, 18 August 1951, p.1.

25. Eddy, *op. cit.*, p.47.

Select Bibliography

Manuscript and main sources are indicated in the Notes and in Chapter 1.

Books, pamphlets and articles on Montserrat

Akenson, D. *If the Irish Ran the World: Montserrat 1630–1730* Liverpool, Liverpool University Press, 1997.

Beasley, C. G. and Schonten, S. A. *Montserrat Cotton Industry Inquiry Report*, Plymouth, Montserrat, Government of Montserrat, 1954.

Berleant-Schiller, R., 'Free Labour and the Economy in Seventeenth-Century Montserrat', *The William and Mary Quarterly*, 3rd Series, Vol.46, no.3, 1989.

Berleant-Schiller, R., 'Land and Livelihood in Montserrat after the End of Slavery' (paper in progress, 1992–3).

Berleant-Schiller, R., 'Montserrat during the Emancipation Process, 1810–1826', in R. Paquette and S. Engerman, *The Lesser Antilles in the Age of European Expansion*, Gainsville, University Presses of Florida, forthcoming 1994.

Blankenship, J. R., *The Wildlife of Montserrat*, Montserrat National Trust, 1990.

Brown, D. F., *A Survey of the Development and Growth of Secondary Education in the Island of Montserrat, West Indies*, c.1969.

Buffonge, C. *Volcano Book 4* 1998 & 1999 Montserrat, The Author, 2001.

Consultant Engineers Partnership, Ltd, *Hurricane Hugo in Montserrat*, UNDP Bridgetown, Barbados, 1989.

Crandall, D. R. and Dyde, B. S. *The Fortifications of St George's Hill Montserrat*, Plymouth, The Montserrat National Trust, 1989.

Demets, A. (Bishop), *The Catholic Church in Montserrat West Indies 1756–1980*, Plymouth, Montserrat, 1980.

Dewar, A. M. *Music in the Alliouagana (Montserrat) Cultural Tradition* unpublished manuscript, University of the West Indies, Barbados, 1977.

Duberry, A., *Folk Medicines of Montserrat and their Use* (Thesis UWI Barbados), c.1979.

Ebanks, G. E., *Montserrat and Its People – A Demographic Analysis*, Georgetown, Guyana, The CARICOM Secretariat (undated).

Engish, T. S., 'Ireland's Only Colony, Records of Montserrat 1632 to the end of the 19th century', bound typescript, West India Committee Library, 1930 (available at the Montserrat Public Library).

Fergus, H. A., *History of Alliouagana: A Short History of Montserrat*, University of the West Indies, Montserrat, 1975.

Fergus, H. A., 'The Early Laws of Montserrat (1668–1680): The Legal Schema of a Slave Society', *Caribbean Quarterly*, Vol.24, nos 1 and 2, 1978.

Fergus, H. A., 'Electoral Behaviour in Montserrat', *Bulletin of Eastern Caribbean Affairs*, Vol.5, no.2, 1979 (UWI Barbados, Institute of Social and Economic Research (ISER).

Fergus, H. A., 'Montserrat Colony of Ireland, The Myth and the Reality', *Studies: An Irish Quarterly Review*, University of Dublin, 1981.

Fergus, H. A., 'Some Problems of Micro States in Micro Parliaments of the Commonwealth Caribbean: The Montserrat Case', *Caribbean Affairs*, Vol.4, no.1, 1981.

Fergus, H. A. 'Montserrat's Days of Lime and Cotton', *Caribbean Quarterly*, Vol.28, no.3, 1982.

Fergus, H. A., 'Personalities in Montserrat Politics: Comments on the 1983 Elections', *Bulletin of Eastern Caribbean Affairs*, Vol.10, no.2, 1984, ISER.

Fergus, H. A., *Montserrat, Emerald Isle of the Caribbean*, London, Macmillan, 1983.

Fergus, H. A., *W. H. Bramble: His Life and Times*, University of the West Indies Centre, Montserrat, 1983.

Fergus, H. A., *Rule Britannia: Politics in British Montserrat*, University of the West Indies Centre, Montserrat, 1985.

Fergus, H. A., 'Constitutional Downgrading for Montserrat: Tampering with the Constitution', *Caribbean Affairs*, Vol.3, no.4, 1990.

Fergus, H. A., 'Tea Drinking – As Montserratian as Goat Water', *Writing Ulster*, nos 2/3 (Northern Ireland), 1991, pp.128–30.

Goodwin, C. M., 'Sugar Time and Englishmen: A Study of Management Strategies on Caribbean Plantations', Doctoral Dissertation, Boston University, 1987.

Government of Montserrat, *Montserrat Development . ian*, 1966–70.

Great Britain, *Montserrat* (Colonial Annual Reports) 1957 and 1958, 1959 and 1960, 1961 and 1962, 1963 and 1964, 1965 and 1966, 1967–1972, London, HMSO.

Great Britain, *The Montserrat Constitution Order 1989*, London, HMSO, 1989.

Hammond, S. A., *Report on an Inquiry into the Organisation and Salaries of the Civil Service, Leeward Islands: Part IV, Notes on the Organization of the Department of the Administration of Montserrat c.1951.*

Higgins, M. D. *Montserrat and Its Irish Connection* (Unpublished Lecture) Montserrat, March 2000.

Irish, J. A., *Alliouagana in Agony: Notes on Montserrat Politics,* Montserrat, 1974

Irish, J. A., *Life in a Colonial Crucible: Labour and Social Change in Montserrat, 1946-Present,* New York, JAGPI Productions and Caribbean Research Centre (CUNY) 1991.

Kirnon, H., *Montserrat and Montserratians,* New York, 1925.

Lang, D. M., *Soil and Land Use Surveys No.22, Montserrat,* UWI, Trinidad, 1967.

Lawrence, G. E., *Thomas Ogarra, A West Indian Preacher,* London, Epworth Press, 1956.

Lawrence, G. E., *Montserrat and its Methodism* (unpublished typescript), Bristol, 1967.

Leeward Islands Government, *Federal Department of Labour: Annual Report 1947* (Advocate Co. Ltd, Printers).

MacGregor, A. G., 'The Royal Expedition to Montserrat B. W. I. The Volcanic History and Petrology of Montserrat with Observations on Mt. Pelè in Martinique', *Philosophical Transaction of the Royal Society of London,* 1939.

Markham, E. A. and Fergus, H. A., *Hugo Versus Montserrat,* Coleraine and Boston, Linda Lee Books, 1989.

Mathurin, O., 'Electoral Change in Montserrat and Antigua', T. Munroe and R. Lewis (eds), *Readings in Government and Politics of the West Indies,* Jamaica, Department of Government, University of the West Indies, 1971.

Mendes, I., 'The Historical Notes of the Early Years of the Island of Montserrat', *The Leeward Islands Review,* 1937.

Messenger, J. C., 'The Influence of the Irish on Montserrat', *Caribbean Quarterly,* Vol.13, no.2, 1967.

Messenger, J. C., 'Montserrat: The Most Distinctively Irish Settlement in the New World', *Ethnicity,* Vol.2, no.3, 1975.

Nugent, N., 'An Account of the "Sulphur" or "Soufrière" of the Island of Montserrat', *Transactions of the Geological Society London,* Vol. 1811.

Pattullo, P. *Fire from the Mountain: The Tragedy of Montserrat and the betrayal of its people,* London Constable, 2000.

Perret, F. A., *Volcano – Seismic Crisis at Montserrat 1933–1937* Washington, DC, Carnegie Institute of Washington, 1939.

Peters, F. E., *A Brief History of Montserrat and Her Recent Hurricanes,* Montserrat, 1929.

Peters, F. E., *The Abolition of Slavery,* Montserrat, 1934.

Petersen, J. B. and Watters, D. R., 'Archeological Testing at the Early Saladoid Trants Site, Montserrat West indies' (paper submitted 17 February 1992 for publication in the Proceedings of the 14th Inter-national Congress for Caribbean Archaeology, Barbados, West Indies).

Philpott, S. B., *West Indian Migration: The Montserrat Case,* London, The Athlone Press, 1973.

Pulsipher, L. M., *The Cultural Landscape of Montserrat, West Indies in the Seventeenth Century: Early Environmental Consequences of British Colonial Development* (PhD diss., Southern Illinois University, 1977).

Pulsipher, L. M., *Seventeenth Century Montserrat: An Environmental Impact Statement*, Historical Geography Research Series No.17, 1988.

Pulsipher, L. M., 'Galways Plantation, Montserrat', H. J. Viola and C. Margolis (eds), *Seeds of Change*, Washington and London, Smithsonian Institution Press, 1991.

Riley, E. H., *Montserrat: Assistance in Reconstruction Post Hurricane Hugo in Montserrat*, British Development Division in the Caribbean Barbados, 1989.

Rules of the Montserrat Trades and Labour Union, Plymouth, Montserrat 1946.

Somerville, D., *The Early Years of Montserrat* (typescript at Montserrat Public Library), 1976.

Steadmond, D. W. *et al.* 'Vertebrates from Archeological Sites on Montserrat W. I.', *Annals of Carnegie Museum of National History*, Pittsburgh. Pennsylvania, 19 April 1984.

Watters, D., *Transect Surveying and Prehistoric Site Locations on Barbuda and Montserrat, Leeward Islands, West Indies.*, unpublished manuscript, University of Pittsburgh, 1980.

Watts, F., *Report on the Agricultural Industries of Montserrat*, London, HMSO, 1906.

Wheeler, M. M., *Montserrat West Indies: A Chronological History*, Plymouth, Montserrat National Trust, 1988.

General sources

Alleyne, S. and Cruickshank, J. K., 'The Use of Informal Medication – Particularly Bush Teas – In Jamaica Patients with Diabetes Mellitus', *Cajanus*, Vol.23, no.1, 1990.

Aspinal, A., *The British West Indies*, London, Pitman & Sons, 1912.

Aspinal, A., *The Pocket Guide to the West Indies* London, Sifton Praed Co. (1907), 1923.

Beachey, R. W., *The British West Indies Sugar Industry in the Late 19th Century*, Oxford, Basil Blackwell, 1957.

Beckles, H. and Shepherd, V., *Caribbean Slave Society and Economy*, Kingston and Jamaica, Ian Randle Publishers, James Currey Publishers, 1991.

Brathwaite, E. K., *Folk Cultures of the Slaves in Jamaica*, London, Port of Spain, New Beacon Books, Revised edn. 1981.

Bridenbaugh, C. and Bridenbaugh, R., *No Peace Beyond the Lines: The English in the Caribbean, 1624–1690*, New York, Oxford University Press, 1972.

Black, J. (ed.), *The Blathwayt Atlas Vol.II*, Providence, Rhode Island, 1975.

Burn, W. L., *The British West Indies*, Westport, Connecticut, Greenwood Press, 1951.

Burns, A., *History of the British West Indies*, New York, Barnes and Noble, 1965.

Coleridge, H., *Six Months in the West Indies in 1825*, New York, Negro University Press, 1970 (formerly John Murray).

Colt, H., in T. V. Harlow, *Colononizing Expeditions to the West Indies and Guiana, 1623–1667*, Second Series, London, 1967 (1925).

Curtis, E., *A History of Ireland*, 6th edn, 1950, paperback reprint 1961.

Davy, J., *The West Indies before and since Slave Emancipation*, London, Frank Cass and Company (1854), 1971.

Deerr, N., *The History of Sugar*, London, Chapman and Hall, 1949.

Dunn, R. S., *Sugar and Slaves*, New York, London, 1973.

Du Tertre, J., *Histoire Générale des Antilles*, Vol.IV, Paris, 1967.

Eddy, A., *In Defence of None*, Basseterre, St Kitts, 1983.

Edwards, B., *The History Civil and Commercial of the British Colonies in the West Indies*, London, 1793 (1801).

Edwards, P. E. (ed.), *Equiano's Travels*, London, Heinemann Educational, 1967.

FCO, *Partnership for Progress and Prosperity: Britain and the Overseas Territories* London, HMSO Cm 4264, 1999.

Goveia, E., *Slave Society in the British Leeward Islands at the End of the Eighteenth Century*, New Haven and London, Yale University Press, 1965.

Great Britain, *Report of Her Majesty's Colonial Possessions*, transmitted with the Blue Books for the Year 1851, London, HMSO.

Great Britain, *Report of the Royal Commission Appointed in December 1882 – Part III, The Leeward Islands*, 1884 C-3840.

Great Britain, *Report of the West India Royal Commission*, London, HMSO, 1897, C.8655.

Great Britain, *Report of the West India Royal Commission* (Moyne) 1938–39, 1945.

Gwynn, A., 'Early Irish Emigration to the West Indies', *Studies: An Irish Quarterly of Letters*, June 1929 and December 1929.

Gwynn, A., 'Cromwell's Policy of Transportation', *Studies*, December 1930 and June 1931.

Gwynn, A., 'Documents relating to the Irish in the West Indies', *Analecta Hibernia*, No.4, 1932.

Gwynn, A., 'The First Irish Priests in the New World', *Studies*, June 1932.

Hall, D., *Five of the Leeward 1834–1870*, Barbados and London, Caribbean University Press/Ginn & Company, 1971.

Harford, J. D. *et al.*, *Reports on the Presidencies of the Leeward Islands Colony for the Year 1936*, Advocate Co., Ltd, Barbados, c.1937.

Higham, C. S. S., *The Development of the Leeward Islands under the Restoration, 1660–1668*, London, 1921.

Johnston, J. R. V., *The Stapleton Sugar Plantations in the Leeward Islands* (reprinted from *Bulletin of the John Rylands Library*, Vol.48, no.1., Autumn, 1965), The John Rylands Library, Manchester, 3, MCMLXV.

Lewis, A., *The Agony of the Eight*, Advocate Printery, Barbados c.1963.

Lewis, G. K., *The Growth of the Modern West Indies*, London, MacGibbon and Kee, 1968.

Lewis, M. G., *The Journal of a West Indian Proprietor*, London, 1834.

Macmillan, W. M., *Warning from the West Indies*, London, Faber and Faber, 1936.

Marshall, W. K., 'Notes on Peasant Development in the West Indies since 1835', *Social and Economic Studies*, Vol.17.

Martin-Kaye, P. H. A., *Reports on the Geology of the Leeward Islands and British Virgin Islands*, Government Printery, St Lucia, 1959.

Miller, E. *et al*, *Foundation for the Future: OECS Education Reform Strategy*, OECS Secretariat, Castries, St Lucia, 1991.

Morrison, S. E., *Admiral of the Ocean: A Life of Christopher Columbus*, Vol.2, New York. Time Incorporated, 1962.

Morse, A. R., *The Quest for Redonda*, Cleveland, Ohio, The Reynold Morse Foundation, 1979.

Oldmixon, J., *The British Empire in America*, Vol.2, New York, Augustus Kelley Publishers, 1969 (1741).

O'Loughlin, C., *Economic and Political Change in the Leeward and Windward Islands*, New Haven and London, Yale University Press, 1969.

Pares, R., *War and Trade in the West Indies*, London, Frank Cass, 1963.

Pitman, F., *The Development of the British West Indies 1700–1763*, Connecticut, Archon Books, 1967.

Ragatz, L. R., 'Absentee Landlordism in the British West Indies 1750–1833', *Agricultural History*, Vol.5, 1931.

Report of Mr. Rodney Gallagher of Coopers and Lybrand on the Survey of Offshore Finance Sectors in the Caribbean Dependent Territories, London, HMSO, 1990.

Sheridan, R., *The Development of Plantations to 1750: An Era of West Indian Propriety 1750–1775*, Barbados, Caribbean University Press, 1970.

Sturge, J. and Harvey T., *The West Indies in 1837*, London, Dawsons of Pall Mall (1838), 1968.

Tyrell, A., *Joseph Sturge and the Moral Radical Party in Early Victorian Britain*, London, Christopher Helm, 1987.

Ward, J. R., *British West Indian Slavery 1750–1834*, Oxford, Clarendon Press, 1988.

Watkins, F. W., *Handbook of the Leeward Islands*, London, West India Committee, 1924.

Watts, D., *The West Indies: Patterns of Development, Culture and Environmental Change since 1492*, New York, Cambridge University Press, 1987.

Williams, E., *Capitalism and Slavery*, London, André Deutsch, 1964 (1944).

Yorke, P. C. (ed.), *The Diary of John Baker*, London, Hutchinson Co., 1931.

APPENDIX 1

Electoral candidates, 1952–96

Allen, C. J	1978(L)	1983(L)
Allen, J. W.	1961(W)	1966(L)
Allen, K.	1961(L)	
Allen, P.	1983(L)	
Allen, R. C.	1973(L)	
Arthurton, P.	1987(L)	1991(L)
Bass, J.	1996(L)	
Blake, J. P.	1966(L)	
Bramble, B.	1983(L)	
Bramble, M.	1978(L)	
Bramble, P. A.	1966(W)	1970(W) 1973(W) 1978(L) 1983(W) 1987(L) 1996(L)
Bramble, W. H.	1952(W)	1955(W) 1961(W) 1966(W) 1970(L)
Brandt, D.	1983(W)	1987(W) 1991(W) 1996(W)
Browne, C.	1991(L)	1996(L)
Browne, I.	1973(L)	
Cassell, J.	1996(L)	
Chalmers, J. B.	1961(L)	1978(W) 1983(W) 1987(W) 1991(L)
Daley, L.	1991(L)	
Dublin, J. S.	1970(W)	1973(L) 1978(W) 1983(L) 1991(L) 1996(L)
Dyer, E. A.	1966(W)	1970(W) 1978(L) 1983(W) 1987(W) 1991(L)
Dyer, M.	1958(W)	1961(W) 1966(W) 1970(L) 1978(L)
Dyer, (Howe) M. M.	1979(W)*	1983(W) 1987(L)
Edgecombe, D. E.	1987(L)	
Edgecombe, E. T.	1952(W)	1955(W)
Edgecombe, J. W.	1952(L)	1955(L)
Edgecombe, W. L.	1961(L)	
Edwards, B. W.	1952(W)	1955(L) 1958(W) 1961(W) 1966(W) 1970(L)
Edwards, J. N.	1966(L)	
Farage, L.	1991(L)	
Fenton, B. E.	1996(L)	
Fenton, D. C.	1958(L)	1961(W) 1966(L) 1970(L) 1973(L) 1978(L)

*By election

Fenton, D. E.	1987(L)	
Fergus, J.	1966(L)	
Grant, F.	1991(L)	
Griffith, R. W.	1952(W)	1955(W) 1958(L) 1966(L) 1978(L)
Howe, C.	1973(L)	
Howe, J. J.	1966(W)	1970(L)
Howes, L. G.	1991(W)	1996(L)
Howes, W. S.	1958(L)	
Irish, J. A.	1983(L)	
Jeffers, V.	1987(W)	1991(L)
Joseph, A. A.	1978(L)	
Joseph, R. G.	1970(L)	1973(W) 1978(L)
Kelsick, E.	1958(L)	1970(L)
Kelsick, M. R.	1958(L)	1961(W)
Kirnon, C. T.	1991(W)	1996(L)
Lake, P.	1966(L)	
Lee, H.	1958(W)	
Lee, J.	1961(L)	1996(L)
Lewis, L.	1991(L)	
Lewis, R.	1973(L)	
Margetson, F.	1978(W)	1983(L)
Meade, B.	1996(W)	
Meade, I.	1996(L)	
Meade, J. H.	1996(L)	
Meade, R.	1991(W)	1996(W)
Meade, T. E.	1961(L)	1966(L) 1978(L) 1978(W)
Meade, W.	1991(W)	
Mercer, H. S.	1952(L)	
O'Garro, J.	1966(L)	
Osborne, B. B.	1987(W)	1991(W) 1996(W)
Osborne, H.	1966(L)	
Osborne, J. A.	1966(W) 1996(W)	1970(W) 1973(W) 1978(W) 1983(W) 1987(W) 1991(L)
Osborne, J. R.	1966(L)	
Osborne, R. E. D.	1952(L)	1955(L) 1958(L)
Parson, C.	1966(L)	
Payne, R. A.	1996(L)	
Payne, D. A.	1973(L)	
Perkins, J. W.	1961(L)	
Phillip, C.	1996(L)	
Ponde, R.	1979(L)	
Ponteen, J. S.	1996(L)	

Ponteen, N.	1991(L)				
Riley, P. R.	1966(L)	1970(L)			
Ryan, C.	1983(L)				
Ryan, Charles	1983(L)				
Ryan, W. H.	1970(W)	1973(W)	1978(L)	1983(L)	
Samuel, R.	1978(L)	1983(L)	1987(L)	1991(L)	
Taylor, D.	1983(L)				
Taylor, J.	1978(W)				
Thomas, V.	1983(L)	1996(L)			
Tuitt, A.	1991(L)	1996(W)			
Tuitt, G. W.	1996(L)				
Tuitt, J.	1987(L)				
Tuitt, M.	1970(W)	1973(W)	1978(L)		
Tuitt, N.	1978(W)	1983(W)	1987(W)	1991(W)	1996(L)
Wade-Bramble, R.	1983(L)	1987(L)	1991(W)		
Walkinshaw, M.	1952(W)	1955(W)	1958(W)	1961(W)	
Wall, J. C. L.	1952(L)	1955(W)	1958(L)		
Weekes, J. J.	1970(W)	1973(L)			
Weekes, J.	1966(L)	1970(L)	1973(W)	1978(L)	
Weekes, R. L.	1996(W)				
Wilson, J. E.	1996(L)				
Wilson, J. W.	1983(L)				
White, P.	1991(L)				
White, T.	1987(L)	1987(L)	1991(L)		

APPENDIX 2

Officers who administered the Government of Montserrat on behalf of the British Government

Montserrat was supervised by the Governor of the Leeward Islands from wherever he resided, but he had a deputy in Montserrat who was styled Deputy Governor or Lieutenant-Governor. The title President, reserved for the senior Council member, should not be confused with the post of Deputy Governor. The President sometimes acted for the Deputy, however, whenever the need arose, especially during an interregnum. In 1989 the title Commissioner was given to the administering officer. This changed to Administrator in 1956, when the Leeward Islands defederated in order to enter the West Indies Federation as separate units. In 1971, the status of the post was advanced to Governorship. Montserrat's first Governor was Mr Willoughby Harry Thompson, CBE, apart from the first three representatives who were loosely called Governors before the Leeward Islands Act of 1671 set up the first Federal Assembly. Although it is incomplete, this is the most up-to-date listing.

1632	Anthony Brisket
1649	Roger Osborne
1665	Nathaniel Reade
1667	Anthony Brisket (II)
1668	?____ Stanley
1668	William Stapleton
1672	Edmund Stapleton
1676	John Carroll
1680	Peter Cove
1687	Redmund Stapleton
1687–95	Nathaniel Blakeston
1695–1700	Thomas Delaval
1700	Anthony Hodges
1710	John Pearne
1713	John Marshall

1715	Thomas Talmach
1722	Charles Dilke
1726	Paul George
1728	John Osborne
1729	Thomas Digges
1768	Michael White
1777	Anthony Wyke
1778	William Mulgrave
1782	Michael White
1782	L. J. de Goullon
1784	Michael White
1790	Alexander Gordon
1827	S. E. Steward
1841–52	Edward Dacre Baynes (President)
1854	Hercules G. R. Robinson
1855–61	Edward E. Rushworth
1862–66	William C. F. Robinson
1867–70	W. R. Pine
1875–83	Neale Porter
1888	J. Spencer Hollings
1889	Edward Baynes
1900	F. H. Watkins
1906	W. Davidson Houston, CMG
1918	C. F. Condell
1922	H. W. Peebles, DSO, OBE
1929	H. H. Hutchings, ISO
1932	T. E. P. Baynes, OBE
1946	Hugh Burrowes
1949	Charlesworth Ross, BA
1956	Arthur Francis Dawkins
1960	Alonzo Wiles, OBE
1964	Dennis Raleigh Gibbs, CMG, CVO, DSO
1971	Willoughby Harry Thompson, CBE
1974	Norman Derek Matthews, OBE
1977	Gwylym Wyn Jones, CBE
1980–84	David Kenneth Hay Dale, CBE
1985–87	Arthur Christopher Watson, CMG
1987–1990	Christopher J. Turner, CMG
1990–93	David P. Taylor, CBE
1993–97	Frank Savage, OBE
2001–	Anthony James Longrigg, CMG

APPENDIX 3

Chronology of major events

1493	Columbus sighted Montserrat on 11 November.
1632	Irish Catholics from St Kitts under Thomas Warner colonized the island.
1634	Dissident Irish Catholics from Virginia joined the new colony.
1636	St Anthony's Church built by Governor Anthony Brisket.
1667	The French captured Montserrat and restored it at the Treaty of Breda. A Carib raid and a hurricane occurred.
1671	Montserrat became part of the first Leeward Island federation.
1672	A massive earthquake occurred on Christmas Day. St Anthony's Church destroyed.
1678	Earliest recorded population 'census'. Population: 3674.
1682	Caribs raided Montserrat carrying off slaves.
1735	Peak year in sugar production: 3150 tons.
1767	Hurricane and flood – Fort Ghaut overflowed and threatened Plymouth.
1768	Planned slave uprising on 17 March, St Patrick's Day.
1773	Hurricane damage estimated at £50 000.
1782	The French captured Montserrat and held it until the Treaty of Versailles, 1783.
1793	Methodist work started.
1816	Hurricane, 16 September.
1834	Slaves 'freed', 1 August.
1837	End of the Apprenticeship System.
1838	1 August, full emancipation of slaves.
1843	8 February, worst earthquake in recorded history.
1852	Lime industry started by Francis Burke.
1852	Elected members in the majority in the Legislative Assembly. A freed man elected for the first time.
1866	Representative Assembly abolished, Montserrat became a Crown colony.
1866	Hurricane occurred.
1871	Federation of the Leeward Islands including Dominica.
1883	St Mary's Chapel built as 'Church of the Emancipation'.
1885	Lime production peaked.
1891	Secondary education began.
1896	Disastrous flood.

1898	Fox riot at Frith's Village connected with illicit distillation of rum.
1899	Destructive hurricane struck the island.
1901	Birth of W. H. Bramble.
1901	Experiment in the growth of sea-island cotton started.
1905	The Pentecostal Church initiated by L. Hurley.
1917	Royal Bank of Canada started to operate.
1920	Montserrat Teachers' Association formed.
1924	Disastrous hurricane struck.
1928	Island severely damaged by hurricane.
1928	Montserrat Secondary School established.
1934	Montserrat won Leeward Islands cricket tournament.
1936	Representative Government reintroduced on a narrow franchise.
1941	Cotton production peaked at 1 175 932 pounds.
1942	Toby Hill riots.
1943	R. W. Griffith elected to Legislative Council.
1945	Government took charge of all primary schools with the exception of the Roman Catholic school.
1949	Steelband started at Ryner's Village.
1950	Major strike in the cotton industry – first in Montserrat.
1951	Montserrat's first away-win in the Leeward Islands cricket tournament.
1952	W. H. Bramble elected to Legislative Council through a new constitution (1951) giving universal adult suffrage.
1952	Radio Montserrat established at Olveston by F. Delisle.
1953	Inquiry into the cotton industry and industrial relations headed by Professor C. Beasley.
1953	Aircraft landed at Delisle's Olveston airstrip.
1955	W. H. Bramble and his Labour Party won a second term.
1956	Change in cotton-planting season from March to September.
1958	W. H. Bramble won a seat to become Montserrat's federal representative.
1961	Montserrat Seamen and Waterfront Workers' Union registered.
1961	W. H. Bramble became first Chief Minister, under a new constitution – Letters Patent 1959.
1966	Radio Antilles started broadcasting (erected 1965).
1966	Her Majesty Queen Elizabeth II and the Duke of Edinburgh visited.
1968	Montserrat reluctantly joined the Caribbean Free Trade Association (CARIFTA).
1970	W. H. Bramble defeated at the polls by his son's Progressive Democratic Party.
1972	Montserrat joined CARICOM.
1973	J. A. Irish formed the Montserrat Allied Workers' Union (MAWU).
1973	Austin Bramble's PDP returned to power at a snap election.

1975	A Speaker (H. A. Fergus), replaced the Governor as presiding officer in the Legislative Council.
1978	John Osborne's People's Liberation Movement (PLM) snatched power from Austin Bramble's PDP.
1981	Flood on 3 September regarded as worst in living memory.
1982	J. A. Irish launched his United National Front Party (UNF) on 25 November.
1982	J. A. Osborne, the Chief Minister, launched his steel boat *Western Sun*, built by himself, on 1 December.
1985	NDP led by B. B. Osborne established.
1988	W. H. Bramble died, 17 October.
1989	Hurricane Hugo devastated the island, 17 September.
1990	Montserrat received a new constitution.
1991	NPP led by R. Meade won the General Elections.
1995	The Soufrière Hills volcano started to erupt on 18 July.
1996	Reuben Meade's NPP lost the General Elections making place for a coalition led by Bertrand B. Osborne, MBE as Chief Minister – 11 and 13 November.
1997	Blackburne Airport officially renamed W. H. Bramble Airport.
	A massive volcano eruption devastated large areas in the east of the island and killed 19 persons on 25 June.
	Bertrand Osborne resigned as Chief Minister pushed by a palace coup, and lawyer David Brandt succeeded him – 22 August.
	The largest and most devastating dome collapse occurred in the south of the island – 26 December.
1998	A total lunar eclipse occurred on 26 February.
1999	Elections Commission headed by Howard A. Fergus recommended 'voting-at-large' in a single island constituency. Nominated membership in the Legislative Council abolished.
	Formal opening of the CARICOM Village by Prime Minister Basdeo Panday of Trinidad and Tobago on 29 December.
2000	Visit of HRH Prince Andrew, Duke of York, his third since the volcanic crisis (others being in 1997 and 1998).
2001	John Osborne's New People's Liberation Movement won the General Elections on 2 April.

Index